Unsavory Elements

Stories of foreigners on the loose in China

Edited by Tom Carter

Unsavory Elements, stories of foreigners on the loose in China
Edited by Tom Carter

ISBN: 978-988-16164-0-1

© 2013 Tom Carter and the contributors

'View From a Bridge' © 2000 by Peter Hessler. Originally published in The New Yorker.
Reprinted with permission.

Cover artwork © Nick Bonner, Koryo Studio & Dominic Johnson-Hill, Plastered T-shirts

Contents

Dedicated to the people of China,
who have enriched our lives with
these page-turning experiences.

Introduction

I almost died in China. Only six months into my first year here I had my first big chance to become a statistic for the U.S. State Department thanks to encephalitis, a viral infection of the brain that can kill within seven days. The symptoms: everything many Westerners might expect the first time they come to China, including headache, fever, confusion, fatigue, nausea... The doctors at the small-city hospital near where I lived were completely mystified until my mother, a veteran emergency room nurse back in the States, instructed them via telephone on how to diagnose and treat my illness.

Having a nice smile holstered and ready to quick-draw in China is always good for foreigners lost in translation, but my American sense of law and order has been less useful. Following a beating by three drunken men at a hotel in Chongqing that nearly knocked the teeth out of my smile, I reported my assailants to the local police. That didn't have quite the response I'd hoped for; they kicked *me* out of the hotel at 4:00 a.m., because it was now deemed "unsafe for foreigners."

Oh, and there was that one time when...

The list of amazing, perplexing or ridiculous experiences for almost any foreigner in the Middle Kingdom goes on and on. Hence this book.

From the moment we step foot in the Middle Kingdom, foreigners are subjected to an extraordinary range of alien experiences, ranging from appalling to exquisite. We contend with seething masses of humanity, accosting stares and shouts from curious Chinese who have never before seen a foreigner and predatory scammers operating under the impression that "all Westerners are rich", as well as the ability to befriend nearly any stranger on the street, the endless variety of Chinese cuisines and a sense of security that comes with being in a country with one of the lowest violent crime rates in the world.

A small but growing contingent of foreigners now call China "home," and those who stick it out seem to actually *enjoy* flirting with fatality under smog-laden skies. And while Chinese emigrants continue to flee their motherland to chase the American Dream, Westerners are arriving in today's China in unprecedented numbers chasing their own dreams.

These foreigners are not always greeted with a welcoming bow. In recent years, as many Western economies have faltered, the collective esteem of Westerners in the eyes of some Chinese people has also fallen from the pinnacle of superstar status. On top of the 220-million-strong "floating population" of migrant laborers, China now also has to deal with over one million foreigners, many of whom are in effect economic refugees. Where we once held our heads high at the rather cool moniker "foreign devils," we have in some cases been reduced to "unsavory elements."

Change is the only constant in China. Yet, the more China changes, the more it stays the same, and our *experiences* as outsiders remain essentially timeless. *Unsavory Elements* was conceived from this concept. Whereas a Chinese host may ply you with endless glasses of machine-grade alcohol at a banquet, *Unsavory Elements* serves a multi-course feast of original writings commissioned expressly for this anthology. This book may fall under the genre of travel writing, but travel is just the beginning of the adventure here. These narratives are also about living, learning and loving in this land, about becoming intimate with Chinese culture. Their contributions contain the candidness of Old China Hands after several drinks at an expat bar, and a closeness usually only found when sharing a cramped hostel dormitory with other unwashed backpackers.

The cast of contributors range from China's most renowned Western writers and other outsiders living in China who have witnessed the nation's dramatic development over recent decades to inveterate vagrants such as myself.

There is a big difference between being tourist and traveler, which Peter Hessler highlights as he tours the bleak border between China and North Korea, and Pete Spurrier who learned how to travel the hard way as a hobo stowed away on third-class trains from Urumqi to Hong Kong. Dominic Stevenson writes of a stint in a Shanghai prison, and Bruce Humes of being hospitalized after a brutal beating. But for every heart-breaking moment that China exacts on us, there is also a heart-warming one, such as Kay Bratt's unconditional love for a disabled orphan, and Kaitlin Solimine's relationship with her homestay Chinese mother.

Many of the authors featured in this anthology got their start as English teachers, including Matt Muller, who compares his career to descending the evolutionary ladder, and Michael Levy, who offers a glimpse into the unscrupulous side of the English teaching business. Indeed, foreigner business people abound in the new New China, like Graham Earnshaw who tells of guerrilla publishing, and Matthew Polly of losing his shirt while trying to sell shirts at Shaolin.

Unsavory Elements has its share of hilarious moments, including Derek Sandhaus' baijiu-soaked banquet gone wrong. But some of the stories were not so funny when they were happening, such as Nury Vittachi's experience of being strong-armed by scammers, and Rudy Kong in the middle of an ice-hockey brawl – with the police. Alan Paul proves a humorous account of a family road trip across Sichuan where patience, an open mind and even more patience are a traveler's most required traits.

Some Western families have settled in China to introduce their children to a new culture, as Aminta Arrington has done, admirably attempting to overcome China's self-imposed social divisions, and Susan Conley, as she and her children use street food as a savory medium to acclimatize. But on the other hand,

Jocelyn Eikenburg talks of how, when it comes to love, interracial relationships don't have it easy against 5,000 years of tradition.

One of the best parts about living in China is the opportunity to mingle with the people, which Dan Washburn does during a visit with villagers in what he calls "perhaps the poorest village in the poorest province in China." As every foreigner here knows, the affable Chinese have the tendency to make their foreign friends feel like superstars, but musician Jonathan Campbell also discovers that being a *real* rock star in China is not always as glamorous as it seems.

Some expats prefer the glam and glitz of China's cosmopolitan cities, on which Susie Gordon reflects during a neon-lit night out in Shanghai, whereas a hardened explorer like Jeff Fuchs prefers to spend his days trekking through the Himalayas of Tibet. Audra Ang witnesses a darker side of China's Tibetan population in Xiahe, and Jonathan Watts pays tribute to an expatriate environmentalist living in the jungles of Xishuangbanna.

China is often a place where the real tends to shade into the surreal, something to which Mark Kitto can attest as he relates how local officials decide to make a statue of him. Deborah Fallows, too, when she and her husband are coerced into writing a confession just for taking photos at Tiananmen Square.

Meanwhile, Mike Meyer muses that the rapid rise of modern Beijing has made it less a city than a drafting table, and my own observation of a young peasant prostitute "who had trouble walking in her platform heels" is probably an apt metaphor for a nation struggling to cope with its development.

To be sure, if you want to hear some good stories about Chinese history, just sit down next to any old-timer and his caged songbird in a Peking park or take tea with a village elder. But for the Chinese-challenged laowai, *Unsavory Elements* offers a contemporary perspective of a nation that, as Simon Winchester predicts in the epilogue, is poised to become the next world superpower.

The stories herein are as varied as the multitude of migrant workers milling about Guangzhou Central Railway Station during Chinese New Year. Yet each reveals as much about China as it does about us, the "unsavory elements" who live here, not only accepting China's cultural eccentricities, but *thriving* in the midst of them.

Tom Carter
Shanghai, China
2013 (Year of the Snake)

Selling Hope

Michael Levy

Michael Levy is an educator, writer, and traveler currently living in Brooklyn, New York, where he teaches high school history. His memoir, "Kosher Chinese: Living, Teaching, and Eating with China's Other Billion", was chosen by Barnes and Noble as the best book by a new author in 2012.

"WE CAN PAY YOU ONE thousand dollars, American," he began.

I was seated across from my boss, Mr. Mao, in a Starbucks in Chaoyang, the throbbing business district at the heart of Beijing. Chaoyang literally means "facing the sun," and that August day made the name feel depressingly apt; the short walk to the Starbucks from the skyscraper that contained *English Yes!* – Mr. Mao's training school – left me breathless. I was tickled by beads of perspiration running down my sides.

"It's hard to say no to a thousand dollars," I replied.

"Yes, but you misunderstand," Mr. Mao quickly interjected. "One thousand dollars *per essay*."

I stopped breathing. I had eighteen students total. Each of their essays would take no more than a few hours. I could be on a plane to Thailand by the end of the week, spend a month at the grandest spa Bangkok had to offer, and still have enough left in the kitty to buy a car when I got back to the U.S.

My sweating got worse as my nerves mixed with the heat. I took a sip of coffee, swallowed, and suspiciously scanned the conspicuous consumers of Starbucks. A teenager in a Bathing Ape t-shirt, bangs in his eyes, thumbing his phone. A table full of businessmen smoking cigarettes and ogling the women who walked past the window. A pair of baristas, identical in height, haircut, eye color, and ennui, leaning against the espresso machine. But no one was listening in. In fact, no one seemed to notice me at all, a rare treat that made modern, middle-class Beijing stand apart from the rest of China.

"The essays can be short," Mr. Mao went on. "Typical admissions essays, to schools you know well, so it is no problem for you. As you know, the students cannot write their essays on their own. Chinese teenagers do not know themselves well enough."

A simple proposition: I would write essays in the names of Chinese students seeking admission to American boarding schools.

A *lucrative* proposition: I'd be earning more per hour than New York lawyers.

And a surprising proposition: I had known Mr. Mao for only a month, but he never struck me as a schemer or a cheat. He was in his mid-30's, with a head that swung lazily back and forth on his neck like the smoke that drifted from his Great Wall cigarettes. He wore an oversized suit, and blinked at me through slightly-crooked glasses. Effete, goofy, and innocuous, he seemed more Paris Hilton than Mao Zedong.

This impression was confirmed each time he gave me a ride in his Infiniti M. "I don't really know how to drive," he'd giggle as he ground the gears and dumped the car off curbs, swerved in front of oncoming buses and cabs, or weaved into crosswalks full of bicycles. One night, while driving together along Third Ring Road, Mr. Mao had leaned over to depress the cigarette lighter and sent the car banking at the same angle as his body. A cement truck weaved wildly to avoid us, missing the car by mere inches. "I really need to practice!" Mr. Mao yelled over the horns.

That car, as with the rest of Mr. Mao's lifestyle, was brand new. He had gotten rich, and gotten rich quick. But like the rest of his generation of Chinese Jay Gatsbys, the source of his wealth was murky.

I knew the money came from *English Yes!* I knew Mr. Mao charged nouveau riche parents in Beijing a handsome fee for access to his elite summer school, a school that offered a high-priced possibility of escape from China's corruption, pollution, and competition. And I knew Mr. Mao was selling hope – the hope of admissions into elite, ivy-covered American high schools. What I didn't know was *how* much he charged Beijing parents, or the particulars of the other "services" he offered them. These finer points were now becoming clear.

"We think this fee is reasonable," Mr. Mao continued, pushing his crooked glasses up his nose. "And you will be doing a great service for the students. They need someone with your qualifications to help them in this final stage of the application process."

The door to the Starbucks opened and a blast of scorching air cut through the room. Two well-dressed women stumbled in, folding up parasols. Parasol Woman Number One was wearing a white, slim fitting dress. Parasol Woman Number Two was in high heels, outrageously short shorts, and a shimmering blouse. Their clothing clung to their bodies. "I'm so hot I could die," one said to the other. Her companion mopped her brow with a purple handkerchief.

A faint whiff of expensive perfume mingled with the smell of coffee, offering the olfactory patina of 21st century Beijing. But these scents could not mask a more visceral and ubiquitous bouquet – my own stale sweat, and the reek of pollution and urine wafting in from the street.

Mr. Mao waited for his answer.

★

Working at *English Yes!* was the cushiest teaching job I had ever landed. In fact, Mr. Mao had hired me because, during the regular academic year, I worked at one such school in New

Hampshire. There, I taught six days a week, coached sports, advised students, and ran clubs. In Beijing, by contrast, I worked just two hours a day, yet I earned enough to live comfortably in a four-star hotel while nesting money away for an end-of-summer tour of Asia. Like any typical Beijinger with a good job, I felt blessed and didn't ask too many questions.

Mr. Mao set me up on the 18th floor of Building Number 8 of the Everbright Office Complex. 18th floor for 18 8th graders. Lots of 8's, a lucky number in Chinese numerology. It was not a coincidence.

"Mr. Mao thinks of everything," Yan Yan told me on the first day of classes. He was tall, earnest, and favored tracksuits, Puma sneakers, and any product made by Apple. He commuted four hours a day to get to the training school and back to his home on the outskirts of Beijing; his mother always accompanied him for the journey. During class, she waited in the lobby of the Everbright Office Complex while their driver waited in the family's BMW outside. When class ended, she would come up to the 18th floor, hand Yan Yan a bottle of cold milk, and whisk him away. Aware of China's lactose intolerance, I once asked her about the milk. "We want him to be the tallest boy in his class," she replied.

I spent the summer teaching Yan Yan and his classmates what it was like to learn in a "Western style classroom." It was a job I took very seriously, and a job I believed in. I knew the power of good teaching and good texts. I wanted my students to question their surroundings and think for themselves.

We had round-table discussions. We read Arthur Miller and Ralph Waldo Emerson. I asked the students to debate, to work in groups, to think independently and creatively. Yan Yan sat to the left of Amy and to the right of Yi Bo in the tight circle I created in our cramped room. We were all elbow-to-elbow at a flimsy plastic table. Mr. Mao had poured a small fortune into his slick education center, but there was no escaping the feeling that we were in a Potemkin village.

It was a village the students hoped to escape.

"I *must* leave China before ninth grade," Yi Bo told me with wide eyes. He was an energetic, overdeveloped 14-year-old with a bit of a mustache. He had chosen the English name Robot.

"I want to go to Saint Paul's School," he told me in a monotone that was befitting of his name.

"That's great!" I responded. "But why that particular school?"

"It is number one in America."

"Number one according to whom?"

He shrugged.

"You'll have to go to chapel every day."

He shrugged again, but I wouldn't let it go: "Saint Paul's is Episcopalian. Students there go to chapel four times a week. It's a Christian school."

"I don't care. I can believe whatever they want me to believe."

Emersonian, Robot was not. At times, this frustrated me. But I also marveled at his ability – typical of post-Maoist Chinese – to ignore all ideology and focus purely on the practical. If Episcopal prayer could get Robot out of China, he would engage in it. And if cheating on an essay helped, he would cheat. Today's morality and beliefs, he had learned, were merely tomorrow's forgotten shibboleths.

Amy picked up where Robot left off: "We need to leave because China's job situation is corrupt, and nothing is certain here." Amy wore her hair in a tight braid and rarely smiled. She was gaunt; a wisp of a girl. She often chewed on her lower lip, obliviously, or perhaps indifferently, leaving it cracked and bleeding. "In America, life is more honest and simple," she continued. "In America, you don't have to suffer."

Our classroom had thick curtains to blot out the sun, and we had a wall-mounted air conditioner. Nevertheless, the tiny room was stifling by the end of each of our two-hour sessions. Amy would scurry out after dismissal and get me a bottle of soda. She was kind, diligent, and as smart as any 8th grader I've met in my 15 years of teaching.

"You'll have many options, Amy," I assured her one afternoon as she handed me an ice-cold cola. I cracked it open and took a long sip. "Your English is fluent, and you have a lot of drive. American schools will be lucky to have you."

She shook her head. "I hope so. But it is difficult for us to compete."

"How is it difficult for you to compete?" I asked, nonplussed. "You're a fantastic student!"

"Exactly. Your schools discriminate against Chinese *because* we are much better test takers than you Americans. So it is not enough for us to be smart. We need something…more."

The something more was me. If *I* would cheat for Amy, she could escape corruption. If *I* would throw out my moral compass, she could head to America to find one. Or something like that.

Yan Yan and Amy left class that day together. Had we been back in the U.S., I might have guessed they were dating. I could imagine Yan Yan reaching over to hold Amy's hand, and Amy blushing. I could imagine them heading off to the mall together, or going to a movie. But this was Beijing. Yan Yan would be chauffeured home and spend the night cramming for the TOEFL. Amy would head off for a few more hours at yet another training school. These were hard working kids.

But hard work might not be enough anymore.

★

Mr. Mao waited for my answer as my mind continued to drift. What could I buy with $18,000? Could I live with myself if I took it? Would he pay me in cash? Could I even carry that much currency back to America? What would Customs say, let alone my conscience?

The baristas greeted the women with the parasols: "Huanying guanglin Xingbake! Welcome to Starbucks!" they cried simultaneously in Beijing-accented Mandarin. Their voices were crisp, but their bodies had the same slump I saw in Robot. Beijing weighed on a person. The summer heat was like a blanket; the crowds of people a constant bodily assault; the corruption palpable; and the pollution a death-sentence.

"Listen," I said, returning my attentions to Mr. Mao. "This is a generous offer. But it's cheating. We would never do this in America."

Mr. Mao smiled. His head drifted slowly back and forth, floating on his neck. "Our students have high test scores," he told me. "They are diligent. They deserve a chance."

"But if I write their essays, they have an unfair advantage."

"I disagree. Your American students get admitted to elite schools because they are alumni, or because they play sports well, or because they have a 'connection.' *English Yes!* knows exactly how it works there."

"The system might not be fair," I responded, "but if I write these essays, it sends the wrong message. It tells the kids that cheating is ok."

Mr. Mao laughed. "Really, Mike, you know they work harder than American students. But if you don't help them, they don't have a chance."

We stared at each other for a beat before Mr. Mao took a deep breath and looked slowly around the Starbucks. Eventually, he spoke, but as if to himself: "Think of Yan Yan. His father was a peasant 20 years ago. Now he has enough money to help his son escape from China. He was at Tiananmen Square, you know, during the disturbances. Doesn't Yan Yan deserve a chance?"

Yan Yan did deserve a chance. But a chance at what? A chance at living an honest life, with honest role models? A chance to escape China? The two possibilities seemed mutually exclusive. For the rich in Beijing, life offered a thin layer of hope wrapped around a rotten core. Perfume masked urine; expensive training schools were filled with cheap plastic tables...

And the only way to get to an honest place was to cheat your way into it.

I recalled what Yan Yan had written about his father's political activities in a homework assignment I had given a few weeks earlier.

Do I think my father is a hero? Yes, but not because he was at the disturbances of 1989, but because he escaped from them and made a life for his family. But this is very difficult in China. There is so much competition and corruption. I am always confused. I think my life will be clearer in America.

"Consider my offer," Mr. Mao concluded. "If it is not you writing the essay, it will be someone else. But it should be you who gives them this chance. Isn't that what every teacher hopes to do?"

EAST OF NOWHERE, SOUTH OF HEAVEN

Alan Paul

Alan Paul is the author of "Big in China: My Unlikely Adventures Raising a Family, Playing the Blues, and Becoming a Star in Beijing." A film based on the story of Paul's Chinese blues band, Woodie Alan, is being developed by director/producer Ivan Reitman. Paul wrote the award-winning "The Expat Life" column for WSJ.com from 2005-09 and also reported from Beijing for NBC, the *Wall Street Journal* and others. Paul's book, "One Way Out: An Oral History of the Allman Brothers Band", will be released in 2014.

"DEAD YAK!" MY 6-YEAR-OLD son Eli was screaming, his eyes wide with fear. My arms were in his pits, his hands gripping my forearms as he squatted to relieve himself. We were miles above sea level, in cold, thin air, surrounded by soaring Himalayan peaks in the remote reaches of Western Sichuan.

Having passed countless yaks over the past few days, but none for many hours, I was sure he was having some kind of childish hallucination, maybe caused by hours in a bus chugging up a crumbling, under-construction road filled with nervous adults pretending everything was just fine.

"*Shhh,*" I counseled. "Just do your thing."

"There he is!" he screamed again, turning to point behind him. Indeed, a rotting corpse lay about 10 feet down a steep embankment, big brown yak eyes open and staring straight ahead...at us.

"I don't have to go anymore." Eli pulled up his pants and

ran frightened back onto the bus. I stood and stared at the yak, making sure I wasn't hallucinating myself. I already felt wracked with guilt for dragging my family, including not only my three kids – aged three, six and nine – but also my in-laws *and* my wife's great aunt and sister, on what was fast turning into a wild-ass trip.

Back on the bus we had hired for this family excursion, I spied my wife Rebecca typing away on her Blackberry. I was equally astounded that she was thinking about work and that she could send and receive messages from east of nowhere and south of heaven. The situation summed up something about China, where cell service never died, but roads sometimes did.

"Becky," I said leaning over her seat, my voice low. "How can you be working at a time like this?"

She raised her eyebrows, but not her eyes, which were still on her little handheld screen. "I'm sending information to the office about where we are and telling them if they don't hear from me for a half an hour to notify the American consulate in Chengdu."

She was, not atypically, a step or two ahead of me. I wished I could have said she was overreacting.

★

I had always wanted my family of five to have genuine China experiences, to see how the rest of the country lived outside the boom town metropolises of Beijing and Shanghai. We took regular trips into the country's vast, beautiful, often primitive and unregulated interior. I loved these journeys and thought they were important for the kids – a crucial antidote to the expat bubble in which we lived in Beijing for the past two years, where our home was inside a walled compound. In fact, we didn't have a choice about where we lived (the Wall Street Journal employed my wife and owned the home) and while it had some real advantages, we worried about our children becoming the expat equivalent of "fu er dai," spoiled, sheltered children – a syndrome that was currently infecting vast swaths of modern Chinese households.

As a balance, we explored parts of Beijing that some of our bubble neighbors never bothered with, and, whenever we could, headed to different provinces, especially in the poorer, minority-dominated Southwest. The problem was, when you go off the beaten track in China, you can hit deep weeds pretty quickly, and it's not hard to fall off the road altogether.

The unknown can be frightening in a society that lacks minimal safety standards. In Beijing, I saw window washers dangling from skyscrapers by a single rope, pedestrians strolling blithely by open manholes, and men welding without masks. As such, we always tried to control what we could (the kids wore bike helmets despite such things being a rare sight here in the bicycle capital of China) and made do with what we couldn't (there was often no choice but to pile the whole family into a seatbelt-less cab).

All of those considerations seemed silly now. How could I square worrying about bike helmets or seatbelts with dragging my extended family on a trip like this? This five-day journey through Sichuan's "wild west" Tibetan region was consistently beautiful and fascinating, but also difficult and often dangerous, culminating in this endless bus ride on a half-built, high-altitude road with no guard rails in the dark of night.

★

We had woken up that morning in a tiny hotel in Dongba, a primitive town in a gorgeous valley hard by the banks of a raging river, and then driven upstream to visit the home of a Tibetan friend of our guide. It was a lovely, leisurely morning that concluded in a small town which was to be the last stop before we climbed up and over an almost 15,000-foot pass to the Wolong Panda Reserve. We walked into a small restaurant and saw a gaggle of grandparents and their runny-nosed progeny sitting on a couch watching TV in a small back anteroom. We said hello; they gawked back in stunned silence.

It quickly became clear that the kids wouldn't be eating much. "Chicken feet...again," 9-year-old Jacob huffed. Instead, he turned his attentions to a plate of watermelon and cantaloupe. It was the kind of finicky eating we had gotten used to on these trips, even as the kids were unconsciously expanding their palettes. At one muddy, outdoor barbecue joint in rural Guizhou, picky Jacob had turned from a veritable vegetarian into an ardent carnivore at the enticement of some local kids with whom he caught "harmonious" river crabs and skipped rocks. But on this day, with only chicken feet to be had, Jacob would stick with fruit and white rice.

Strolling through that dusty little town, I watched the faces of the old Tibetan women in their traditional blue smocks and headdresses light up when they saw my three blue-eyed, curly-haired moptops. The kids' presence in such places opened a lot of doors for us, drawing people to our family, inviting us to join them for meals or take tea. The friendly exchanges often began with a request to take a photo with our children, but sometimes dissolved into pure chaos as more and more strangers crowded around jostling for a picture, or even just a glimpse of the "xiao laowai," "little foreigners." Many people, both Chinese and foreigners, have remarked that they couldn't imagine taking such journeys with young children, but we found these experiences enlightening for all of us.

Chris, our English-speaking guide and a Sichuan local, said we had "about three more hours" before we reached Wolong, including about 10 clicks on a bumpy road. We piled onto the bus in a jovial mood. Just outside of town, we started ascending a twisty mountain road mangled by construction and reduced to one lane – but still hosting two-way traffic. With no flagman, our driver, the calm and competent Wang, had to keep his eyes locked ahead, ready to pull over in an instant. I asked Chris if this was the "bumpy" road he had mentioned and he nodded yes, though nothing in his manner was affirmative.

At one point, Driver Wang pulled up side-by-side with a passing bus and, in a Sichuan dialect, had a long, friendly conversation with the other driver.

"The road is like this all the way," Chris translated for us after some prodding. He was giggling, not out of glee but out of nervousness, as the Chinese have the habit of doing.

My heart sank but we pushed on, slowly gaining elevation. We passed thousands of migrant workers and had to stop frequently for various hindrances: the tractor blocking the road, with just three workers shoveling sand and unwilling to move until the wagon was full…the idiotic car that drove into a ditch backing away from us, necessitating an hour-long delay while said workers watched us try to lift the car, none offering to help without significant payment.

Anna spent hours watching Dora DVDs (I defy Dora and her trusty Map to explore Sichuan), while Jacob and Eli were happy that we were giving them total Gameboy freedom; the same electronic distractions which had driven us crazy when the boys wanted to stay on the bus at Buddhist temples and scenic overlooks were now a welcome alternative to the bored restlessness and tantrums that might have been.

"When we get back to Beijing, I'm going to sneak into school and rip up all the workbooks for all the kids, who will thank me," Eli suddenly exclaimed.

He was in a British Montessori school and the daily workbooks drove him insane. I tried to explain how he was learning, and reminded him that he usually loved school, but Eli just sighed and said, "You just don't understand life, dad."

"Some of the kids would be mad at you, Eli," Jacob countered in my defense.

"No!" Eli insisted, then: "Really? Why?"

"Well, literacy is the hardest subject in my class and a lot of kids hate it – but I love it."

Jacob was admirably trying to make Eli see that not everyone would feel the same as him, but Eli took it more liberally.

"I'm not you, Jacob," he pouted.

It was time for dad to step back in. "Eli, you're different, of course," I said. "Everyone's different, especially at an international school in the capital of China with kids from 40 countries. That's what Jacob's trying to say. Some kids might thank you for liberating them from literacy, but some might actually *like* the workbooks. And even though everyone's different, you and Jacob and Anna are more alike than anyone."

"Our BNA is almost the same, Eli," affirmed Jacob.

"It's DNA," I corrected. "But yes."

Eli stubbornly shook his said. "You're nothing like us, dad. You're totally different."

"Why?"

"Number one, you're forty! And number two, you're bald."

Eli looked at me cock-eyed when I burst out laughing, grateful for this sweet distraction.

Our bus pushed forward, our guide reassuring us "we're almost there," the same mantra we had been hearing for hours, until coming to a halt at a cement barrier blocking the road – all the more maddening because just behind it laid a newly paved section. Instead of gliding onto it, we were forced to slowly drop two feet to the left onto a rubble-strewn lane. There was a precipitous drop off to our right. My chest tightened.

We finally reached the snowy summit of Four Girls Mountain and asked Driver Wang to let us out to stretch our legs a bit. The four majestic peaks, reaching over 20,000 feet, loomed above us. I hoisted Anna onto my shoulders, while Rebecca trailed, holding Eli and Jacob's hands. Together we gazed out over corkscrew switchbacks cut through a barren, rocky landscape stretching to the horizon. It was simultaneously awesome and insane to be in this spot as a family, though, for a flicker of an instant, the lone explorer in me longed to be out there alone with just a 4x4.

★

As darkness fell, we no longer saw road workers, only the glow of their large white tents that we passed every few hundred yards. I imagined them on the other side of those tents, smoking cheap cigarettes, drinking erguotou – and cursing that rich foreigner who refused to pay them to help lift a car out of a ditch.

By now, the battery for every electric device we had was dead. Anna was asleep with her head in Rebecca's lap. Eli was making up horrible horror stories with his grandpa Hal, while Jacob and Grandma Ruth made up a new game, "Sichuan Yahtzee," allowing the bangs and bumps of the road to roll the dice. When Anna awoke and started bawling, Grandma Ruth improvised marvelous riffs on traditional fairy tales, mercifully keeping the kids entertained for hours while I lapsed into a fog of anxiety.

"Dad," Jacob suddenly yelled from up front, "Who was the seventh dwarf again? We've got Grumpy, Sneezy, Happy, Doc, Sleepy and Dopey."

"How could you forget Farty?"

It was at nine o'clock that night when we burst into cheer at the sight of a sign that read, in English and Chinese, "Welcome to Wolong, Home of the Pandas" – but we were not at the hotel yet. We were still on a rubble pile and the road in front of us was a gaping hole.

As I stood there bitterly looking down into that hole, silently damning New China's incessant construction, I felt my face growing warm and wet. It was blood gushing from my nose. The dust, dryness, altitude – and stress – had gotten the best of me. I pressed a towel to my face as Wang spoke to some scurrying workers.

"Only one driver for machine," Chris said, indicating the huge backhoe sitting by the side of the hole, "and he's eating, or sleeping. They trying to get him. His name is Lu."

Based on past responses from the roadside workers I was not brimming with optimism. But within minutes, someone *did* emerge from a tent and, waving at the bus full of foreigners, climbed aboard the backhoe and began furiously filling in the crater. My favorite childhood book, *Mike Mulligan and the Steam Shovel*, came to mind…except now Mike was a migrant Chinese named Lu with a cigarette dangling from his mouth. As Lu put the last load in and patted it down, we cheered and waved back at him.

"Good news!" Chris exclaimed as our bus rumbled into gear. "I called hotel and they agreed to keep hot water on whole extra hour so you can take shower!" He seemed surprised that we weren't more enthusiastic.

We finally arrived at our hotel at half past 10. Some of the in-laws went to eat at the hotel restaurant, which had stayed open late for us, but all I wanted was a beer. After the kids showered and went to bed, I filled a tub and grabbed two giant bottles of room-temperature Tsingtao. I sat in the tepid, graying water sipping tepid beer and entering a buzzy bliss. Listening to my kids deeply breathe in a well deserved sleep, I reflected on our day. The "three-hour drive" had taken nine-and-a-half; the "bumpy road" was really a calamity of construction; our guide had been too petrified of losing face to forewarn us of the truth; our hotel thought they were doing us a favor by giving us hot water…

And yet, there was no place I would have rather been.

★

About a week later, over dumplings at our Beijing kitchen table, I asked Jacob if he had been scared on that endless bus ride.

"A little."

"Why? What were you scared of?"

"Bus very wide. Road very narrow. Road very high."

"Ah yes," I said. ""But what were you actually scared of?"

He looked me right in the eye and illustrated a bus falling off a cliff, his right hand raising high into the sky and then turning to plummet through the air. I took a bite of dumpling and smiled.

STATING THE OBVIOUS

Michael Meyer

Michael Meyer authored the book "The Last Days of Old Beijing: Life in the Vanishing Backstreets of a City Transformed." His writings have appeared in *The New York Times* and *Time Magazine*, among other outlets. He received the Whiting Writers Award, and a Guggenheim Fellowship. His next book, "In Manchuria: Life on a Rice Farm in China's Northeast", is due out in 2013. He teaches English at the University of Pittsburgh and literary journalism at the University of Hong Kong.

BEIJING APPEARED. BEIJING VANISHED in a brown cloud. Beijing reappeared. Beijing vanished in a brown cloud. Things were as they had been: for three thousand years, the city churned through a cycle of Made, Disassembled, and Rebuilt.

The airplane banked. Through the window I caught another glimpse of the green screen of mountains, the open curtain of cropland, and a smudge on the horizon. I looked for a skyline. I saw only haze. We glided over a thin strip of concrete. A tractor rolled through the gauntlet of trees lining both sides. They were the only trees in sight, and they were all the same height, standing in two rows that receded into the smudge.

At the arrivals gate, a man with salt-and-pepper hair and glasses held a sign with my name. Mac ("as in Macintosh") was my assigned host. He was a local. I reacted accordingly, going through the routine I'd perfected the past two years as a Peace Corps volunteer in the countryside: fawning over the introduction, saying I'd heard so much about him, how nice it was to meet at last, how hard he must work as the school's business manager, so sorry for troubling him for having to fetch me, and, oh, had he eaten?

Mac's mouth became a bemused, tight-lipped bend. It was the look one made when fending off an excited dog, wondering what sort of person raised it, and how to get away.

I kept yelping. "What's your Chinese name? Don't worry, I'll be able to pronounce it. I've spent two years in Sichuan!"

Departing the airport, we merged onto the billboard-lined expressway and into a swarm of Santanas. Nothing looked Chinese.

"Where's Tiananmen?" I wondered. "Are we going past it?"

Mac waved out the windshield at the brown cloud. "We're going a different direction."

"But I was told our school was near everything."

"It's near many things. It's near the Summer Palace, the Old Summer Palace, Peking University, Qinghua University." He saw my face fall. "Trust me, the air is much better out there."

I sat meekly in the sedan, which slowed – but never actually stopped – for the horizontal stoplights, and stared out the window at people flying kites from the patches of grass between flyovers. In the sodium-white sky, they bobbed amidst the ocean of open pits and bamboo scaffolding and swirling dust. Neon signs flashed from the side of the road: *Asian Games Village, Meat Pie King*. A sign pointed to the Great Wall Expressway. Around us rumbled blue Liberation trucks, loaded down with sand, oil drums and migrant laborers clutching shovels.

I had arrived on a drafting table, not a city. Here, airport, here cropland, *here* – running graphite along the edge of a ruler – the highway into town, here the city itself, at the heart, the Forbidden City and Tiananmen. Around *that* the city wall. Don't want a wall? All right, let's erase it. There! A ring road in its place. The Second Ring Road. These X's mark the old gates. They'll be intersections! And *here* – the hollow hiss of sharp pencil on paper – a *Third* Ring Road. Why stop there? Let's make a Fourth. One day a Fifth! Now, we'll need some axis roads in between – the cutting echo of the pencil's point – we'll get rid of all this *old* stuff. Say, how about a subway?

The car kept going. I grew nervous. It seemed awfully far. "Last road," Mac assured me. We hung a right and faced a well-lit, four-lane boulevard, divided by a median planted with grass.

"This is Shangdi," Mac announced.

"Like God's place?"

For the first time he laughed. "It sounds like it, but it's not the same Shangdi. It's the High Technology and Information Zone. The tourist bureau says the moon above Beijing shines brighter because of the signals beaming from here. You can see the stars."

There were no people. There were no stoplights. There were no vehicles. It looked like a canvas, not a neighborhood.

Mac stomped his foot, activating the stairwell light, and deposited me in my contractually provided home: two eight-foot-by-eight rooms. I brushed away a mound of sand from the window sill. The grains spilled atop an empty bookshelf, then onto the bare concrete floor. In the refrigerator I found pickled radishes, cans of Tsingtao beer, and a brick of fresh tofu. The glass-enclosed patio held two clotheslines and more mounds of sand.

A map of Beijing hung on the door. My eyes began at its center, the Forbidden City, followed the blue ovals that were its bordering lakes, and moved diagonally to the broad patch of green and blue in its top left corner, the old and new Summer Palaces. The diagram's uppermost northwest corner ended at the Qinghe River. I was off the map and in a tiny concrete box.

The humid August night affixed me to the bed sheets. I opened the patio door and its windows. A thin coating of sand covered the concrete I had swept just two hours before. Beijing was being swallowed by an encroaching desert.

I lay on the bed, regretting the decision to come.

★

Sunbeams seared the bed at five in the morning. Then I heard the sound, Beijing's rhapsody-in-do: the thunk-thunk-thunk of sledgehammers, the tinking of chisels, the rumble of trucks. I swept away the fresh-fallen sand from the sill and leaned out a patio window. Below, groups of grannies in sleeveless shirts sat gabbing on stoops, a child attempted to ride a training-wheeled bike, and a garbage collector in a white surgeon's mask pedaled a flat-bed tri-wheeler.

I laced up my skates and wheeled to Shangdi's welcome arch. A woman called, "Butian, buyao qian! If it's not sweet, I don't want money!" Muddy oranges and apples piled atop her cart. She watered the fruit, sluicing off the dust that continually coated it.

On the corner, mirrored in the ice-blue windows of the vacant New Technology Center, a spry elderly man fluidly stabbed at his reflection with a tai qi sword. Three teenage girls sat in his shadow, fumbling with their own rollerblades. Unlike in the provinces, here no one called me laowai, nobody shouted a three-octave H-ell-O!

I pushed onto the boulevard. Its new, hard asphalt was ice-slick, and created a speed that helped keep my pace with the one empty bus clattering alongside me. A maze of dirt-lane hutong led to siheyuan, four-sided courtyard homes. I passed a park where a man stooped to chat with a pair of ducks in the pond. The sky was open and blue. The bus driver invited me to grab his bumper, and I let him pull me along, stopping at a market below the elevated Great Wall expressway.

I bought some breakfast and chatted with the vendor, a stout jolly man with white, cropped hair to match his threadbare tank top. "You talk like a Sichuan person!" he laughed. "This is Beijing. We speak the nation's Chinese here."

A row of blue trucks rumbled through the construction's clamor. It was only 6:35 in the morning.

"I studied English in middle school," the vendor continued, switching into a staccato voice. "Gah-ud morn-neen tea-ah-che!

"Tea-ah-cher. Tea-cher?" He lapsed back into Chinese. "Why did my English teacher say 'tea-ah-che'? She was from Sichuan. Sichuan people can't talk."

In dialect, I spat, "Fuck you looking at, moron?"

The man's belly rippled from laughter. "Very good! You sound just like a true Sichuan person." He refilled my bowl with soymilk. "You know, Sichuan people call shoes 'children.' Ridiculous! You like douzhi? What's douzhi? It's what Beijing people drink. I'll get you a glass. Sichuan people don't drink it."

As I sipped on the green bean juice, I understood why. A chicken foot tasted better than the dreggy liquid. At my asking, the man pointed me towards Tiananmen Square. All I had to do was follow the traffic and aim for the smudge in the distance. I weaved between rows of red taxis; it would have been faster to skate along their rooftops.

When the traffic began hugging the curb, I moved to the paved-stone sidewalks, ducking underneath shuttlecocks flying between racquets in a morning round of elderly-people's exercises. They were the least of my worries; drivers fed up with the congestion jumped the queue, and onto the curb, to reach an intersection via sidewalk. The badminton players and I scattered out of the way like startled pigeons.

In a decade of skating, I'd never fallen and didn't wear a helmet. After two hours in Beijing, I'd stumbled through a pile of manure, over a crate of smashed beer bottles, and off a bumper of a swerving miandi. Then I fell, windmilling onto the grass median between the traffic and bike lanes. I looked back to see what got me. I'd never seen road kill in China; there wasn't anything left to run over. Yet there it was, an unfortunate buttermilk snake, stretched flat in the morning light. I looked closer: an unrolled condom.

At the Jishuitan subway stop, I turned east and then south at the Arrow Tower by Deshengmen Bridge, into a back-alley maze of traditional hutong and the West Lake. From here it was a placid, car-free skate along the lake chain – Back Lake, Front

Lake, North Lake – towards the white dagoba that poked above the tree line in Beihai (North Sea) Park. The Forbidden City's high red walls glowed in the morning sun. The air changed to heavy and wet.

"Tiananmen Square, which all people of nationalities of China yearn for," announced the sign. I clunked down stairs, under Chang'an Jie, Eternal Peace Avenue, and back up the other side. It was the only way to enter the area. The tunnels were an effective way to limit access to the square. The sign warned, in Chinese and English, that Tiananmen Square must be kept "solemn, silent, clean and in good order." To these ends, a few activities were prohibited:

Parade, assembly, speech, writing, distributing, posting, hanging and spreading of words and propaganda materials.

Picture-taking and kite-flying weren't on the list. Nor was skating. So I pushed off, excited to race across the world's largest plaza, over eight football fields long and five across. The wheels barely got going before hitting a divot between paving stones. I lifted up and tried again. Nothing. The spaces between stones were wide and deep.

Across Eternal Peace Avenue, Chairman Mao's portrait stared. As did the crowds of tourists moving past, cat-calling "laowai!" and "H-ell-O!" in southern accents. Locals didn't hang out in the square.

An old man renting kites pointed to the sun. "Too hot."

I liked that; an introduction to the Beijing conversation opener of stating of the obvious. I nodded and sat down to write in my journal, breaking one of the posted rules. A shadow fell across the page. I looked up at a middle-aged man in a yellow mesh baseball cap.

"You are writing."

"I am writing," I echoed.

"What are you writing?"

"Words."

"See them?" The man pointed to a group of young men milling about. "Bianyi. Be a little careful," he warned, pulling at his clothing.

The men he'd pointed to looked exactly alike. Each had a crew cut, a nondescript face, a short-sleeved white collar shirt tucked into tan slacks, and thick-soled black shoes. Each carried a rolled-up newspaper. Every now and then one would talk to it, hold it to his ear, then speak to it again. A man who looked exactly like him would approach, point to someone, then saunter in that direction.

I dug out my small red Chinese dictionary to look up bianyi. I guessed yi was part of yifu, clothing, since the man had tugged at his shirt. Bian had several homophones. I settled on "ordinary and everyday." Ordinary clothes. Plain clothes! It was the second word Beijing taught me, after douzhi. I turned to the man renting kites and pointed at the look-alike men. "Bianyi?"

He nodded. The point of wearing plain clothes was to be surreptitious, to infiltrate by stealth, and these guys were pros. A bianyi would spot a gathering of more than four people. He'd sidle up to it. The group would finish snapping grandpa in front of Chairman Mao's portrait and wander off towards the Monument to the People's Heroes. The bianyi spoke into his newspaper. A different bianyi canted behind them. The tourists asked him to move out of the way of their photograph.

★

By nine o'clock, it was too hot to remain in the square. I rolled along the sidewalk that bordered the Forbidden City's southern wall. People stretched out on stone benches. I went to sit on one when a man fussed, "Wait wait wait!" He unrolled a *People's Daily* and draped a page over the stone. "Sit on that, it's cleaner."

The man stood beside a homemade cart of two bicycle tires, a platform, and a rusty oil drum that spilled a sweet aroma.

"Hongshu," he announced. I shook my head. I didn't understand. He fished with tongs and produced a roasted yam, wrapping it in a square of newspaper. He mimed peeling back the skin and taking a bite.

How much did I owe? He took it back and weighed it on a hand-held scale, the same kind my postman had used in Sichuan. Two yuan. I bought another, and a cob of roasted corn from the vendor beside him. Traffic hummed behind the trees that shielded us from Chang'an Jie. Another man, walking in relief against the red wall, pitched ices. "Yi kuai yi ge'r, yi kuai yi ge'r! One for a yuan. He called out loud and quick, his Beijing 'r' as thick and chewy as the yam.

I rolled its steaming, sweet pulp from one side of my mouth to the other, too involved in not burning my tongue to notice the shadow and breeze that crept over rooftops and down the hutong. Above us, The Hand surveyed the current lines and turned its pencil on end. *Erase.* The instinct overruled nostalgia, aesthetics, tradition. *Erase.* It looked down on the avenue toward Xidan – over the closeness of the crowd, the cluttered storefronts. *Erase.* The lines came quickly, and straight. Here a bank, here an office tower, here an underground shopping mall, here a widened intersection, nowhere shade. Disperse, separate, shunt everyone inside to air-conditioned sameness. *Erase.* After the lines became concrete, a person could sit at the Dairy Queen outside Book Mansion, look up, and have no idea what city he was in. They all looked so alike nowadays. Or did Beijing always look like this? It was so hard to remember.

Around us, indifferent men and women sprawled on the benches atop *People's Daily*, smearing yesterday's events with today's sweat. A drowsy male voice asked for the time. "Ten minutes to ten."

Down in Sichuan, outside my old apartment, the campus vegetable market was packing up. The dough sticks and soymilk got tossed in the slop bucket, and dollops of pork and onions went into lunchtime dumplings. "Building Socialism," the college's first class, let out. A pinched voice was ringing from the loudspeaker, reading the day's headlines from "our nation's glorious capital, Beijing."

Now I lived here, where the news was made.

Paying Tuition

Matthew Polly

Matthew Polly is the author of "American Shaolin" and "Tapped Out." A Princeton University graduate and Rhodes Scholar, he spent two years studying kung fu at the Shaolin Temple in Henan, China and his writings have appeared in *The Washington Post, Esquire, The Nation*, and numerous others. He is currently working on a biography of Bruce Lee for Penguin Books. He lives in New Haven, Connecticut.

"THERE IS NOTHING MORE useless than a poor laowai," said Leader Liu, the Chinese Communist Party official in charge of the school I attended.

Since I was the only foreigner within 500 miles *and* I was going broke, I was pretty sure he was talking about me. I was a student at the Shaolin Kung Fu Center, which was built by the Henan provincial government next to the famed Shaolin Temple, the birthplace of kung fu. My teachers were monks who broke bricks and boards with every part of their bodies. I trained seven hours a day, "eating bitterness" (chi ku) while suffering daily beatings at the monk's calloused hands and feet.

It was brutal, awesome, and surprisingly expensive.

I had arrived at the Shaolin Temple expecting the windswept monastery from the 1970s American television series *Kung Fu*, starring David Carradine. What I discovered instead was a tacky tourist trap. The government had turned the venerable, 1,500-year-old village into a Kung Fu World, a low-rent version of an Epcot Center pavilion. At the Shaolin Kung Fu Center, the monks gave daily performances of their martial skills to the throngs of tourists. After watching a particularly breathtaking display of talent far superior to anything in a Hong Kong flick, I inquired about becoming a student and was led to a back room.

Leader Liu, wearing not an orange monk's robe but a grey suit, white silk socks and plastic dress shoes, smiled greedily at my interest and told me what was required to become a student of the modern Shaolin Temple: $1,300 per month for room, board, and tuition. I exhaled deeply (that was almost all the money I had on me), signed over thirteen $100 American Express Travelers Cheques, and began my training as Shaolin's very first American disciple.

★

After three months at Shaolin, I was running dangerously low on funds and realized that, at my current burn rate, I'd never make it to through a full year of training, which had been my goal. Confessing my situation to one of my monk instructors with whom I'd built up some guanxi, relationship, he basically told me that $1,300 per month was the Sucker Laowai Price.

I should explain here that there are no fixed prices in China. It all depends on who you are and how strong your guanxi is with the other party. There is the Chinese friend price (deep guanxi), the Chinese friend-of-friend price (shallow guanxi), the Chinese stranger price (no guanxi), the smart laowai price (he knows what the real Chinese price is), and the sucker laowai price (usually 100-200 percent higher than the smart laowai price).

It took seven days of bitter negotiations with the school's communist leaders – during which I pled poverty and thus earned Leader Liu's epithet as a "useless foreigner" – to bring down my monthly fee to the Smart Laowai Price of $550.

Even at the reduced rate it was still going to be tight, and being called useless had stung my pride. I decided I needed to start earning. But how? My only marketable skill was the ability to speak English, but none of the monks could afford to pay for lessons. Imports were a non-starter; China is the world's factory and has little need for (nor can it afford) most things made in the West. So, like many other aspiring Western entrepreneurs, I focused on China's burgeoning, dirt-cheap manufacturing industry. Exports would be my salvation.

After years of performing for local crowds, the Shaolin monks had begun to take their act on the road, touring in Japan, America, and Europe. To enhance their subsistence-level government wages ($30 per month), the monks had begun to pack their suitcases with kung fu tchotchkes to resell on their trips. A $12 Shaolin sword would go for $100 in Tokyo, and a monk only needed to sell four to double his annual income.

I settled on t-shirts. One of the most popular tourist items was a series of shirts with hand-painted images of the Shaolin monks in kung fu poses. They retailed for $3 a piece at Shaolin, and I figured I could get them wholesale for $2. Crappy concert tees in America sold for $20. These were *hand-painted*! I was certain they would fly off the shelf. So my only question was: How many to buy?

This is where I made my first big mistake. Instead of estimating how many t-shirts I could reasonably expect to sell, I calculated how much money I wanted to make, and worked backwards from there. With tuition and plane tickets, I calculated that a year in China was going to run me fifteen grand. If I sold 1,000 shirts, I could cover all my expenses with several thousand to spare.

I looked down at lucky number 18,000 on my notepad and saw that it was good. It made my heart swell and my head spin. I could afford to travel around the country. I could slip a little extra money to my teachers. Leader Liu would be forced to give me face. And I could prove to my father that dropping out of college to run away to the Shaolin Temple hadn't been completely foolhardy.

But then I started fantasizing. If one bird in the bush was this beautiful, how much better would two birds be? $18,000 was okay, but not nearly as good as $36,000. All I needed to do was sell 2,000 t-shirts.

How hard could that be?

★

Within two days of mentioning to one of my teachers that I was interested in buying 1,000 hand-painted Shaolin shirts, a local factory owner, Mr. Chen, was at my hotel room. As lethargic and inefficient as China's state-run industry is, its private businessmen are the polar opposite. It was as if Mao had cast a 40-year spell over the country, putting its merchant sensibility to sleep, only to have its people's innate industriousness wake up all at once.

One of the first things I had learned during my stay was that the Chinese love to negotiate. They love it so much that even after an agreement is reached they'll often reopen negotiations just so they can do it all over again. Americans, on the other hand, love making deals and view negotiating as a necessary evil; a means to an end. The Chinese know this about Americans, which is why they like to string out negotiations, thereby frustrating their American counterparts, to get a better deal for themselves. Fortified with this knowledge, I was intent on giving the impression of infinite patience.

"Come in, come in, come in, Mr. Chen," I said in Mandarin. "I am honored to meet you. My teachers tell me what a successful businessman you are."

"Where? Where? Where?" he replied repeatedly, the Chinese manner of politely brushing away flattery.

In preparation for Mr. Chen's arrival, I had laid out a pot of tea, a bottle of Chinese booze, a pack of cigarettes and other customary sundries with which to entice him.

"Here, here, here, take a cigarette," I offered. "They are Marlboro, an American brand."

"Ah, ah, ah! Take, take, take one of mine," he said as he

grabbed my cigarette with his left hand while flipping open his own pack with his right. "They are 555, a British brand."

Having successfully navigated the Exchange of Cigarettes introductory ritual (while also establishing we were not the kind of riff-raff who smoked cheap Chinese cigarettes), we moved to the Toasting Phase. I poured some baijiu, the Chinese rice liquor that tastes and affects the digestive system like Liquid Drano, into two thimble-sized shot glasses.

"Empty cup," I announced, knocking back the rotgut.

I poured us each another shot.

"No, no, no," he whined. "My stomach is tender. One is enough."

"Oh no, you can't drink just one," I smiled. "You know the saying, 'A man cannot walk on one leg.'"

Mr. Chen's eyes lit up. "You are a China expert!"

"Where? Where? Where?" I replied, politely brushing away his flattery.

We settled down and shifted to small talk. I asked him about his factory. He asked after the health of my parents. The point of this part of the game was to see who could go the longest without bringing up the business at hand. He was the first to blink.

"So I have heard said that you want to buy a thousand tee-shirts."

"Well that depends on the price," I said.

"You know they are $3."

"That's the price the merchants sell them for. I want the price you sell to them."

"$2.50," he countered.

"You are joking, right? I hear they buy them from you for $1."

"Who speaks such fart words?" he asked, feigning indignation. "Tell me his name and I'll strangle him to death."

"Everyone tells me this," I said, fibbing. The merchant I had bribed (for $30) had told me the wholesale price was $2.

"Because you are my new American friend, maybe I could give them to you for $2.25."

37

"You are too kind," I replied. "And because you are my new *Chinese* friend, I could pay $1.10."

"Impossible," he scoffed. "I would lose money on each one. It would be like you snuck into my house and stole from me. $2.15."

"I'm buying 1,000 shirts. You will save money by making and shipping them all at once instead of a handful to this merchant and a handful to that one. $1.15."

And so it went for the next five hours. I was aiming for $1.50. He didn't want to drop much below $2. At various impasses I would pour us each two shots of baijiu. The rural Chinese in Henan Province mixed alcohol and business like you wouldn't believe. Perhaps as a result, they also had a charming nationalistic blind spot: they honestly believed they could out-drink everyone else on the planet. As an Irish-American who outweighed them by 50 pounds, I had come to find this both amusing and useful.

By the time Mr. Chen reached $1.75, his face was beet red. I was at $1.30 and still mostly in control of my faculties, but starting to slip over the edge. It was time to drop my final card.

"What if I buy *two-thousand* t-shirts?" I asked. "Is your factory capable of handling such a large order?"

The implied insult sobered up Mr. Chen, as did the possibility of doubling his gross profits. Very quickly we settled at $1.50 and shook hands. He left and I collapsed on my bed, feeling triumphant until the room started spinning.

★

A single t-shirt is so lightweight and, when folded, so compact. 2,000 t-shirts...not so much. This was the horrifying realization that came crashing down upon me two weeks later when Mr. Chen and four workers carried in box after massive cardboard box of hand-painted Shaolin shirts – 35 boxes in total that filled a third of my room. I should have balked. I should have reopened negotiations. But I still believed the situation was salvageable.

As I mentally hesitated, I opened several boxes at random to pull out the shirts at the top to check their quality.

"You see, they are good," Mr. Chen grinned, a tell-tale giveaway in China of nervousness.

But I could see nothing wrong with them. I put the t-shirts back in the boxes and pulled out $3,000 cash. We shook hands again. He left. I collapsed on my bed and the room started spinning, even though I'd had nothing to drink.

Crisis management time. Clearly 2,000 shirts were too many for me to personally carry on one of the monks' international tours. But each tour was usually 25-people strong: 18 performing monks, three or four leaders from the school, one translator, and the remaining spots reserved for regional Communist Party officials with whom the school needed to curry favor. If I could convince a dozen or so of the monks to carry a suitcase filled with t-shirts, then I'd be back in business. Of course, I'd need to pay them upfront or cut them in on the backend, but with $36,000 in expected profit I could afford to be generous.

The following Saturday when my training ended, I hired a minivan to take me to Zheng Zhou, the capital of Henan Province, for $100. After the three-hour ride that nearly ended several times in a tragic multi-car accident, I walked into the city's first ever multi-story department store, filled with peasants, many of whom were dumbfounded by the array of consumer goods on display, and found the floor that sold suitcases.

"How many of the extra-large ones do you have?" I asked one of the young women working there. The appearance of a 6'3" foreigner wearing a PLA-style winter coat and speaking Chinese with a slight Beijing accent blew her mind. She gasped, covered her mouth, and fled. I tracked down a floor manager and was told they had fifteen suitcases for $20 a piece. I handed over $300 and carted them off to my rental van.

It was not until I got back to my room and started transferring the t-shirts from the boxes to the suitcases that I discovered why Mr. Chen had appeared so nervous. While the top half of the boxes were all large and X-larges, the bottom half were smalls – and when I say small I mean Chinese Small, which is the equivalent of American Toddler. I was the owner of 1,000 baby tees that I'd be lucky to unload for $10 a piece.

Oh how I wailed and gnashed my teeth. I screamed and cursed Mr. Chen's 18 generations and vowed to violate their graves. But there was nothing to be done. China had a strict mai zhe zifu, buyer beware, policy. And to be fair, I had never stipulated sizes. I thought I had played him by boozing him up and getting the price down to $1.50, but it turned out *I* was the sucker at the mahjong table.

I didn't have much time to feel sorry for myself because I faced a bigger problem. The monks had been hired to tour America again, but they were having trouble getting visas. The previous tour, their first ever, had ended in political scandal: two of the monks had defected. It was a heavy loss of face for the Chinese government. Their propaganda office had for years been heavily pushing the argument that life for Chinese immigrants in America was awful. The most popular show currently on Chinese television was *Beijingers in New York*, about a Chinese couple whose marriage and lives were destroyed by unscrupulous Westerners. Towards the end of the miniseries, the Chinese husband, furious that his wife had been seduced by her American boss at the sweatshop where she worked, railed against the entire round-eyed race with this memorable line:

"Do you know why Westerners are so hairy? Because when we were human, they were still monkeys."

Leader Liu spent month after month trying to pay off the right official to secure visas, but eventually abandoned the American deal and secured an offer to tour around Southeast Asia. The change in destination weakened my argument that I should be included on the tour as the translator, so I let it be known up the channels that led to Leader Liu's ear that I'd be willing to pay for my own plane tickets. He let it be known back down them that I was bu shou huanying, unwelcome.

You don't climb up the Communist Party hierarchy, even to a lowly local level of Shaolin Kung Fu Center leader, by turning the other cheek. ChiCom officials never forgive and never forget; they will spend years or decades patiently waiting to revenge a slight, to cross a name off their Enemies List. Out-negotiating Leader Liu over my tuition in such a public way had caused him to lose face, the worst thing you could do to a Chinese. He knew I'd bought thousands of t-shirts to sell (everyone did, because everyone in Shaolin knew everyone else's business), and he purposely wasn't going to do anything to help me sell them.

Now I was well and truly going to lose my shirt. Banned from all Shaolin tours, there was no way I could sell a thousand shirts for $20 a piece. To cut my losses and stop throwing good money after bad, I probably should have burned them or at the very least given them away as charity, but I was young, dumb, and bullheaded.

I found a Chinese moving company that drove them over the spotty back roads that connect Zheng Zhou to Beijing, and another company that packed them in a container ship for San Diego, where American officials held them up for three month until I paid the bribe (otherwise known as "Customs Duty"). From there I had them shipped to my parent's home in Kansas, where my father took one look at the fifteen suitcases in his basement, one look at his prodigal son, shook his head, and didn't speak to me for a month.

I didn't blame him. Including all the shipping expenses, the total I had spent on those 2,000 t-shirts had surpassed $7,000.

★

My only bit of luck during this epic moveable farce was Gene Ching. He was the Asian-American editor of Kung Fu Magazine and an executive in the company's martial arts catalogue sales business. We had met at the Shaolin Temple and I had done him a number of favors: setting him up with the right teachers, negotiating his tuition, etc. In short, we had deep guanxi. When I told him my t-shirt tale of woe, he saw a way to repay me.

"I can afford to go up to $5 per shirt," he said.

"For all of them?" I asked, desperately.

"No," he laughed. "The small ones are unsellable, but I'll take the 1,000 large and extra-large ones."

Much later, I retold my story to an older Taiwanese businesswoman, a friend of my parents. She smiled and patted my hand when I had finished.

"Do you know what the Chinese slang is for someone's first business venture?" she asked. "We call it 'Paying Tuition,' because you always lose money, but you learn a great deal in the process."

REFRAINS FROM WASTERFUR SCARCITY

Matt Muller

Matt Muller joined the United States Marine Corps in 1994 and later received his B.A. in English from The College of William and Mary in Virginia, rode his bicycle across America, went to and flunked out of medical school, and wound up in China teaching English. His writings have appeared in *Mala: The Chengdu Bookworm Literary Journal*. Matt is presently based in Sichuan.

ONE DAY IN CHINA I found myself squealing like a pig.

I was playing a simplified version of charades with a classroom full of indifferent high school students, but it was a tough crowd and we had gotten off to a shaky start after my attempt to actually teach them something meaningful had been vetoed by the head Chinese teacher.

"Play Games!" she commanded me in shrill authoritarian-nese. "Sing songs!"

In fact, I am a university teacher and don't normally play games or sing songs with my students. I had been grading final exams the day before when the dean of the university phoned for a favor (Translation: somebody asked him for a favor so I had been farmed out to his favoree; favors and guanxi, it seemed, are what keep China plastered together). This is how I found myself playing the role of various animals, including pushing my nose up, grunting and oinking.

Thankfully, my latest rendition caught the students' attention. Girls stopped texting on their mobiles, and boys ceased roughhousing. Both groups took just enough time to look up and shout "pig!" in unison. Then they went back to whatever they were doing.

"They're very clever," I said, turning to their teacher. "They must have an excellent teacher." My tone dripped with a sarcasm I was certain she found inaudible.

The next 10 minutes whizzed by in a blur as the teacher flipped through a stack of picture cards. Each magic card transformed me into a frog, a duck, and a cow. By some feat of thaumaturgy, I even managed to turn an ordinary chair into a flying bicycle, which I rode around the room. But that archfiend of classrooms, Boredom, soon materialized. It stalked the children. One by one they fell prey to it.

The Chinese teacher – a celestial maiden with skin as fair and pure as a tube of mercury-free skin whitener – showed me the next card: Rabbit. I froze.

"Don't be shy, just have a try," she said, smiling. This must of have been one of her teacher slogans.

My heart had skipped when she smiled. Fine, your highness, I had wanted to teach. But if I can't have that, then I'll have you. Looking into her double-lucky lidded eyes, I hoped to make a connection. Her brown eyes remained professional while encouraging me to enjoy her. No flash photography or touching allowed. But the cocksure American in me insisted that could be changed.

We jumped to the next card. Dog. Pavlov's dogs came to mind, reminding me to exercise self-control of my salivary glands as I my eyes pranced over her body. I asked her to skip that one, too.

Then came Cat. A flash of inspiration: to crawl on all fours, rub up against the teacher's legs, growl like a great cat of the Serengeti and lick the erogenous zone behind her knees. The class full of noisy students faded away far off into the hazy distance as I contemplated my next move. I could already taste her black fishnet stockings and smell her leather boots. Then I would wander up to her inner thigh...

Each card turned me into something bestial, but I discarded

my impulses as a single white male in China and decided on something more appropriate for this audience. So I meowed and made a clawing motion at some phantom menace. The class gleefully shouted the answer, blissfully ignorant that they had almost learned the true definition of what it means to be "*so open*," as the Chinese often describe Americans.

And so the game continued, my students improving their vocabulary while I rapidly descended the evolutionary ladder. And I wondered, for perhaps the bazillionth time this day, something all foreign English teachers in China inevitably find themselves asking at least once:

What the hell I was doing here?

★

It was a damp, wintry day in the city of Chenzhou. Despite being only a hundred miles north of the Tropic of Cancer, this city of five million lost souls was shrouded in a cold brown fog. The sun appeared only once or twice a month in the form of an ochre smudge. Ivyl, my escort for the day, waited for me at the university's front gate. The original plan was drive by car, but Ivyl said the traffic was so horrible that we would instead have to take a motorcycle taxi. It was, she ascertained, the only "meaningful" way we could fight through the gridlock, weaving through an apocalyptic territory of construction yards, barricades, and a highway choked with cars, buses, and trucks spewing fumes.

Ivyl's casual assessment did not jive with my own. I had served four years in the U.S. Marines, and I knew her plan was a recipe for suicide. Perhaps in some parts of China this would be a relatively safe gamble. I had even resorted to this method of travel in the last city I lived in, Changsha, as a kind of thrill ride. The adrenalin rush had been exquisite; there is nothing like hugging the waist of the Grim Reaper, his jaw clamped down on a Double Happiness while whizzing through, by, against, and around traffic. That Scooter of Death had had a velocity of 10 near-death experiences per mile.

But that was Changsha, a second-tier city. This was Chenzhou, a fourth-tier city with third-tier aspirations. Walking would greatly increase our chances of survival.

"I don't ride motorcycles in Chenzhou," I said, gesturing at the gridlock and cacophony.

"You do not have to *ride* it," she replied with a saccharin, face-saving smile. "You just have to sit on it."

She probably thought I wasn't being very manly, which meant I was losing face. But as an American, losing face was not a problem.

"We'll walk," I decided with finality.

So we trekked to the private school beneath a cadaver-gray sky. Chenzi Highway was the only road downtown. The green hills on both sides of the road were being ripped apart in an orgy of destruction and construction. Drivers blasted their horns with wanton abandon. Amongst hundreds of shambling wayfarers, I seemed to be the only one who flinched at every sound, sticking fingers into my ears, protecting myself. Some horns seemed to be weaponized. These were not your typical sound-making devices. Their cars were equipped with sonic cannons. Each blast pulsed through you like an abusive parent ripping you out of the cradle and shaking you furiously, rattling your brain to and fro. This was Progress.

Accompanying Ivyl and I along the side of the highway were vendors with weathered faces. From time to time they would make futile attempts to sell steaming bowls of hot and spicy noodles, baked sweet potatoes, or fresh fruit to starving vehicle passengers. Other pedestrians bore baskets of goods hanging from a bamboo stick balanced on one shoulder. Mothers with bundled-up babies strapped to their backs pushed carts of dried meat. One of them leaned into some sort of wagon with swiveling office chair wheels. It looked like an old popcorn cart, except its machinery had been gutted and its windows brimmed with something that was definitely not puffy white popcorn. Instead there something else that was brown and glistening. I focused on the Chenzhou chainsaw massacre going on around me, asking myself: *What the hell am I doing here?*

Behind me, there was a gasp of pleasant surprise. Turning around, I saw Ivyl pointing at the cart. Time slowed nearly to a standstill. There they were. Instead of popcorn there were severed heads. They had been stripped of fur. Black eye sockets leered from behind the glass windows. Each head grinned with an overbite. This was happening all over China: bunny genocide.

"Rabbit head!" Ivyl confirmed. "Do you want snack? It is very delicious."

I turned away, watching others wade through the mud and smog. Men in camouflage pants, Mao jackets and conical straw hats barked into cell phones with one hand while hauling sacks of rice or live chickens in the other. Other people heaved and puffed in the cold while exhaust belched from the tailpipes of black spit-shined sedans, buses packed like sardine cans, and trucks hauling pigs and coal crept down Chenzi Highway.

The city itself had a Walmart, several KFCs, and McDonalds franchises, all signs of Chenzhou's gloriously futile ambition to become "The Tourist Capital of China." But the rest of the city was an eyesore – the kind contracted from gonorrhea after waking up in a KTV and rubbing the sleep out of your eyes. All around us, white bathroom-tiled apartments, clothing stalls and noodle shops were sprouting upon land that had been used as landfills.

I pointed to either side of the road where high-rises with Grecian columns stood empty and lifeless. Large billboards showed glowing, light-skinned Chinese family units enjoying "Mid Level Luxury."

"Why doesn't anyone live there?" I asked, utterly mystified.

Ivyl looked around, blinking her eyes. I couldn't help but wonder if she even saw what I was seeing.

"Yes," she finally agreed, "it is verry wastefur."

It took a moment to process her Chinglish before continuing the conversation.

"But what is the cause? Why don't people live in them, instead of those houses over there?" I pointed to a batch of crumbling houses with slate tile roofs, glassless windows, and laundry hanging in the cold wet morning. Grandmothers chased after waddling toddlers. Every square inch of ground seemed to be planted with seasonal vegetables. A month from now this all would be demolished. Luxury high-rises and sterile boutiques would be thrown up in their place.

"China is still developing," Ivyl answered curtly, looking away.

We finally made it to the choke point where vehicles drove carefully around a solitary police officer supposedly directing traffic. His eyes were glazed. I had seen this before when I had served in Monrovia, Liberia. There, homesick Marines bored witless wanted nothing more than to be unleashed. Or perhaps this officer had inhaled too much diesel fumes? Who did he piss off, I wondered, to have been stationed here?

Like he must have been doing, I myself wondered yet again, *What the hell am I doing here*? Today's excursion would supplement my lowly teaching income with a couple hundred yuan, a salary that expats in Shanghai scoffed at but went a long way here in this dingy city of southern Hunan province. I could feel my rising resentment of their "Mid Level Luxury," so I quickly reminded myself that, if nothing else, I was sacrificing myself on the altar of Education. After all, I was a philologist. Or was it logophilist? I couldn't remember which. But this is exactly what we lovers of words did to earn our bread and butter. Just as symbologists (at least the ones in the movies) foiled dark conspiracies in an effort to decipher ancient codes, I contended with monomaniacal motorists so that I could share my love for words and literature with the Chinese. At least, that is what I told myself to make my life meaningful.

Today my students would learn some new vocabulary. Tomorrow they might learn a Celine Dion song. Maybe one day they would be reading *Huckleberry Finn*. And perhaps if they were lucky, within the next decade they would find employment at Pizza Hut, taking orders in English from demanding foreign tourists. As a pioneer in the Wild, Wild East, I was laying down the railroad for freedom and democracy. But that was just another thing I told myself to get through my own misery.

The truth was that teaching in China was a career path as dismal as the Chenzi Highway.

★

Teaching English literature at a Chinese university is a coveted position, for everyone knows how easy university teachers in China have it. Unfortunately, its salary correlates with this bias. What's more, Chinese students viewed college not as an institution of higher learning, but merely as a kind of post-Gao Kao afterlife where shell-shocked victims could recover from the exam. It was a place to have a good rest.

On the flipside were the Chinese public high schools. The teachers there were diligent; their salaries were shackled to exam scores. So of course they didn't just teach. They also stood watch from the podium, and strode along the aisles with a wood ruler in hand searching for shirkers. Productivity was not a problem here. Anything besides this hard labor was by definition selfish individualism. Chinese teachers baited their workers with the promise of heaven: once the students aced the Gao Kao, they could finally attend college and have a nice four-year vacation.

So here I was teaching at a Chinese university. It wasn't teaching so much as damage control. While there were always exceptional students, most fell into three major categories: those who slept in class; those who gazed into their cell phones; and those who at least turned forwards, but their eyes had an unfocused, detached lifelessness; the classic "thousand yard stare" of a trauma survivor. Almost all of them lacked any concept of homework. Either that or they pretended it was an idea too foreign to comprehend. Instead of homework, they slept.

And when they weren't sleeping, Chinese college students spent their time in smoky internet cafes playing online role-playing games. In another era, they would have wasted away in an opium den. There was no actual learning done in Chinese universities. Like Boxer, the cart horse from *Animal Farm*, most would be shipped out to a glue factory – themselves becoming glue, that other magical ingredient that holds China together.

Today's teaching gig wasn't just a way to earn some spending money. It was also a chance to observe pre-Gao Kao students in all their misery. The Gao Kao was the Mount Qomolangma of all exams in China – a nationally administered test that determined not only which college students got into, but also railroaded their whole lives. Students who were accepted into universities in Beijing or Shanghai went on to stressful and meaningless careers of prestige while those stuck in provincial-level colleges would be relegated to jobs at said fast-food franchises. Whatever college they went to, most were destined for a life of harmonious desperation. Everybody knew it was a farce. Yet whenever I sought more information, I was shut down with a solid: "China is still developing."

When we arrived at the private school where the dean of my university had loaned me out for the day, Ivyl introduced me to the head teacher, Daisy. That is when I noticed two things. First, the head teacher made me want to do something I have long since abhorred: sing. I felt like taking up more space, stretching my arms and legs. I licked my lips, suppressing an urge to pounce upon her.

I shook these thoughts away, realizing another thing: the room was full of teenaged high school students, half of whom were boys totally oblivious to the lovely Daisy. How could this be? It was as if they could not see her. Instead, they were gaping elsewhere: at each other, their cell phones, and me.

The first order of business, Daisy implied, was to "entertain" the high school students. I frowned at this; I guessed there would be no real teaching done today. My role as a foreign English teacher in China was as empty as those "wastefur" luxury high-rises:

My presence improved the school's image, but nobody was interested in putting me to any good use.

Everybody saw my ineffectiveness when I informed Daisy I didn't know any good songs, not even the "Merry Christmas" song. The class went silent. It was as if a needle skipped off the record of my life. Somebody in the back snickered. Daisy's brown eyes narrowed: how wastefur, they seemed to admonish.

Hoping to salvage the situation, I told her I could tell stories. It was my last ditch effort to redeem myself. But I had to think fast. The students were waiting. And they weren't just waiting; they were starving for deliverance. Though I had recently taught a semester's worth of sanctioned literature, other stories came to mind: *Nineteen Eighty-Four, Brave New World, Lord of the Flies...* Maybe I could toss them into the wok and stir-fry a fable?

Somebody yawned audibly. A boy hawked up a lugie. Time was running out. I cast a net out into the sea with all my strength, fishing for something to say that would save us all. Somebody else began clipping his finger nails. Snip. Snip. Even Daisy paced to and fro behind me, her boots promising hot sex as they echoed upon the granite floor: clipop, clipop, clipop.

Then I made a split second decision to just tell the Story of Myself:

"A long time ago, in a beautiful country far, far away..."

"Wait!" Daisy snapped from behind me. "Do you understand him?" she said at the students.

There was a wave of head shaking. The teacher told me to slow down, simplify and use present tense verbs. These were high school students?

"Okay," I agreed, "Where was I? Oh, yes. There is a boy. The boy dreams. He wants to go to another country..."

"Maybe they still do not understand you," Daisy interrupted again.

"You mean they don't understand *me*? Or they don't understand how somebody could dream of going to another country?"

Daisy flinched. "Another country?" she repeated, frowning and rubbing her temples.

I decided to trudge onwards. "And there is a cat," I said, redoubling my effort to speak Hemingway-nese. Besides, adding an anthropomorphic cat would make for a cool side kick. I also revised the rest of the story to incorporate the words they had just learned. Improvise, overcome, and adapt. Ooh-rah! And then the cat and his boy would journey to the animal farm in the center of the fucking earth. But first, I needed to hook my audience.

"The cat is *the* cat in the hat..."

Pleasure rippled from the class as soon as I mentioned this. Finally! They took the bait.

"The boy and the cat want to go to a new world..."

I lost them again. Many began looking around in confusion. Others began fidgeting with their cell phones. Perhaps it was time to give the boy and cat some swords, and something to use them on.

"Maybe you should hurry," said Daisy.

Boredom came like an overdue earthquake. You could hear its growl in the student's restlessness. The school's foundations seemed to tremble. Drywall crumbled down, dusty at first, and then like a flurry. Soon boredom would shower down upon everyone, a sign of the building's imminent collapse. If only I had some magical guanxi that I could sprinkle upon the walls, then everything would be all right. But this was no Harry Potter movie. This was real life. It was up to me to lead them to safety. I lifted my proverbial torch. Follow me!

"The man and his cat sail across the ocean. They have adventures. People meet them. Some are bad. Most are good. The end."

The students clapped. The Chinese teacher smiled, leaning forward with widened eyes. The children were safe. And maybe I would get the teacher's phone number. All the while they would never know that the hero and his cat had also taught a village of munchkins the secret alchemical process of separating quicksilver from baby milk, or had watched as wingless, corrupt bureaucrats from the cosmic center idled as a species of aristocratic, fire-breathing capitalists invaded from the ragged circumference of the universe. Those would be tales for another day...or maybe a special bedtime story for my new favorite Chinese teacher.

But now it was time for another game. It was the "Learn Chinese Game." It was also known by its traditional Chinese name: "Civilize the Foreign Pig!" All the students got in a line. At first I was amazed by this. Like wildlife of any sort, orderly queues are seldom, if ever, seen in China. But then to my horror, the line encircled me. One by one, each student would enter the circle, instruct me, and then go back to their seats. All the while the noose tightened.

"How do you say, 'good morning' in Chinese?" I asked the first student in line. This was a great opportunity to learn some Chinese and impress the celestial maiden of my dreams.

"No, that's too easy," Daisy chided.

"How about, 'Will you be my girlfriend?'" I asked, ignoring the students' laughter and glancing sidelong at Daisy. It was a struggle to keep my own eyes from going down on her.

Annoyance stomped across her face. "No, that is not very useful in everyday life."

And that is how I learned to play "Civilize the Foreign Pig!" It was a game about living in China. At first the students stood in an actual line in front of the pig and proceeded to impart the wisdom of great thinkers from Confucius to Mao Zedong upon me. The only thing missing was a dunce cap.

The kids in the back of the line quickly lost their patience, as Chinese people in the backs of lines have the tendency of doing, and soon ran riot. A boy pulled his mouth open and let off a blood-curdling scream; meanwhile other boys started playing "PLA Soldiers versus Uyghurs" (kind of like "Cowboys and Indians" in America). Girls turned on their music players and added pop music to the rising din. In a way, it sounded like the Chenzi Highway. The offspring of bourgeois Chinese had transformed the lifeless classroom into a jungle island *Where the Wild Things Are*, shouting, singing, laughing and dancing around the spitted foreign pig. I heard a fly buzz while Daisy stood by, either anesthetized or indifferent to the disorder.

A boy came over and consulted with Daisy in Chinese. I tried to read their expressions. They were plotting something, I just knew it. Both the teacher and her student had donned their hunting masks.

"He will teach you," said Daisy.

The boy said some words. Many words. There were many words strung together in a singsong rhythm seamless and undecipherable. The teacher had to check her translator app before explaining to me that it was a famous Chinese expression that meant something like, "Vertigo is not supper, nor is it an essay, painting, and so on."

"Wow, *that* sounds useful. Who said that?"

The teacher grimaced, sucking air through her teeth with a hiss. "I do not know the English name."

So much for stalling. Instead of shedding light on this mystery, they went over it again, one homophonetic syllable at a time. We did this several times. My eyes must have had the distant far off look of one who has dissociated. Meanwhile, somewhere in the dark recess of my mind, an ominous voice informed me, "You're traveling through another dimension, a dimension not only of sight and sound but of mind…" The room spun and I heard The *Twilight Zone* theme song. Please, God, let that be somebody's ringtone.

"Do you understand?" said Daisy.

"Absolutely."

China was still developing. And so was I. I had spent my first five months in China struggling with the language's four different tones and pronunciation of characters once unknown to me. It became a wall my speech organs were powerless to climb over. Plus I was tone deaf. At least, that was my own high school music teacher once said.

What I wanted to explain to the Chinese teacher but didn't was that I am an imaginative learner. Not to be confused with "visual learning", my style is actually a disability. Normal people learn by hearing or seeing. Some learn by doing. A few can even learn by osmosis. Me? I needed an adult female wearing a tight sleeveless cheongsam mini-dress to help me learn Chinese. All my senses would have to focus; otherwise I would end up knowing nothing. Tracing each Chinese character upon the small of her back with my index finger was only proper way to begin a lesson. It would not be enough to see where the teacher's tongue quivers between her teeth as she makes a certain buzzing sound. No, I would need to feel and taste how it's done.

That is what I wanted. But it is horrifying to see what a little piece of gold can do to destroy a fantasy world. As soon as I noticed that Daisy was wearing a ring, I lost all motivation to learn Chinese. It was as if she had become not just invisible, but distasteful. She might as well be just another faceless bureaucrat, wingless and corrupt.

★

I concluded my class by giving the students an opportunity to interrogate me, an activity that all Chinese love second only to mahjong. This passion for interrogation harkened back to the struggle sessions of the Cultural Revolution. Little did I know, a breath of fresh air was about to pass close to my orbit.

But first, I got the usual algorithmic checklist asked of foreigners in China: Do I know how to use chopsticks? Do I like Chinese food? Do I play basketball? How much do my clothes cost? This of course led to questions about the quantity of cash and girlfriends in my possession. And then finally: Why did you come to China?

All was not lost. A girl of around 17 years of age – let's call her Clarisse – hopped forward, eyes wide as if sensing danger. She clutched a Buddha hanging around her neck with a braided red string. By now, the classroom had descended into utter chaos. Both my escort and the head teacher were on their cell phones, themselves oblivious to the way I had been throwing meaningful glances at the exit. Nobody was paying attention. We might as well all be idling on Chenzi Highway.

I remembered Clarisse from the beginning of class. Students had been asked to introduce themselves and tell me their hobbies. Clarisse stood out amongst them. While most supplied rote answers about sleeping, eating, and playing video games, and identified themselves with joke names or poor but telling translations of their Chinese names (Demon, Blue Sky, etc.), Clarisse seemed to have chosen one with care. And unlike her peers, she said that she actually enjoyed writing and reading, having just finished the Chinese translation of *Harry Potter and the Prisoner of Azkaban*.

Clarisse said something that was mostly incomprehensible to me. It was as if her English had degenerated since my arrival. I was only able to pick out three words from her question: "war" and "poor people." I asked for clarification, but then the head teacher said something in harsh authoritarian-nese. She bore down upon us, black boots stomping.

"Hey, wait a minute. She has a question," I said. It was one of those oppressive moments in Communism when conversations were secretly monitored to "maintain harmony" and preserve stability. Otherwise, who knows? Maybe a word will start an earthquake, an earthquake for some, at least; but a new world for many others.

The teacher ignored me. Hands clenching, she stared down Clarisse. The little girl blushed. She looked down to hide it and was about to go back to her seat. But this time I would get want I wanted.

"Clarisse, wait…" I think I knew which war and which poor people she was talking about: America's war. Now *that* is something we all need to talk about. This is why people need to learn how to communicate with each other.

I gave Clarisse a metaphorical tip of the hat for venturing beyond the borders of the Mediocre Kingdom with such audacity. The Chinese were slowly but surely learning the easiest way into a foreigner's heart is to sow the seeds of conflict. There was hope for this generation yet. For a moment at least, there was a sky lantern floating upwards into the smoggy night.

I scrambled to piece together an answer for her. My own military service came to mind, as well as that of my cousin, whose blood now mingled in the sands of Central Asia. How could I put this simply? How do I explain things like friendly fire, collateral damage and drones to an insulated Chinese teenager? How do I explain the unexplainable? I might as well explain Chenzi Highway.-

Would she get it if I said that I don't support the war but I support our troops? Now there was a good start. That refrain heard so often across the Pacific had been corrupted into a meaningless, thought-killing euphemism – perfect for a Chinese classroom. I felt anger rise up and course through me. It was a rebellion. Then I crushed it with a new armored slogan more powerful than all the previous slogans I have heard before: America is still developing.

Then again, maybe I had read too much into her question. Had Clarisse said "wall" and "pool peopre"?

Clarisse sat down at her desk. Her gaze fluttered around the room from the doorway to the clock and to the windows. Beyond the cage-like bars, traffic blared on into the smog of life in this country.

"Maybe it is time for you to say goodbye." The head teacher's voice was now shrill. "The students need to have a rest."

"Clarisse," I shouted over the pandemonium on my way out, catching her eye. "No matter what happens, you just keep reading and writing. Keep asking questions. And keep asking yourself: 'What the hell are you doing here?'"

The Shoe

Kay Bratt

Kay Bratt is an author and advocate of orphans in China. After founding a volunteer group and working in a Chinese orphanage for over four years, Kay was inspired to publish her memoir, "Silent Tears; A Journey of Hope in a Chinese Orphanage." In China, Kay was honored with the 2006 Pride of the City award for her humanitarian work. Now living in the United States, Kay does volunteer work with An Orphans Wish (AOW) and writes Asian-inspired fiction aimed at raising awareness of issues that affect women and children in China.

KAY HURRIEDLY FINISHED DRESSING the last child and tucked her under the thin coverlet. The toddler girl, called Hei Mei because of her dark countryside complexion, stared up at Kay with lonely eyes. Patting her head, Kay smiled reassuringly, but wished she had something to leave her with to pass away the rest of the long afternoon – a toy, stuffed bear or anything to hold with her tiny fingers or give her something to look at other than the institutional-white concrete walls and water-stained ceiling.

Knowing it wasn't to be, she instead focused on the positive: that today the children would sleep in clean beds and wouldn't need to filter their breaths through the overpowering stench of illness and waste. Though the children were sometimes distressed by the harsh process of the bath itself, the weekly washings and "clean linen day" brought a freshness and diversion to the usual monotony of institutional life. Kay touched the tip of Hei Mei's nose, blew her a kiss and, with one more backward glance at the rows of dark heads tucked into the many cribs and beds, she headed for the door.

In the shabby kitchen area, Kay used a pair of pliers to turn on the rusty spigot, then washed under a pitifully thin trickle of water. With many of the babies suffering from mysterious rashes and fevers, this water was her only protection against bringing unwanted viruses home to her own family. But with no soap available and only one grimy towel lying on the counter, all she could do was shake the water droplets from her hands.

She thought what a huge difference it would make to regularly have soap and clean towels available but reminded herself she wasn't here to judge; instead she'd continue to help where needed and try to make a difference in whatever small ways she could. It had only been a few months since she'd followed her husband to China for his job relocation, and just getting permission to volunteer in the orphanage had been difficult. After finally finding something to do to combat the severe homesickness she battled, she didn't want to jeopardize her position by over-stepping her boundaries.

★

Stopping at the door to replace the worn slippers with her own shoes, Kay grabbed her bag and entered the hall. Usually she would return home at this time, but not today. With a renewed burst of energy, she walked gingerly down the recently-mopped stairs to the second floor where the older children shared a large room, and where Xiao Gou would be waiting.

"Where is Xiao Gou?" she called out in a singsong voice, moving closer to the room, knowing the child could hear the distinguishable sound of her Southern-accented American voice through the echo of the long, empty halls.

The wide smile that welcomed Kay when she turned the corner told her the little girl had not forgotten the promise made the week before. There, perched on one of the wooden beds in the rows of many, Xiao Gou waited patiently. Borrowing a wobbly but functioning stroller from the orphanage, they left the building to the chorus of Xiao Gou's little friends calling out goodbye. Surprisingly, the children didn't show any jealousy; only genuine happiness for Xiao Gou's chance to leave the orphanage for a grand adventure.

Kay waved goodbye, wishing she could take them all, but glad for the continued permissions to have Xiao Gou in her care without a chaperone. After her tirade against the nanny the week before, Kay knew she was lucky to even be permitted to see Xiao Gou at all. But she'd do it all again because she was done tolerating the humiliation heaped on that child; she was finished holding her tongue to allow them to "save face."

It all came to a boiling point the week before when Kay came in and found Xiao Gou sitting on the dreaded bowl for the second time in a week, her pants taken and her nakedness displayed for everyone to see. Xiao Gou was obviously embarrassed – shame was evident in her reluctance to make eye contact – her tiny bottom wedged in the bowl and resting on a pile of her own waste. When Kay witnessed her look of defeat, she lost all self-control and told the nanny what she thought about her so-called toilet training method.

It had taken a translator and an impromptu meeting with the director, but that nanny would never again give Xiao Gou grief about her inability to control her bowels. It also didn't go unnoticed that Xiao Gou had looked on with an expression of pride at Kay's outrage. It was a tense moment but one that showed Xiao Gou that she mattered – and that there was at least one person left who'd help her fight her battles.

Now Kay tried to forget that event and pledged, for this day at least, to keep an optimistic attitude. Settled into the car, she passed Xiao Gou a bottle of water and stared down at her impish face. Despite everything she'd been through, the child's resilience amazed her. The car accident that had turned Xiao Gou's life upside down had resulted in her ultimate abandonment, and, sadly, her mother and father had not seen her since they had up and walked away from the hospital intensive care unit two years ago.

Despite the obstacles, Kay was committed to fighting for Xiao Gou to be approved for adoption. However, the same parents who had abandoned her also refused to give guardianship to the government. Without the official guardianship, Xiao Gou could be held in the orphanage her entire childhood, unable to ever join a family. With the grim possibility that Xiao Gou may never be allowed to be adopted, Kay spared the child from any unfounded optimism and changed their routine from the comforts of a home visit to small excursions into the city.

★

After half an hour of winding through brutal traffic, the driver finally maneuvered the car to the curb and put it in park. He popped the trunk, got out and retrieved the stroller, setting it on the sidewalk. Kay climbed out and draped her bags over the handles, then returned for the girl. Settled in the stroller and smiling ear to ear, Xiao Gou's outing began.

Traversing the bustling streets of China is not easy for anyone, but the challenge is made infinitely greater for a Caucasian woman accompanying a physically disabled Chinese child. After several years in China, Kay should have been used to the many stares and nosiness of passing strangers, but the honest truth is that no foreigner can ever fully become comfortable with this custom; for her and for Xiao Gou, the lack of privacy was a constant hindrance to their limited time together. On the streets, people with disabilities are blatantly pointed at, talked about and even assaulted with intrusive questions about their physical impairments. But 6-year-old Xiao Gou possessed a strong stubborn streak and simply refused to answer or acknowledge them.

Pushing the stroller behind a young couple hand-in-hand

with their own little girl skipping between them, Kay smiled her approval for their ignoring the age-old preference for a boy and instead choosing to treat their daughter like a precious jewel. Xiao Gou, on the other hand, intently stared at the other girl's pink frilly dress and long pigtails, then insecurely ran her hand through her own institutional-style chopped locks and straightened the fabric of her cheap, one-size-too-small dress.

Just like everywhere else in the world, McDonalds restaurants are a local favorite here and always packed full of people. Using her elbows and a determined expression, Kay finally made it through the packed streets to the restaurant, up the stairs and to the register. She unbuckled Xiao Gou and placed her on the counter to choose her lunch. Finally served, Kay juggled the tray and pushed the stroller to an empty table. What would normally be a 15-minute "happy" meal expanded to almost 45 minutes as Xiao Gou took her time to savor every bite of her little feast, dipping the nuggets into her sauce with her dainty fingers.

When she finished, Kay pointed to the colorful McChildren's area and asked if she wanted to play. With her approval, Kay picked her up, carried her to a red block and set her down, then returned to the table to watch.

Xiao Gou murmured a hello to a couple of girls climbing around her. They stopped playing and stood staring at her, without returning her greeting, obviously struck by her disability. Xiao Gou looked over at Kay as if she wanted to cry. The curiosity from adults hadn't upset Xiao Gou, but disapproval from her own peers appeared to be breaking her heart.

After a few minutes, Kay could see that the cold, distant manner of the other children was ruining the fun, so she told Xiao Gou it was time to go. With her purse looped around her neck, a diaper bag over her shoulder, Xiao Gou perched on her left hip, and the stroller clutched in her right hand, Kay clunked down two flights of stairs while trying her best to avoid tripping over the two street children who pulled on her pants begging for money.

Further down Walking Street, Kay pushed Xiao Gou past the open children's shops, chuckling at her oohs and aahs of all the pretty things she saw in the windows. Despite her circumstances, Xiao Gou was still a girly-girl at heart.

At a shoe store, they found a pair of sandals they both agreed on. As they moved around the shop waiting for the salesperson to retrieve her size, Kay realized they had once again accumulated a crowd of curious onlookers. When she stopped, they stopped; when she moved, they moved. The saleswoman at last returned. As Kay bent in front of Xiao Gou to fit the shoe on her, the crowd closed in.

Kay and Xiao Gou were emotionally close enough that, even in spite of the language barrier, the child could sense what Kay was feeling without her ever saying a word. As strangers peppered them with questions, Xiao Gou shooed them away as if they were pesky flies. But the more she tried to push them away, the more they closed in tightly until Kay felt flustered and light-headed from the lack of air.

Kay hurriedly put the first shoe on Xiao Gou and bent around to get the second shoe. With the second shoe in her hand, she glanced around to give the inquisitive people a reprimanding look as she felt around for Xiao Gou's other foot. Reaching wildly with unsuccessful efforts, she finally looked down for it and then it hit her – there *was* no other foot.

Xiao Gou has only one leg.

In a moment of shocked realization at her inexcusable blunder, Kay looked up at Xiao Gou to find her wearing an amused smile and staring down at Kay's fumbling hands. Their eyes met and they both broke out in loud laughter at the inside joke no one else shared. Kay shook her head in amazement at Xiao Gou's resilient sense of humor as she held the extra shoe.

The laughing increased as Kay tried to negotiate a 50 percent discount by buying only one shoe from the shoe clerk. Despite her tough bartering, the woman refused and Kay bought the pair, but left one behind in the certainty that if she brought a pair of new shoes back to the orphanage, they'd quickly disappear. With only one, Xiao Gou had a small chance of keeping it for herself.

★

One hour and one new, frilly pink dress later, it was time for Kay to return Xiao Gou to the Social Welfare Institute. With the inevitable in front of her, Xiao Gou pouted the last few miles. Kay sighed and comfortingly told Xiao Gou she'd be back again in a few days, but nothing Kay said would take away Xiao Gou's dismay of returning to the orphanage.

Finally arriving at the orphanage, Kay carried Xiao Gou in and left her at her desk in the classroom. Kay bent to kiss her goodbye but in her disappointment at being left again, Xiao Gou turned her face away. Kay ignored the slight and stuffed two cookies into Xiao Gou's pockets for later, a gesture the small girl usually appreciated. But in her goal to lash out, Xiao Gou reached for the sweets and threw them to the floor – quite a sacrifice to a child who would probably go to bed hungry.

With no other way to comfort her, Kay waved goodbye. As she headed to the door, she turned to see Xiao Gou dangling her sparkly new sandal around to draw attention from her peers. Kay walked to the gate as the sound of Xiao Gou chattering about her adventure rang in her ears. It wasn't much, but she was glad to have given her something to hold onto, some small piece of joy to lighten her burden of institutional life.

Pushing aside these heavy feelings, Kay trudged down the alley to her waiting car. So very tired – emotionally and physically – she climbed in and leaned her head against the headrest, closing her eyes to hide the sadness she buried deep within. Not sure how much longer she can continue her fight for the children or how much more of her there is to give, she pledged to keep going until she no longer can.

Communal Parenting

Aminta Arrington

Aminta Arrington is the author of "Home is a Roof Over a Pig: An American Family's Journey in China." She has an M.A. in international relations from Johns Hopkins University School of Advanced International Studies and studied at Waseda University in Tokyo. Aminta and her family lived in Shandong province for four years, teaching at Taishan Medical University at the foot of Mount Tai. They now live in Beijing.

ONE SATURDAY AFTERNOON I was taking a much-needed nap on our couch when Katherine buzzed me on the intercom.

"Mom, Xue Hanshao and Grace got into a fight. Xue Hanshao said she wouldn't play with Grace. Then Grace hit her, and Xue Hanshao started to cry. And...well...can you just come down?"

I sprinted downstairs into the courtyard. The four girls were lined up waiting for me. In the center were Katherine and Bing Bing; on both ends were Grace and Xue Hanshao, wearing matching offended looks.

"Grace, did you hit Xue Hanshao?" I asked. Grace immediately burst into tears.

"Ayi, Auntie," began Xue Hanshao, "Grace hit me right here. It hurt."

"Xue Hanshao," I said, "Grace should not have hit you, I'm sorry. But did you say some words that hurt Grace?"

Xue Hanshao looked down at her feet.

Katherine interjected: "Mom, Xue Hanshao also said something else. She said that Americans said Chinese people were dogs." Katherine looked at me quizzically.

Immediately I remembered the sign that supposedly hung in front of a park in Shanghai during the early days of the twentieth century:

No Dogs or Chinese Allowed

I had heard that though widely accepted as fact, there was no evidence that such a sign ever existed. I knew this must be what Xue Hanshao meant, but I didn't know how to fix the rift that it had created.

★

For over a year we had been living in Tai'an, a small city in Shandong province at the foot of Tai Shan, one of China's most sacred mountains. My husband and I taught at the university; our three young children all attended the local kindergarten. We walked to school, we bought groceries, we played in the park, we explored our new surroundings. But we were removed from realty. The foreign teachers' building where we lived was supposed to act as a "safe haven" from the tumult of daily Chinese life, but it sometimes felt like a lonely outpost.

We naively thought Katherine, Grace and Andrew would quickly make friends in their kindergarten. That was not the case. The amplified childhood world of sight and sound simply made them feel their foreignness more keenly. The neon flashing Chinese characters and sing-song Mandarin tones seemed to prevent them – even exclude them – from participating. The hyper-structured nature of Chinese kindergarten didn't help them assimilate, for there was simply no time for play. Even recess had been "harmonized."

"Have you made any friends in your class?" I hopefully asked our oldest, Katherine.

"Mom," she sighed with youthful exasperation, "I can't make

friends here. They speak Chinese; *I* speak English."

"Katherine, we do live in China. You aren't going to make many English-speaking friends here."

She just blinked at me.

"Besides, you can speak some Chinese."

She didn't bother to reply. She clearly thought, as all children think of their parents, I just didn't get it.

★

Mr. Jia, our minder who busied himself around our courtyard so the university could keep track of the foreign teachers, had been helping the children learn Chinese.

"What color is this?" he would ask in Shandong-accented Mandarin, pointing to Andrew's trousers.

"Lanse! Blue!"

He repeated the question, this time pointing to Grace's red shirt.

"Hongse!"

In this simple, nonthreatening way, my children eventually learned their colors in Chinese. And just as Mr. Jia enjoyed following the foreign teachers around, the children enjoyed following Mr. Jia around while he watered the plants or plucked a chicken before dinner, learning some Chinese along the way too.

It was on a pleasant Saturday afternoon that Mr. Jia brought some crabs for the kids to play with. He put the crabs in a basin of water, which resulted in squeals from our children. Katherine noticed two neighborhood girls peering into the courtyard, clearly curious about what the foreign children were looking at.

"Pangxie," Katherine announced proudly, repeating the word for crab that Mr. Jia had just taught her. Curiosity overcame decorum, and the line between foreign and Chinese was breeched. The two girls shyly entered the courtyard.

"What are your names?" I asked.

"Bing Bing," answered the quiet one, her hair pulled neatly back into a ponytail.

"Xue Hanshao," answered the second. She wore fancy clothes, all ruffles and fur and sequins, the theatrical accoutrements to a dramatic personality.

"This is Katherine and Grace," I said.

A shy exchange of "ni hao" followed.

The girls circled around the basin, poking at the crabs and squealing when the crabs tried to pinch back. "Watch out for the big crab, he's trying to climb out!" "He's pinching my stick!" "He won't let go." "I think this one's getting mad." "This is fun."

And just like that, afternoons were no longer spent ensconced in our apartment.

"We're coming down right away," Katherine and Grace would answer in increasingly fluent Mandarin whenever Xue Hanshao and Bing Bing came into our courtyard and buzzed the intercom. Then they would scurry away to put on boots and coats to go play hide-and-seek in the bamboo grove, throw rocks into the dirty pond in the park or just run up and down the streets shouting "kuai dian! hurry up!"

Friendship with Bing Bing and Xue Hanshao transformed Katherine and Grace from otherness to sameness. And since Chinese was now their default language of play, Katherine and Grace spoke to each other nearly always in Chinese as well, even inside our home in the foreign teachers' building.

★

Xue Hanshao's mother ran a small business, more of a cart, really. She stocked up on sundry items needed by university students – toilet paper, socks, long underwear – then positioned her cart by the student dormitories to peddle her wares. Her spot allowed her oversight of the comings and goings of the entire campus. If I couldn't find the girls, I'd just go find Xue Hanshao's mother.

"Have you seen Katherine and Grace?" I asked one day.

"They're picking flowers by the track," she answered, pointing to the gravel track that was usually overgrown with weeds.

I walked over and saw four heads bent over flowers, looking at ants and digging holes in the dirt.

"Eeeeek!" screamed Xue Hanshao. "Get that bug away from me!"

Grace waved the spider on a stick in Xue Hanshao's face like a magic wand.

"Auntie," Xue Hanshao said, seeing me approach, "Grace is being mean."

"Grace, don't tease. Be nice. Girls, say goodnight to your friends. It's time for dinner."

One day, Katherine said to me, "Mom, Xue Hanshao said she doesn't have any toys. Does she really not have any toys?"

"Maybe you misunderstood," I said, and thought no more of it. After all, Xue Hanshao did have a flair for the dramatic.

But when Xue Hanshao invited the girls over for her birthday party, Katherine remembered. "Mom, I really want to give Xue Hanshao a Barbie…just in case she really doesn't have any toys."

We went shopping together, and Katherine and Grace picked out a doll suitable for Xue Hanshao: one with lots of ruffles on her dress. It wasn't actually a Barbie doll, but a Ba-Bee doll (only knock-offs were available), but the girls were satisfied that they had the perfect present.

The girls came home from the party excited. Excited to have been with their friends and eaten birthday cake. Excited to have finally been invited into their friend's home. But later Katherine pulled me aside.

"It's true Mom. Not a single toy. I looked."

And yet not having toys did not equal not having fun. The campus was a perfect childhood world of trees to be climbed, alleys to be explored and crumbling walls that made perfect balance beams. In fact, there was so much to do that my children's toys sat unused; they were just clutter in our tiny apartment.

Why play with inanimate toys inside a compound, when China is alive with voices and faces.

Bing Bing's parents had also set up a fruit stall near the student dorms. Her dad rode off in the early hours, returning with boxes of oranges, apples, and bananas perched perilously on his motorcycle. Bing Bing's mom, with her hair pulled back in a ponytail like an older version of Bing Bing, managed the money and the scale. In winter she'd be bundled up, shivering, her fingers protruding from her gloves as she put fruit in plastic bags and weighed them, only stopping to walk quickly home and fix lunch.

I often bought fruit from Bing Bing's stand: tangerines to ward off sickness as the cold of winter began to set in; pomelos and pears and apples. Stopping by her fruit stand was part of my daily routine.

"You look tired," she often said.

I am tired, I thought. Teaching full-time…parenting three kids…trying to cope with life in a new culture with no dishwashers or cars...

"You're also busy," I replied, and it was true. 12 hours a day, seven days a week at her fruit stand, with only short breaks to prepare meals for Bing Bing, her husband and her father-in-law.

We talked of our hometowns, hers a small village a few hours away, mine a small town so many worlds away. Our new life in China was as much for my husband and I as it was for our children, but I knew her life had but one singular purpose: to give Bing Bing a chance at a better education and a better existence.

In the spring the girls climbed the trees on campus, filling up with delicious yellow cherries. Grace loved climbing cherry trees. It combined together her two great pleasures: monkey bars and eating.

In the fall our girls left the kindergarten and began attending the local primary school, often walking to school with Bing Bing and Xue Hanshao. After school, they'd play together until we called them in for supper or homework.

"Katherine and Grace, hurry up, dinner's ready!"

"Just ten more minutes," Katherine called out.

"Not ten more minutes. Now!" I answered.

"Bing Bing is the exact same," her mother said. "She never listens when I call her." She came and stood next to me, her hands on her hips. "Bing Bing!" she suddenly screamed. "You come too! Hurry up!"

This communal parenting brought me out of the privacy of our foreign enclave and into the public life of the community. Here, parenting was everyone's responsibility; all adults were "aunties" and "uncles." But it was through Bing Bing and Xue Hanshao that we had been allowed to enter into this social structure, and eventually given our own place in it. And now, a sign in some park distant from us in space and time was threatening this.

★

"Xue Hanshao, Americans didn't say that Chinese were dogs," I assured her. "It's not true."

"No, it is true," the little student asserted back, "My father told me."

Now I was in a difficult position. How could I contradict her father, the tall affable gentleman who always greeted us with an enthusiastic English "Helllloooo"?

"Well," I sighed, "even if it were true, there are a lot of Americans, and most of them are good even if one said a bad thing. Just like there are a lot of Chinese, and even if one does something bad, that doesn't make all of them bad, and it doesn't make you bad. Besides, China and America are good friends."

She nodded her head, but I didn't know if I convinced her. After all, why should she believe me over her own father? I turned my attention to Grace. It took some coaxing, but she finally came around and apologized to Xue Hanshao.

"It doesn't matter," said Xue Hanshao. Katherine and Bing

Bing both gave Xue Hanshao pointed looks. "I'm sorry too," the little princess finally relented.

That night I researched online the *No Chinese or Dogs Allowed* sign. The park in question, Huangpu Park, is located at the end of the Bund in Shanghai. From when it was built in 1868 to 1928 it had various signs at the gate with various lists of regulations. Most often, the first regulation stipulated its intention as a park exclusively for the foreign community. Another regulation said no dogs or bicycles were allowed. But scholars said they found no evidence for the popular belief that a *No Chinese or Dogs Allowed* sign ever existed.

However, in a memorable scene in the 1972 movie *Fist of Fury*, an Indian Sikh guard, pointing at a *No Chinese or Dogs Allowed* sign, refuses Bruce Lee entrance into the park. Lee stands by while first a foreign woman with a dog, and then – the ultimate insult – a group of kimono-clad Japanese, are allowed to enter. Lee kicks the sign off the wall, meets it in mid-air, and in one dazzling kung fu kick, smashes it into pieces. And that is perhaps why, regardless of scholars' findings, in the popular Chinese mind the sign *did* exist.

And frankly, sign or no sign, we have to admit that the underlying sentiment – that the Chinese were inferior – was likely present. For there was a time when Western powers, with their imperialist thoughts and actions, treated the Chinese with little dignity. This sign, allegedly posted at the turn of the last century, was merely a symbol of previous humiliations. Yet here it was casting its long shadow over a Shandong playground in 2010, forcing my seven and eight-year-old daughters to answer for events of a hundred years past.

Chinese have a fundamentally different relationship with their history than we Westerners. History is a subject we study in school. But wars took place in faraway lands. Our individualism means that our collective history, as Americans, is once removed from our identity. World War I and the Great Depression and the Smoot-Hawley tariff are events in history books. They are studied, they are even interesting, but they are not that connected to who we are.

Not so for the Chinese. History here is not book knowledge. Rather, their history is carried along with them as they walk along the way, an unseen burden, an invisible shadow; unconscious, and therefore, powerful. We Americans read about history. The Chinese experience it like reaching back into their own memory.

Katherine, Bing Bing and Xue Hanshao began playing a game in the courtyard. Grace was interested, though she still sat broodingly on my lap. A few minutes later Xue Hanshao approached.

"Grace, won't you come and play with us?"

Grace was off like a flash and the four girls scampered off together as children do, whether in the East or West, their differences quickly forgotten. I wondered if Americans and Chinese would always have to remain watchful of history's long shadows. Perhaps so. Unless Xue Hanshao's and Bing Bing's generation doesn't pass the story on to their children.

EVERY THOUSAND YEARS

Dan Washburn

Dan Washburn is Managing Editor at the Asia Society in New York. Dan worked as a freelance writer out of Shanghai from 2002 to 2011. His writings have appeared in *The Atlantic*, *The Economist*, ESPN.com, and other publications. In 2005, he founded the popular website Shanghaiist. He is currently working on a book about the development of golf in China. Dan lives with his wife in Brooklyn.

THERE ARE NO GUARDRAILS on the road to Qixin. And there is only one other way to the top of the mountain – a four-hour hike. It was February, and the ice and snow from Guizhou's winter storms had recently melted, leaving the famously treacherous cliff-side dirt road even more rutted and muddy than normal. But it was passable, by local standards at least, for the first time in weeks. And so we stood in the bed of the dump truck, gripping the rails tight, bracing our bodies as the vehicle lurched back and forth like a rowboat in rough water.

After more than an hour of winces and white knuckles, we could finally see over the top of the mountain. The road had nowhere else it could go. Terraces gave way to the severity of the land. Barren tree trunks jutted out of large bleached boulders. It was clear we were arriving at our destination. This was where Zhou Xunshu grew up.

For the past year, I had followed Zhou from province to province as he competed on the China Tour, the country's fledgling (and now defunct) professional golf circuit. The goal was to tell Zhou's remarkable story – he went from peasant farmer to security guard to self-taught golf pro in less than a decade – through a series of magazine articles, and eventually a book. To tell the tale correctly, I needed to see where Zhou came from.

Zhou was fine with this, but it was clear he had no desire to join me on the trip. A word Zhou often uses to describe his childhood is ku, or bitter. "Some people have memories from their childhood…I don't," Zhou told me. "We'd get up and hike to school and come back and work in the fields. We did this every day. Who wants to remember that?"

And so I went to Zhou's village – two days and four modes of transportation from my home in Shanghai – without Zhou.

★

Qixin, stuck on the side of a remote mountain, elevation 6,000 feet, is perhaps the poorest village in the poorest province in China. There is no way to prove this, of course, but there's also no denying that life in this tiny collection of crude stone homes is harsh and antiquated. People here aren't starving anymore, as was the case in years past, but a stay in the village easily conjures up centuries old images of the American frontier. It's a simple, gritty existence.

I was greeted by Zhou's father, a slight and smiley old man who wanted nothing more than to make this stranger feel at home. He brought out some short wooden stools and arranged them in the courtyard near stacks of firewood and bundles of drying tobacco leaves, and then two smaller plastic stools, on which he placed a bowl of local walnuts ("from the tree just over there") and a plate of fresh apples.

"I am just very excited," he said with a thick local accent. "You went through so many hardships coming here. Thank you so much for coming. Thank you so much. Our only concern is that the living conditions here are not good enough for you."

Zhou's father moved slowly, his legs riddled with rheumatism and hyperostosis, but he was chatty and animated. His dialect was often hard to decipher, but he spoke just as much with his body and face as he did with words and phrases. In contrast, Zhou's mother barely said a word. Her husband chatting away, she went about her business preparing the evening's meal, picking the stems off of a clutch of wild mushrooms. Her silver hair was tucked inside a light gray stocking cap emblazoned with the word PING, an American brand of golf equipment.

Also joining us was Zhou's eldest brother, known as First Brother among family members. There was something about him, perhaps his pompadour-esque poof of jet black hair, which reminded me of a 1950s greaser. He took long intense draws on his Huangguoshu cigarettes, named after Guizhou's famous waterfall, the largest in China. And he was determined to drink alcohol with every meal.

"You know, Zhou was going to become a police office," First Brother said.

This came up several times during my stay in the village. Zhou may be a professional golfer, he may be the most successful person to come out of Qixin, but for some he's still the family member who was supposed to become a police officer, and failed. Police officer is a concept Zhou's family, especially his parents, could understand. It's a concept they knew their neighbors would understand. Golf was different. It was strange. It was foreign. It was completely new.

How can you impress your friends with your son's job when even you don't understand what he does?

★

There is no refrigeration in the village. And after the brutal winter of 2008 there was almost no fresh produce, either. When it snows heavily, as it did this winter, no vehicles can access Qixin and even the simplest items are a luxury. Villagers must lug heavy bags of rice up the mountain on foot and family cooks need to get creative with the same nonperishable, and very familiar, ingredients every day.

The colorful array of dishes laid out before us, however (I counted 10 courses) belied the forced culinary uniformity of the season. The menu was explained to me: "This is fried potato slices. That is tofu. That is fried wheat gluten. That is rice noodles. Those are pig's ears. That is larou. That is also larou. And that one, too." Preserved pork, three ways.

I had to pace my consumption cannily, because each time I finished what was in my bowl, someone would immediately fill it up with something else. "Eat more," they would say. "Eat more pig's ear!"

Sometime between serving numbers six and seven, the faint warble of recorded music could be heard from somewhere in the darkness beyond the house.

"Ah, the power is back," First Brother said. "Good."

It wasn't long ago that life without electricity was simply Life. Qixin didn't get wired until the mid-1990s. Bowls overflowing with food were also a relatively new phenomenon. Nearly everyone seated around the table remembered when there was barely enough to eat.

"Before, only when celebrating festivals or having friends visiting could we eat meat," First Brother said. "Nowadays, we can eat meat any time, every day. Before, drinking beers – no way. Drinking rice wine – no way."

That was certainly no longer the case. First Brother raised his glass of beer in my direction.

"Before we did not know each other, and now we do," he said. "So we are friends. Ganbei!"

This was the first of many toasts I would receive from First Brother. Often we were the only two drinking. This was especially true at breakfast.

We never sipped. It was always ganbei, dry the glass. We started with beer, a rather unmemorable lager from Henan province they purchase at the market down at the bottom of the

mountain, 180 500-milliliter bottles at a time. We then graduated
to a dubious local moonshine made from corn sold at the market
for just three yuan per liquid pound.

Finally, during our last night together, First Brother brought
out a bottle he received from his wife's brother-in-law. It was filled
with a pinkish brown substance and hundreds of tiny flecks of…
something. It was called yaojiu, medicine alcohol, and First Brother
claimed it contained 25 different medicinal herbs that could "cure
problems with your lung, liver, kidney, spleen, and bones."

"This is the first time we meet," he would say. "We are so
grateful."

Ganbei!

"From our grandparents' generation until our next generation,
it is impossible to have the chance to have a foreigner come to
visit us."

Ganbei!

"In our hometown, this is probably a chance every thousand
years that you come to our home. We are very happy. So drink
more. This is our Guizhou people's custom. You are our friend
coming from far away."

Ganbei!

"Today, you came to visit our home and I am very excited.
This is something not even money can buy."

Ganbei!

"You are my best friend, and it is not easy for you to come all
the way here to be friends with us."

Ganbei!

"Okay, my friend. Finish this corn wine and I promise I won't
give you any more."

Ganbei!

★

Qixin in the winter is absent of color. The ground is brown,
the sky is grey, the trees are bare, the houses are covered in dust.

The only splashes of color come from the villagers' clothing, but even that is muted; it's hard to keep anything clean here for long. When Zhou was a child, he used to bathe in a river near where he watched the oxen graze. That river has since run dry. Now, villagers wash themselves in large basins at home. First Brother said most people bathe about once every 10 days.

On my second day, I walked through the village and arrived at a landing overlooking the valley, which was still partially obscured by fog. The terrain was dry and brittle: tall yellow grass, white rocks, naked trees. This is where, as a child, Zhou would take the family oxen to graze. This was where he, before he ever heard the word "golf," played a golf-like game with a wad of paper and a long-handled sickle.

There were four village boys on the landing ranging in age from seven to eleven. Their cheeks were rosy, their clothes covered in dirt. They looked like a gang of Chinese Huckleberry Finns, "fluttering with rags," long blades of grass held between their teeth. I asked the boys if they knew who Zhou Xunshu was. They all said yes. Have you heard of golf? They all said no. Soccer? No. Basketball? No. Yao Ming? No. The Olympics? No. Do you know what sports are? One of the boys brought up the morning calisthenics they performed at school and asked, "Is that a sport?"

We returned home to find First Brother preparing a chicken for slaughter. This was a special gesture in my honor. Normally, the family would only kill a chicken for Spring Festival, the biggest holiday of the year.

A cigarette heavy with ash dangling from his mouth, First Brother held open the beak of the chicken while his wife poured a clear liquid into its mouth from a white bowl.

"Rice wine," he said. "That will make the chicken taste better."

We crowded around the huolu (literally "fire oven"), a coal-burning stove that also serves as dinner table. During my brief stay in Qixin, I had been asking so many questions – personal questions – and my hosts had answered every one. They had treated me like family. But the thought occurred to me: Did they even know what I was doing there? Zhou is not the best communicator.

"No, Zhou Xunshu did not tell us," First Brother said, raising his glass of beer in my direction. "Ganbei!"

"It was my fifth uncle who called and said someone is coming to visit, but he did not say who," First Brother's son said. "And he called my uncle in Bijie and my uncle in Bijie called the village."

"When they learned someone was coming, did you think it was strange? Did you wonder why?" I asked.

"When you got here, I was wondering why," First Brother admitted. "But we are friends now. I do not care if my youngest brother called or not. As long as you are my friend I will treat you the same way."

"Do they want to know why I am here?"

"I never thought about it. We welcome friends no matter from China or abroad."

I told the family about my research, about the magazine articles, about the plans for a book.

"Good!" First Brother said. "Before I did not know, and now I know. I will not change my mind for three, five, eight, 10 even 100 years. I will always welcome you. Nothing else I can say. You come here, you are my brother!"

★

The roosters rise before the sun in Qixin. So do the people. It was 6 a.m., my final morning in the village, and I was greeted by the sounds of the birds and breakfast. As the cattle lowed beneath me, I opened my room's back door and stared into the darkness. Silhouettes of leafless trees slowly took shape. The mountain was waking up.

Neighbors were joining us for the morning meal, and First Brother (not that he really needed one) took that as an excuse to break out the alcohol.

"Let me pour some corn alcohol for you," First Brother said.

"What time is it?" I asked.

"I like alcohol," he said. "Gan yi bei, drink one glass. I wish you a nice trip."

The neighbor, a man who looked to be about the same age as First Brother, had been staring at me since we sat around the huolu. He finally turned to First Brother and asked, "Where's he from?"

"Meiguo," First Brother replied. "America."

The neighbor, still studying me, paused and cocked his head to one side. "They look like Russians, don't they?" he said.

The neighbor's wife presented me with a bag of hard-boiled eggs.

"One more glass of corn wine!" First Brother insisted. "For your journey. Ganbei!"

The mountain road was said to be slippery that morning, and so too the path leading to the road. But that didn't stop a dozen or so people from seeing us to our ride: a dusty red dump truck with a bed full of dried corn stalks.

Zhou's father slipped his bare feet into a pair of untied basketball sneakers. Zhou's mother wore slippers. And they carefully shuffled along, navigating down the muddy, sloping trail.

"Is his leg okay?" I asked. "Should he be coming all the way down with us?"

"It's no problem," First Brother's son assured me.

Zhou's father took my hand, and we walked to the truck together.

"I am so happy you came to see us," he said to me. "I will never forget you. Thank you so much."

The old man hugged me, and tears came to my eyes.

"We feel bad you come all the way here and we did not treat you well," Zhou's mother said "You need to forgive us for not treating you well enough. We're sorry."

"Thank you," Zhou's father repeated.

"We're sorry," his wife said again.

"Thank you."

"We're sorry."

They repeated this chorus as I climbed into the truck and took my place amongst the corn stalks.

The truck grunted to life. I gripped the handrails tightly and braced my body for the turbulent ride ahead. Zhou's parents were smiling wide and waving.

"Wish you a nice trip!" Zhou's father shouted.

I let go with one hand and attempted to wave back. The truck lurched forward, and I almost fell into the person beside me.

WATER, FOR LI-MING

Kaitlin Solimine

Raised in New England, Kaitlin Solimine has considered China a second home for almost two decades. While at Harvard University, she wrote and edited *Let's Go: China*. She was a Fulbright Fellow in China and an excerpt from her first novel, "Empire of Glass", won the 2012 Dzanc Books/Disquiet International Literary Program award. Her writings have been published in *Cha: An Asian Literary Journal*, *The Hairpin*, *The Places We've Been* among others.

WHEN LI-MING DANCED with the other retirees below the overpass of Beijing's Second Ring Road, her arms fanned and her head lolled as if swimming the breaststroke. When she cooked her famous sweet and sour chicken, the wok's sauces seethed and bubbled like rapids. When she was a teenager, she dreamed of freestyle stroking alongside the great Chairman in the wicked current of the Yangtze. As a Sent Down Youth in Jiangxi Province, she nearly drowned in a flood that overturned her farm tractor.

When I met Li-Ming in Beijing, she insisted I teach her 13-year-old daughter Chenxi how to swim. She said Chenxi needed a big sister like me to show her the strokes because Li-Ming herself never learned. I'd only known Li-Ming for an hour. I was only 16. It was my first time outside the U.S. and this exuberant water-loving woman was to be my mother for five months as part of a high school home stay program.

The first thing Li-Ming said to me was an instruction in Mandarin: "Ni jiao wo 'Mama'," "You call me 'Mama'." I did.

As a haughty teenager, I thought one mother was enough.

Nevertheless, I quickly learned Chinese mothers don't give you a choice: they embrace you with both arms, dictating how you'll eat your food (voraciously – not one rice grain spared) and when you'll wake up each morning (at the crack of dawn – to the sound of a seething tea kettle and CCTV's monotone morning news).

Back home in the U.S., I prided myself on my independence: my mother seldom asked where I was headed when I hopped on my bicycle, or who I was calling when I picked up the phone. But as Li-Ming's "daughter," I was suddenly (and inexplicably) obedient and gracious. She did not so much demand this as she inspired it; when Li-Ming walked into a room, swimming with her wide arm gestures, speaking in her singsong voice, everyone turned to watch. She was someone you were innately compelled to be near; her love, your ultimate goal. Little did I know that Li-Ming had more love to give than I'd ever known.

That's the thing about Chinese mothers: hidden behind their maternal expectations and critical diatribes are women who will fight to the death for you. As soon as I called her Mama, Li-Ming would be my strongest ally for the only months I knew her.

★

My first day living with Li-Ming's family, I was tossed into her turbulent household, where meals were a shared-dish affair and everyone finished their bowls to the last grain of rice. Li-Ming's parents, in for the autumn from Guilin, lived with us, so the three-room apartment had a cramped, elderly air. The walls were decorated like in a curiosities shop: a street map of Beijing, an eye chart, a calendar two years out of date. In my American home, every room had a purpose (the dining room for *dining*, the living room for *living*), but in Li-Ming's home, each room served several purposes: the dining room where we ate at the communal table was also the living room (a futon backed the wall and an old TV sat on a hutch) as well as a bedroom (the bed where Li-Ming and her husband slept was feet away from the kitchen table, bordering the room's only window).

At the cramped table cluttered with dishes, Li-Ming repeatedly said, "You're not eating enough, Katie." Her husband, my Chinese father who I called Baba, nodded in agreement as Li-Ming spooned another heap of pork and peppers into my bowl.

On application essays to the home stay program that placed me with Li-Ming's family, I'd written I wanted to live in China to seek a deeper understanding of the language and culture I'd studied in New Hampshire for two years; in reality, I was testing my independence, challenging my ability to survive outside the comforts of my American home.

I got more than I'd signed up for. We lived in a cramped, humid Soviet-style apartment block beside a community of Beijing's old (now demolished) hutong alleyways. Here, old men sat slumped on street corners, pushing mahjong tiles atop makeshift tables. Siheyuan courtyard homes were shrouded behind tree-tall brick walls – the only view of their inhabitants were the old taitai who teetered on once-bound feet to the shared toilets near Rending Lake Park.

In the distance, Deshengmen Tower and the now non-existent city wall that once extended from it, reminded residents that this part of the city was once the purview of only bureaucrats and royalty. Bicycles, bells jangling, jostled down the neighborhood's narrow streets, clamoring for space alongside exhaust-spewing buses and breadbox taxis (so called for their shape).

At night, lonely and wondering what I was thinking boarding the series of flights that led me here, I cried myself to sleep to the sound of late night commuters arriving home; they'd park their bicycles in the apartment complex's communal courtyard, then plod upstairs. The six-story building, which had no elevators, was built in the early 1980s for the workers of the local danwei, work unit, a then state-owned electrical engineering company whose factory floors were just blocks away. The entire campus once housed factory workers; neighbors would walk to work together, sending their children to the same local elementary school. Living here was like finding a village within in a city.

As I slept, my new Chinese "sister" Chenxi lay just an arm's length away on her matching twin bed. I'd never felt so far from home (at this time the Internet and mobile phones had not yet reached China). On top of that, I was a finicky eater suddenly forced to gnaw on pigs' knuckles and avoid the maggots that wriggled into the family's stock of rice.

Then there were the more *feminine* issues. When I got my period that first month, I asked Li-Ming where to buy tampons in Beijing. I found the word in my Chinese-English dictionary, translating it for Li-Ming with simultaneous pride and embarrassment. But Li-Ming shook her head feverishly, her short hair bouncing.

"No, Katie! You cannot use 'tampons' as you call them!" She said the Chinese word like it was foreign. "No. No. No. No virgins use tampons!"

I didn't dare tell her I'd already lost my virginity. The next day, when I returned from school, there was a stack of "sanitary napkins" on my desk. I later learned the only place to buy Western-style tampons in Beijing was the Friendship Store near the Silk Market; I'd sneak off after school to make my elicit purchase, then hide the contraband in my drawer.

By Mid-Autumn Festival, I was helping Li-Ming before dinners, sculpting meticulously folded dumplings, tossing pinches of sugar into her stir-fries. During these moments I indulged her with stories of my life back in the U.S.: a childhood spent on the wide front lawn of my New Hampshire home, summers swimming against the Atlantic's chilled tide.

She, too, shared stories of her youth: how she'd read poetry outside the guarded gates of Zhongnanhai and attended school with the children of China's communist elite. But she never fit in among these elevated ranks; in middle school she'd worn her jacket inside out to test if the teachers would notice (they did; she was promptly scolded).

There was, I soon realized, a buried misfit hidden within Li-Ming, a girl desiring to live a life much larger than her childhood in China allowed. As a teenager during the Cultural Revolution, she and her fellow Red Guards were sent to Jiangxi Province to learn the ways of peasants. She was a "barefoot doctor" who birthed pigs, milked cows, checked the pulses of donkeys. She loved every minute of it, her city skin quickly shed for the ways of the villagers. In another life, she'd have been born on a farm (as a farm girl, surely she'd know how to swim).

She was also a woman who lived for spontaneity. One misty Sunday morning, she woke Chenxi and me early, insisting we spend the day hiking in Beijing's Fragrant Hills. We all piled into a taxi, our first time leaving the city by a transport other than bicycle or bus. At the White Cloud Temple where we'd begin our day, Li-Ming asked me to pull the hood of my raincoat over my head, synching the ties such that my face barely showed.

"Today you are truly my daughter! My *Chinese* daughter!" she exclaimed, laughing.

"What do you mean?" I asked in a muffled voice.

"*Shhh*," she shushed, holding up her finger and instructing me to stand far from the ticket booth; she was determined for me to enter the complex as her Chinese daughter – the foreigner entrance fee was nearly 10 times that of the Chinese price!

I watched as she handed over the cash, then returned to me, an extra bounce in her step.

"Am I Chinese now?" I asked from behind the veil of my hood, but she didn't need to hear me. She smiled victoriously, wrapping her arm around my shoulder and laughing loudly as we passed through the front gate.

I remember laughing with her, the feeling of a strangely defiant success, but I recall nothing of the temple or what we saw in the damp, disappointingly *un*fragrant hills. All that mattered, despite how unexpectedly I'd fallen back into a familiar role, was that I had entered the temple that day as a Chinese daughter – Li-Ming's, nonetheless.

★

Weeks later, after finishing another multiple-dished dinner, Li-Ming told me she wanted me to see something at nearby Deshengmen Gate. As usual, I couldn't protest her request. Then again, I'd come to love our unexpected adventures and was eager to know what tonight's would bring. We readied for the November air with woolen hats and gloves, the requisite neiku long underwear I hated that Li-Ming always insisted I wear, lest I catch cold. Together, we bicycled to an underpass of the Second Ring Road beside the old City Moat that once prevented foreigners from entering the city's heart.

As we approached, I heard cymbals clashing, drums pounding an incessant beat. Li-Ming could barely wait for me; she quickly locked her bicycle to a lamppost and I skipped to catch up. On a poorly lit square beside the moat, dozens of older women danced in a coordinated fashion, waving red, orange, green, and purple fans into the coal-choked night sky.

"Take this," Li-Ming insisted, handing me my own red fan from a stack atop an empty bench.

"But I don't know how to dance!"

"Of course you do!" she said encouragingly. She was already following dancing women who snaked around the perimeter in a choreographed tango line.

I unfurled my fan, looking for a place to enter. In the far distance, a collection of old men sat on stools providing the musical accompaniment, like a band in a 1930s Shanghai dance hall.

"Just shake your hips and stomp your feet! It's easy!" Li-Ming's fluttering voice insisted from somewhere, but I couldn't see her red hat; here, everyone was the same height, wore the same winter hats, had the same shortly cropped hairdo of Chinese female of middle-age.

In other circumstances, on other continents, I may have thrown down my fan in exasperation. I may have felt incapable of doing that which I didn't know how to do. But I could hear Li-Ming's carefree laughter enticing me from within the circle of women. I raised my fan above my head, followed the steps of those around me, and, for a few minutes of dancing, forgot who I was.

★

Before I left her home, Li-Ming gave me a photo album filled with images of our months together. On its cover, she penned this poem:

时间虽流逝	*Although time flows along,*
记忆永留存	*Our memories will forever persist.*
中美隔万里	*China and the U.S. may be thousands of miles apart,*
爱心的相连	*But our hearts are always linked.*

Less than two years later, Li-Ming passed away after a quick battle with cancer.

★

Chenxi, without much of my assistance, delivered in her promise to her mother: she was a commensurate swimmer, capable of flaunting every stroke – breast, freestyle, butterfly, back. Over the following two decades, I returned to China, keeping my promise to Li-Ming to remain linked to the country and her family. On my visits, I'd fall back into old habits: finding myself finishing my dishes at Li-Ming's old kitchen table, falling asleep in the same room as Chenxi. Within years, Chenxi found her way to the United States for studies and work; eventually, she and Baba walked down my wedding aisle, and I hers. Chenxi and I have swum alongside each other in pools and oceans all over the world: in China, Hong Kong, California, France, New Hampshire, Costa Rica...

But Li-Ming: she never learned how to swim. She loved the water as much as she feared it.

Since Li-Ming's death, I've returned to her home in Beijing dozens of times, living with Baba and Chenxi for as long as several months per visit. One night, sleeping in the exact same bed as always, I dreamt that Li-Ming and I were walking together in nearby Rending Lake Park, a place we often visited together. The air was misty. Willows dipped into the manmade lake's drained basin. Li-Ming wanted to stop at a fruit stand to buy a watermelon. She insisted, once we bought it, that I eat a slice, and I awoke to the taste of that sweet, fleshy fruit on my tongue, honeying my cheeks.

When I opened my eyes, Baba was there, clapping his hands in his customary morning greeting and opening the shades to let in the dawn.

"Time for breakfast!"

"I'm not hungry," I said.

"You must eat breakfast," he insisted, as all Chinese insist.

"I saw Li-Ming in my dream last night."

Without batting an eye, he asked, "What did she say?"

And so I told him, hoping not to disappoint him with the banality of my conversation with his dead wife. But Baba quickly smiled and laughed, as Li-Ming would have.

"She always knows what's best," he said, before shuffling down the hall to the same door Li-Ming used to burst through each afternoon, holding plates of food and insisting, time and time again, that I needed to eat, that I teach Chenxi how to swim, that America must be a large, empty place with so few people, that she was my Chinese mother forever, and that, in the way water is equally dissipating and buoying, we were so lucky, yet fated, to meet.

Invasive Species

Jonathan Watts

Jonathan Watts is the author of the eco-travelogue "When a Billion Chinese Jump: How China Will Save Mankind – Or Destroy It." He was formerly the Asia Environment Correspondent for *The Guardian* and president of the Foreign Correspondents' Club of China. Currently based in Rio de Janeiro, he covers developments related to both the loss and rebuilding of the Amazon.

I NEVER MET JOSEF MARGRAF. The alchemist, ecologist and orchid farmer died a few months before I visited his extraordinary forest home in Xishuangbanna in the spring of 2010. But the short time I spent in his afterlife continues to resonate years later and half a world away.

It was an awkward time. Josef had suffered heart failure at the relatively young age of 56. His wife and young daughters were still mourning, but also slowly trying to move on and continue with Josef's work. Unintentionally and briefly, I became part of their transition. The experience changed me too.

It was pure chance that I was there soon after his sudden death. If I believed in fate, I might have felt chosen in some way to carry on his mission. Others who were in that special place at that remarkable time told me they felt the same. Josef's passing created an emotional and intellectual vacuum that sucked in anyone with a sense of responsibility, adventure or romance. Basically, anyone with a China dream.

'Geography is destiny,' it has been said. There's some truth in that. But we can also move. I've learned over the years that where you are can change who you are – or, at least, how you are seen and what opportunities you are given. It certainly changes your perspective. I guess that is why travel stories are so compelling. It is probably also why so many foreigners see China as a chance not just to reinvent themselves, but to reshape the world. Josef was such a person. I used to think I should remain an observer.

★

A mixture of opportunism, whimsy and rubber had taken me to their semi-tropical southern corner of China. A few days earlier, I had been in Kunming, the provincial capital of Yunnan, for two different stories: the worst drought in living memory (it had rained as soon as I arrived) and a "cancer village" (where my assistant and I had been thrown out by the authorities).

With those jobs done, the weekend ahead and knowing how rarely I was in one of my favorite provinces, I felt I couldn't miss the chance to visit Xishuangbanna. By Chinese standards, it was relatively close: a mere 300 miles to the south. The flight was available and inexpensive so I decided to make a speculative trip. If I found a story, I would claim it on expenses. If not, I'd be paying just a few thousand yuan to see a part of the world that had come to fascinate me.

I had just finished writing a book about China's environment that had left me in a gloomy state of mind, but also hungry to learn more, particularly about alternatives and solutions. During my research, Xishuangbanna had come up again and again. Two important references – Ma Jun's *China Water Crisis* and Judith Shapiro's *Mao's War on Nature* – cited the clearance of virgin forest in the area for rubber plantations among the country's greatest ecological disasters. Still weightier significance was placed on the region by polymath Mark Elvin, who wrote a tome on how Xishuangbanna had become the last holdout for wild elephants in China. These great beasts had once roamed in vast herds as far north as Beijing, but millennia of Han agriculturalism had cleared their forest habitat, leaving just a few dozen left in the border region. It was a last refuge for biodiversity, minority culture and, I hoped, alternative ideas. There was always a better chance of finding those on the fringes. Boundaries and borders tended to be rich veins of change.

I flew into the regional capital, Jinghong, around noon and took a taxi from the airport, across the Lancang (better known outside China as the Mekong), into the city. It struck me as hot, humid and shabby. There were few signs that this had once been the capital of the Tai kingdom, which 500 years earlier had encompassed much of Thailand and Burma. Today, it was merely the seat of government for China's Xishuangbanna Dai Autonomous Prefecture.

Like almost everywhere in the country, it was undergoing a construction boom. New hotels, restaurants and a shopping complex were being built along the riverfront in a modern re-imagining of Dai architectural style. Jinghong was trying to nurture a tourist industry. But the dominant economic force by far was rubber. Seeds of the latex-producing trees, Hevea brasiliensis, had been collected from Latin America by British botanists and first planted in Asia in the 19th century. In the 1950s, the plantations had spread over the plains of Xishuangbanna at the prompting of Mao Zedong. Now, high commodity prices were driving this invasive species up into the highlands. That was what I had come to write about.

My assistant had arranged an interview with a local woman who was known as the most outspoken critic of the monocultures. Minguo Li-Margraf had a formidable reputation, but she was surprisingly hesitant on the phone. She explained that she had not met anyone outside the family's inner circle for some time because her husband, Josef, had recently passed away. But the issue of the plantations was close to both of their hearts, so at the very least she would arrange a guide, and she *might* even speak to us. It would, she said, depend how she felt when we arrived.

The guide, a member of the Dai community, took my

assistant and I across a Mekong tributary to a rubber plantation and showed us how it was almost devoid of life. We walked for an hour or two in the shade provided by the thick canopy that would look from the air like a dense green forest. Underneath, however, it was eerily empty except for workers collecting the latex that dripped down the gashes cut into the side of the trees.

Locals referred to the plantations as "green deserts" because they sucked up so much water and nutrition from the soil that almost nothing was left for any other species. From a short-term economic point of view, this monoculture was eminently logical. Longer-term, it was an unmitigated disaster for the region's fertility and diversity. The consequences had started to be felt in changing weather conditions, pollution from insecticides and herbicides, and complaints from other Mekong nations about falling downstream water volumes. Our guide didn't want to get too deeply into the politics. For that, he recommended I talk to Minguo.

By the time we got to the house, she was ready to talk. This may have been because she too was a former journalist as well as an environmental campaigner and so realized the importance of a comment. More likely, it was because we were guests and, as Minguo later conceded, the mourning process could not go on indefinitely. She appeared somber, but possessed of a powerful spirit. I guessed she was in her late 30s or early 40s – around the same age as me. She was attractive.

I passed on my condolences and tried to be sensitive and professional by keeping the conversation on the subject of the plantations, but that was evidently too confining. Hesitant at first, her train of thought sped from science to fate to reminiscences about her husband. She was a smart, strong communicator who talked passionately, albeit in occasionally awkward English, about their efforts to find an economic alternative to the plantations, but this appeared to be mixed with somewhat half-baked new-aged beliefs, grand claims that stretched credibility, and a focus on a German who was unlikely to be of interest to a

British audience.

It was not the China story I was looking for. But whenever I attempted to steer the discussion back on the rubber track, Minguo looked put out that I had failed to grasp the greater significance of what she was telling me. By the time the interview ended, I was genuinely intrigued, but frustrated too. We had touched on so many topics yet no more than scratched the surface of most of them. Maybe sensing my feelings, she said it was time the wider world learned more about Josef's work. Perhaps she was also glad of the chance to talk to someone outside her circle of grief. I was invited back that evening.

★

Night had fallen by the time my taxi found its way back up the winding, steep, now poorly illuminated backstreets and dropped me once again outside the green double gates of the family home. It seemed different from the daytime. Now the threshold sharply delineated two very different worlds. Walking across, I felt like I was passing from the street to the forest, from artificial light to natural dark, from near silence to an orchestra of frogs and insects.

This was Josef's realm. It was also a bank for the seeds, samples and ideas the German scientist had picked up on his journeys through Yunnan. A biologist by training and a collector by habit, he boasted to friends that this single garden was home to more species than all of Germany. I could believe it. The private jungle stretched into the darkness without visible end. I needed a guide with a torch to lead me from the gates, down a steep path, past the orchid nursery and into the family's home.

I had been impressed by the building during the day. Made of local wood and indigenous thatch, spacious but unobtrusive, decorated with local crafts and simple ceramics, the Dai-style residence was as elegant as any I have seen before or since. The construction relied on pillars more than walls with broad decks at the front and back that left it open to the elements. At night it was hard to tell where the house ended and the forest began.

A child of extraordinary poise came to greet me. A Eurasian with long, dark hair and inquisitive, intelligent eyes, the girl could not even have been 10 years old, but she met this tall, bearded, foreign stranger with the self-assurance and courtesy of a high-society hostess many times her age. Speaking English with a slight German accent, she introduced herself as Linda, told me her mother was still getting ready so she had been sent down to help me pass the time.

As the adoring father of two slightly older Eurasian daughters, I was struck by both a sense of familiarity and difference. This child, with her maturity, precision and congeniality, was so unlike my own or any of her generation that I had met in Beijing, let alone Tokyo or London.

"Do you want to listen to some music?" she asked. "What do you want to hear? If you don't tell me, I will play Bach. *I* like Bach."

She then disappeared into an adjoining hut and, suddenly, a recording of the Brandenburg Concertos was echoing through the forest. I was entranced. The experience was so other-worldly that I felt like the character in a novel; The Magus came to mind.

Her mother appeared soon after with a younger and equally beautiful daughter, who was introduced as Wanda. Minguo was more relaxed than she had been earlier. We chatted as the children played. Minguo said her daughters had developed such a strong bond that they played hide-and-seek not by looking, but by using their hands to sense where the other was. Even as their mother, she said, it felt spooky. But there was reason why they were so close.

Linda and Wanda had never set foot in a school and had barely any contact with other children. Josef had taught them himself: math, history, botany, literature, German and English, while their mother had taught them Chinese. He did not approve of television or computer games. Their interaction with the outside world was through travel and the many visiting professors, diplomats, businessmen and wanderers who came to study and while away the evenings on the terrace – as we were doing – talking and drinking. As a result, most of their friends were not elementary school classmates but postgrads and PhDs.

As with the forest garden and his home, Josef had not just refused to conform to modern norms, he had substituted them with values of his own. I might have been skeptical if I had not seen the enviable results with my own eyes. This was radical parenting and home building. My respect for Josef – and Minguo – was growing.

He was an impulsive romantic too. Minguo told me Josef proposed the first day they met. It was at a reception for the Peruvian ambassador. They talked and hit it off despite a difference in age and culture. He serenaded her on the piano and then asked for her hand. Soon after, they married; he gave up his old life as a program manager for the German development agency and they bought the 10,667 square-meter plot of abandoned rubber plantation on the banks of the Lancang-Mekong where we were now sitting. They restored the forest, built a home and created a family according to a set of mutual beliefs that blended Western science, Eastern philosophy, modern ecological thinking, local traditions and some esoteric and original concoctions of their own.

My cynicism kicked in. A hodge-podge of ideas, a new young wife, a sudden change – weren't these the symptoms of a middle-aged crisis, especially among expats? I was the same age as Josef had been when he proposed, so I knew the urges. I had seen them in friends. I had felt them myself.

But Josef had not acted rashly. Rather, Josef appeared to have looked back at what life had taught him, made some big decisions, and then planned carefully how to put them into practice. This was no fluke. Nor was he selfishly thinking only of himself. His concerns had always been ecological. A doctor of biology from Hohenheim University, Josef discovered and named several species including a variety of ginger in China, a fish in the Philippines and a banana near his home in Xishuangbanna. He was a respected environmentalist who had initiated and managed multi-million dollar programs for the German development agency and the European Union. But he refused to be bound by bureaucratic thinking.

Minguo explained that Josef was disillusioned with conventional approaches to conservation. After decades working with government institutes, aid programs and environmental NGOs, he could see that even the best-managed programs were failing. It was no longer enough to protect key habitats by fencing them off, because that ran up against calls for development and smacked of hypocrisy coming from a Europe that had long since cleared most of its forests for farmland. Instead, he believed the best way to fend off industrial monocultures was to nurture the value of biodiversity beneath the canopy. With this 'use it or lose it' approach, private companies could join hands with local people and governments to strengthen the net of forest care providers. He made a name for this strategy: "rainforestation." After a pilot project focusing on the Golden Lotus dwarf banana (a spectacular plant with hundreds of golden petals that is considered sacred in Buddhism) proved a success, he expanded to 100 other species.

With Minguo as his collaborator and liaison with the local government, Josef took over a mountainside that had once been a rubber plantation, he picked and mixed from his extensive seed bank to re-grow a bio-diverse forest that could pay back the investments with orchid fragrances, honey, mushrooms and other marketable items. He had found partners in the French fragrance industry and German Embassy. In a sense it was an attempt to inoculate the forests with the virus of commodification so the natural environment could build up antibodies that would allow them to survive capitalism. It was also a search for the philosopher's stone of the environmental movement: a way of turning base economic instincts into ecological gold.

But he died before he found that formula and was now buried on the same mountain where he had planted three million seeds.

★

Minguo poured some honey wine. It was no ordinary home brew. She told me Josef had distilled it in the laboratory where he practiced alchemy. I did a double-take. What?! Once again, I felt I was in a different world. How could there be an alchemist in the 21st century? In Yunnan of all places. And German to boot. What piece of literature were we acting out now, Faust?

I wondered if I had misheard or whether something had been lost in translation. But no, Minguo showed me the paper Josef had written on his efforts to combine the sorcery of the ancients with the science of the moderns: first, he noted, he would mix plant samples with water, honey and yeast in two glasses to create a "spirit" and a "soul," which would then be blended in a single glass and left to calcify for a year to allow for their "development under the full influence of planetary constellations." The resulting elixir or arcanum was tested by both personal experiment and in a laboratory in Europe. It was unconventional. Josef knew that. He seemed to revel in breaking boundaries. I was incredulous, but fascinated.

The short paper, titled *Signatures*, was the last thing Josef wrote. A gospel of sorts, it amalgamates Western scientific training, modern ecological thinking and economic pragmatism with references to medieval alchemy, the history of calculus, morphogenetics, quantum physics, a fascination with the Daoist treaties of his adopted home and decades of field research, particularly into his beloved orchids. Like the essences he was constantly mixing in his home laboratory, it was as though years of research and thinking had started to coalesce into something that he felt was of enormous value to mankind. Reading a draft that he intended to submit for publication, I wondered it he had a presentiment of his death (he had suffered a heart attack five years earlier) and decided to condense his studies over decades into a coherent theory that would live on after him.

Written in excellent, but not always perfect, English, the draft overflows with ideas and the excitement that Josef clearly felt when making intellectual connections that spanned centuries and continents, such as the historical link he traces between the hexagrams of the Daoist I Ching, Jesuit priests, Leibniz, the binary system and the fractals of Chaos Theory.

At its heart is a challenge to Charles Darwin's Theory of Evolution. From years of studying orchids in Yunnan, Josef had come to believe that the Victorian scientist's concept of natural trial and error failed to fully explain how plants and pollinators interacted.

To elaborate, Josef cites the case of an extremely rare type of orchid, Sunipia cirrhata, which has only one pollen per flower. He surmises this is spread by a remarkable series of coincidences: First, the orchid releases a honey-like fragrance even though it has no honey. This smell attracts a bee that draws closer to the flower. The bee, in turn, draws a predator hornet. Finally, the hornet attacks the bee, which disturbs the flower sufficiently to release the pollen. Josef was doubtful that this series of events emerged through pure chance. Rather, he felt the plant sensed at some level how the insects behaved.

Unlike Darwin, he believed "change is not gradually evolving but instantly complete," and it is not random but in resonance with existing patterns and fields. Josef also posited the existence of "intentions," such as the "understandable wish of an orchid to get pollinated." That sounded a lot like lust, but there was more to it than that.

For Josef, this was a matter of efficiency. "There is no waste in time nor life for evolutionary changes. Ecosystems, which waste their energy and risk their species through Darwinian mechanisms of waging the war of selecting the fittest, seem meagerly equipped to cope with change," he wrote. "If this observation is correct, we may have substantial influence on the design of our own presence."

It struck me that Josef's theory was the opposite of Christian Creation theory: if he was right, nature is not the master plan of a god on high, but the outcome of an infinite interplay of intentions. This was closer to Daoism or Pantheism than a Judeo-Christian religion. But it was far from passive. In this world of constant biological revolution, change could be shaped by intention.

This was an immensely empowering message. But *Signatures* was no agenda for dictators or individualists. It emphasized the importance of sensitivity to the environment. When things click, Josef, citing the work of Alfred Sheldrake, writes that is because intentions are in tune with "morphic fields."

Before I entered Josef's home, I could not have told you what a morphic field was. But that night talking to Minguo I felt the phenomenon very strongly.

Morphic fields are habitual manifestations that are left behind by every expression of life. In other words, even after flora and fauna decompose, they continue to leave a trace of their behavior on other species. These may be so tiny as to be indistinguishable, but the combinations of millions of such interactions shape habits and habitats. Similarly, when humans die, they leave an afterglow of routines, thoughts and feelings that family, friends and neighbors have picked up and passed on. These habitual – or morphic – fields act as guides for evolution. They influence views of what is possible and desirable. They also shape, shift and blur the boundaries between this and that, us and them, even between life and death. They are ghosts.

It was not necessary to believe in spirits to sense Josef's presence. Less than three months after his death, his presence was still very evident in the home he had built. I looked at his framed portrait – a collage of plants, tendrils, leaves and branches that together formed his features. I walked through his laboratory, drank the honey wine he had fermented, and talked, as he used to do, late into the night with Minguo while breathing in the scent of their garden and watching their daughters play.

By the time I left, I was no longer sure if I had been inside Josef's mind, or he inside mine.

It was not an obvious "China story." Perhaps it was something bigger.

★

Working and wandering around China for almost a decade, I had enjoyed many memorable nights, but few were as thought-provoking and inspiring. I am not sure why. The unexpectedness, perhaps, or the exotic setting. Certainly Minguo's enchanting company and the alchemical effect of the wine. Maybe even Josef's morphic energy and my own feelings of sympathy, curiosity, admiration and empathy.

Josef and I had much in common. Both of us had left our European homelands for Asia, married, and raised daughters in China. Both our jobs focused on the environment and both of our beliefs had been influenced by Daoism. Then there were small coincidental similarities. My paternal roots were also German. I too had proposed very soon after meeting my wife. I would have been writing my book in Beijing at the same time that Josef was drafting *Signatures* in Xishuangbanna. Having read his work, I guess we had come to some of the same conclusions, namely that:

Borders between species, people and nations are transient, and connect as well as divide; individuals can create opportunities for change on both sides by crossing those borders; the key to successful change is sensitivity towards that which is indigenous (in other words, the ability to read morphic fields) and, in the long run, diversity will always be more resilient than monoculture despite the current unsustainable trends in the opposite direction.

There was also much in Josef's approach that I found less convincing: *Signatures* was a remarkable work based on decades of fieldwork and an intimate understanding of botany and biology, but it probably lacked the empirical evidence to stand up to scientific peer review. So too with his approach to rainforestation, which (I guess he would admit) was imperfect. Not everyone can live in a forest garden. Not every forest can be saved by fragrance companies. And while, a more harmonious balance between the economy and the environment is essential, there are immense risks in commodifying ecosystem because the market is not guided by good intentions.

Moreover, whatever good intentions Josef – or I, for that matter – might claim, weren't we too part of a kind of invasive species? Orientalists had come and gone for centuries, imposing and projecting their hopes and fears on Asia. Europeans had brought the rubber trees and monocultural practices to Asia, just as they had brought in many of the political, economic and scientific ideas that developed or distorted China's society and environment. Why should our legacy be any more positive?

That, I think, is the fundamental issue raised by *Signatures* and brought home to me on that unforgettable night in Jinhong. What morphic fields do we leave behind after we move on? What values, what offspring, what environment? In that regard, I think Josef has achieved more than any foreigner I had met. Certainly more than me – the observer. While I was living the life of a Beijing expat, he was restoring a forest in Xishuangbanna. While I collected quotes and wrote stories, he gathered seeds and planted trees. Friends considered him a sage. Certainly, he had gone deeper than anyone I had met in trying to meld Western and Eastern thought and then putting those Daoist-Ecological values into practice.

Judging by his home, his family and his work, Josef spent his last years living up to his belief that those who wasted their time and energy fighting a war of natural selection are meagerly equipped to cope with change. Instead, and perhaps typically for many Germans of his generation, he was looking to the future by making up for past wrongs, in this case those committed by humanity through industrial monocultures.

Josef Margraf became the foreigner who reintroduced indigenous species to China. This outsider did not just adjust to life on the border, he reshaped, restored and ultimately was subsumed in the faraway land he made home.

PLAYING IN THE GRAY

Graham Earnshaw

Graham Earnshaw was born in England and has lived most of his adult life in China as a journalist, businessman and publisher. He speaks Cantonese and Mandarin, and his translation of the Jin Yong kung fu novel "The Book and The Sword" into English was published by Oxford University Press. Graham is also the author of "Life and Death of a Dotcom in China", "Tales of Old Shanghai", and "The Great Walk of China."

I CLAIM TO BE the first person ever to have played the kazoo on the Great Wall of China. I was also lead singer in China's best rock 'n' roll band in the late 1970s and early 1980s; it was the best because we were the ONLY rock 'n' roll band in China. And, for several weeks, I was publisher of the first independent English-language newspaper to be published in Shanghai since the communist takeover of the city in 1949. China provides me, as an outsider, with the opportunity to do so many things that would be impossible in what might be called "the real world." That's one of the things I like about it.

It was the mid-1990s, a time of huge change in China, and particularly Shanghai. There was a monumental opening underway, a new linkage between the formerly separate worlds of foreigners and Chinese in that city. The degree to which in those days Shanghai, and indeed the whole of China, was segregated is hard to understand now, but it was a stark gulf; Chinese people could not even enter the apartment building I lived in then without enduring a grilling from the guards at the gate.

I dropped into Shanghai's heady vortex in late 1995 and immediately set up a website called Shanghai-ed, surely the first city portal website in the country in any language. You can see various incarnations of it by visiting the wonderful Wayback Machine on the Internet. It became the model for various other ventures, including a failed dotcom website venture I set up with a number of friends called ChinaNow, which in turn launched the careers of many people but ultimately died in the dotcom crash of early 2001.

An entrepreneur named Kathleen Lau was running an English-language magazine in the southern city of Guangzhou called *Clueless in Guangzhou*, presumably an oblique reference to a movie of that era, Sleepless in Seattle (Guangzhou was still widely called Canton in English at that time). Or perhaps a linkage between the hit movie *Clueless* and the city of her birth. Whatever. Kathleen and an associate, Mark Kitto, visited Shanghai sometime in 1997 to look at setting up a monthly publication there, and my partner, Tony Zhang, and I lunched with them to discuss some kind of cooperation with the Shanghai-ed website, but the discussion came to nothing. They were looking to do a monthly format similar to the *Time Out* listings and reviews magazine model. An American named Scott Savitt had pioneered the idea of grey-market, foreigner-run publications in China in the early 1990s with Beijing Scene, which ended up being closed by the authorities because it was outside the standard control framework and maybe also because it was making money. Same problems we had in the end.

My partner Tony Zhang and I were running a company that published the Shanghai-ed website, did website construction plus a number of other advertising and marketing activities. Operating in the interstices of communist China society was at once exhilarating and uncertain. There were no rules. Or rather, there was only one rule: that nothing is allowed. But the corollary, which reveals the true genius of China's love of the grey – in contrast to the black and white of the West – is that everything is possible. Nothing is allowed but everything is possible. It's just a matter of finding the right way to explain what you're doing.

★

After that lunch with Mark and Kathleen, Tony and I headed back to the office in a taxi.

"What do you think?" he asked.

"I think we should not let these Johnny-come-lately, fly-by-night arrivistes set up in our town without any competition," I replied through a broad smile. Yet another adventure was about to begin.

We planned out our own publication, and after much discussion fixed on a name for it: Shanghai Buzz. We chose a weekly format, largely because I felt more comfortable with that given my news agency background (although it turned out to be an error). The first issue came out in early July of 1998, a week or so before Kathleen and Mark's magazine, which was called *Ish*. *Buzz* was to last for seven issues before it was closed down by the authorities.

Sure, it was illegal. It had no publication license, its content was not reviewed by the Propaganda Bureau ahead of publication, and we had no right to print or distribute. But we did it anyway.

The editor was an American girl named Erica Lewis who originally joined our company to work on content for the Shanghai-ed website. We all threw ourselves into the process as if the world was about to end. Producing a weekly publication, as anybody who has tried it knows, is both exciting and exhausting: no sooner have you finished one issue than the next is bearing down upon you. We raced around Shanghai gathering information for articles and selling ad spaces along the way. The city was experiencing an explosion of new restaurants, nightclubs, exhibition spaces…everything. In those far-off pre-Internet days, Shanghai's foreign community of a mere

10,000 people or so latched on immediately to such alternative publications, and both the *Buzz* and *Ish* gained market traction surprisingly quickly (there was another monthly publication in the market called *Shanghai Talk* which had been in existence for a few years, licensed out of Hong Kong with some semi-official connections).

> *"Hello Shanghai,"* stated our launch editorial. *"Welcome to the first issue of the Shanghai Buzz. It is central to this newspaper that we see Shanghai as being one of the world's great cities. It was once the fifth largest and most powerful metropolis on the face of the Earth, and we believe it is destined to recover its position at the top of the table of urban rankings -- sooner rather than later. The rate of change here has rarely ever been matched anywhere. If there's any place which has a buzz to it, it's Shanghai. Hence the name. Regardless of our place of birth, we at the Buzz all feel a great sense of belonging in Shanghai. We see this newspaper as being produced in Shanghai by people in Shanghai for people in Shanghai. This is the city of dreams. It always has been. This newspaper is one of our dreams."*

That sense of continuity with Shanghai's past was important for us. We were aware that we were not the first bunch of foreigners to publish a newspaper on the edges of Shanghai society. It had been done in the 19th century, and also during the city's "golden age" of the 1930s, when Shanghai had also been a magnet for raffish foreigners such as us.

Every element of the process of producing *Buzz* was new and difficult, and of course, exciting. Erica and I made up the content as we went along. On top of the standard fare of restaurant reviews, fashion news and hotel information, we emphasized wherever possible the connections to Shanghai's colorful past.

At the time, I channeled the musings of a woman of questionable repute named May-May, who considered herself to be the queen of Shanghai's nightlife. Starting in 1996, she revealed excerpts from her diary on the Shanghai-ed website, commenting several times a week on the characters and developments in Shanghai's demimonde.

Boys and girls!" she squealed in one typical report. "This is May-May with a special edition of my diary entitled for the occasion -- the May-May Annual Shanghai Nightlife Work Report. Doesn't that sound grand??!! It's almost as if I have a job. Well, of course, I do my pets, although not in the sense that the word is usually used by all those poor people who get up somewhere between 7am and 8am every morning. My job is more of a mission. A calling, if you will. To sum it up in just a few words: I am the night nurse feeling the pulse of the city of Shanghai. Isn't that a fabulous concept??!!!! My uniform is somewhat briefer and more revealing than that of most night nurses, but the city doesn't seem to mind."

It was in effect a blog, before the word "blog" had been invented, and as soon as blogs *were* invented, May-May quite rightly stopped doing one. She was given a column in the Buzz, and I will take the opportunity of quoting from her statement in the first issue as it very accurately conveys the madness of the moment:

"May-May Comes Out!!!" shouted the headline on page 3 (May-May was much given to exclamation marks). *"Boys and girls!!! This is so exciting!!!! Here I am, outside cyberspace for the first time, writing a weekly report on the developments in the ever-changing nightlife world of Shanghai for this new newspaper!! The Shanghai Buzz - what a cute name -- it suggests a sting in the tale, which I am assured by the editors will be there. It's not easy keeping up with the many changes to the World of the Night here in Shanghai, but I do my best. It feels like a mission, but someone has to document the extraordinary developments in the glittering underbelly of the city. And it might as well be me, my loves!!!*

"Shanghai's nightlife has changed so much in the past few years. Many people say the city is returning to its decadent past, but my Aunt Daisy, who was once arrested in an illegal gambling den in the International Settlement, says it's nothing like it. But forget the tired old comparisons with the 1930s. And also the comparisons with the more recent past too. Shanghai 10 years ago had nothing that you could call "nightlife." All I remember is gloomy, dusty tree-lined streets lit by dim lights, empty except for a lonely cyclist heading home. And that was 9pm!!! Is this the same city? It seems hard to believe. Bars and restaurants now open and close with dizzying speed. The size and sophistication of the nightspots we have on offer in Shanghai beats anything they have in Beijing. Maybe we don't have as many nightlife places here as in Hong Kong, but we make up for that with atmosphere and depth. Just about every night, I am out making the rounds of the bars and restaurants, keeping up to date on the changes, and starting next issue, I'll be giving you all the latest gossip. At least, all the gossip I dare to reveal!! I try to pass on as much juicy information as possible --a lot of what I hear is best left unsaid. But if you see me in a bar, do come over and say hello, and I'll whisper a few scandalous tales into your ear!! Byeee!!!"

The name Buzz was in fact Tony's idea and came basically from Shanghainese — the words for newspaper in the local language is pronounced "Baw-zi", which is pretty close. Aunt Daisy was a wonderful old lady named Daisy Kwok, who was born in Australia in 1908 and moved to Shanghai in 1912 with her father who was setting up the Wing On Department Store. She stayed on in the city through all the intervening years, lived long enough to see the return of the foreigners and died in 1999.

For venues and marketing companies, the *Buzz* and *Ish* represented an entirely new channel for contacting the market, and it worked well. So well, in fact, that one state publication in Shanghai, the *Shanghai Star*, started to feel threatened. They presumably tapped into their guanxi with the Shanghai government's news and publications department, but, for a time, nothing happened. This was partly due to sheer puzzlement on the part of the communist officials, and partly due to a contretemps in progress at the time between Shanghai propaganda authorities and Beijing-controlled China Daily (which was the publisher of the *Star*), both eager to control the only official English-language newspaper in the city. The city eventually solved the problem by founding *Shanghai Daily* and getting all the *Shanghai Star* staff to defect. A few years later the *Star* faded away.

Design and printing of the *Buzz* was a real challenge. At the time, Macintosh computers and the software needed for page design and layout were much harder to find, and harder to use, than today. It was technically illegal for anybody in China to design a publication, let alone print it, without official Communist Party approval, but we managed to find a flexible Chinese individual named Vincent who ran a design studio in an old industrial building in the south of the city who was willing to take on the task in spite of the risks. In the end, after the newspaper was closed down, I understand he was 'reprimanded' by authorities for having worked with us.

Printing was another problem for the same reasons, but Tony, as he did with many problems, found a solution in the grey. We printed approximately 5,000 copies of the first issue, then 10,000 of all subsequent issues. The distribution was done largely by the staff, with bales of newspapers being dropped by taxi outside various bars and restaurants around town. At the time, there were no clear regulations with regard to such a publication and venues were generally eager to take them in for display, and customers were eager to read them. The entire print run of all issues disappeared almost instantly.

Tony arranged for us to run all our little businesses from an office nominally owned by a businessman from a village in Guangdong who had suddenly hit it very big making television sets (using a brand name that led consumers to mistakenly believe they were imported Japanese products). I had dinner with this man one night at the Portman Hotel and, to celebrate our newfound partnership, he ordered the very best champagne, poured glasses for myself and himself, toasted raucously, drained the champagne in one draught, then turned the delicate champagne glass upside down on top of his head.

Then one morning, the Shanghai Publications Bureau, which controls the licensing and distribution of all magazines and newspapers in the city, paid a visit to our office. I was not there, nor was Erica. But Tony was, as well as our advertising director, an American named Ron Glotzer, who hid in Tony's office. No good could come from the officials seeing a foreigner in the office that day. Tony met with them in the conference room. The conversation went basically like this:

Publication Bureau: "You don't have license, you must stop publication."

Tony: "*Shanghai Talk* and *Ish* don't have licenses either."

PB: "That may be true and we are checking into the situation of all publications."

Tony: "If they continue to publish, why can't we?"

PB: "Anyway, you don't have a license, so you must stop."

Tony: "But the publication is aimed at the foreign community, contains nothing sensitive or political, and is purely a community service publication."

PB: "We have no problems with the content of *Buzz* at all, it is simply a matter of the license. And another thing. We understand you have foreigners working on the publication. Is this true?"

Tony: "Well, we have a couple of foreigners who act as consultants, and we also have a couple of interns."

Push an issue into the Chinese gray, and it just meanders off course like a dud torpedo. The two key words there were "consultant" and "intern". The potentially-explosive issue of employing foreigners was dropped and the officials left. Tony phoned me to pass on the news. His take was that this was negotiable, and that we would find a way round the problem. And in a way, we did, but not using the name "Buzz."

★

Due in large part to the non-confrontational way in which Tony dealt with the Publication Bureau, and the way in which the *Buzz* content never overstepped any sensitive lines, we were never fined for having published an illegal publication in China, although we had of course broken every relevant law. Being weekly, we had no time to figure out an alternative. Mark and Kathleen at *Ish*, with the extra flexibility of a monthly cycle, put out their next issue as an advertising supplement and finally figured out a way to find an official sponsor.

The *Buzz* was in many ways a mess, but it had a vibrancy that was undeniable. We had a ball producing it, and that sense of fun found its way into the newspaper. Plus, of course, it was the first independent weekly English-language newspaper to be produced in Shanghai since the communist takeover in 1949. What a blast.

While the venture failed spectacularly and suddenly, it led on to another venture which was a cooperation with an official publishing house in Beijing for the publication of a weekly news and weekly travel magazine in Shanghai. That project lasted almost a year, and again we ended up so profitable that it was in effect eased out of our grasp by our partners who thought they could maintain revenues on the basis of awful content, and of course that did not work. It ended in a court case that both I and they won and lost in different ways. But that's another story.

VIEW FROM THE BRIDGE

Peter Hessler

Peter Hessler is a staff writer at *The New Yorker*, and the author of a trilogy of books about China: "River Town", "Oracle Bones", and "Country Driving". His most recent book is "Strange Stones: Dispatches from East and West". Originally from Missouri, he now lives in Cairo, Egypt.

ON MY THIRD DAY in Dandong, I woke up at two in the morning with a thief in my hotel room. It was a midrange Chinese hotel, ten dollars a night, and Dandong was a midrange Chinese city, the sort of place you wouldn't pay much attention to if it weren't across the Yalu River from North Korea. But having North Korea five hundred metres away changed everything. Dandong promoted itself as "China's Biggest Border City," and the riverfront was lined with telescopes that could be rented by tourists, most of whom were Chinese hoping to catch their first glimpse of a foreign nation. The telescopes had signs that advertised: "Leave the Country for Just One Yuan!" For nine more, you could catch a ride on a speedboat and get a closer look at the North Koreans, who, during the heat of the day, swam in the shallows off their riverbank. On days deemed auspicious for getting married, it was a Dandong tradition for Chinese newlyweds to rent a boat, put life preservers over their wedding clothes, and buzz the North Korean shore.

There was a lot to think about in Dandong, and that was probably why I had forgotten to close my window that night. Because my room was on the second floor, I'd thought I was safe from intruders, but I hadn't noticed the foot-wide ledge that ran just below the window. Nor had I bothered to put my money belt and passport under my pillow; instead, I'd left them on a dresser, along with my camera, my wallet, my reporter's notebook, and a pair of shorts. The thief was scooping everything up when I awoke. For an instant, neither of us moved.

I sat up in bed and shouted, and he turned and ran for the door. I chased him down the hallway, wearing nothing but a pair of boxers. We rounded a corner, skidding on the tile floor. I caught him at the end of the hallway, by a stairwell.

I hit him as hard as I could. His hands were full of my belongings, and every time I punched him he dropped something. I slugged him and my camera popped out; I hit him again and there was my money belt; another punch and my shorts flew up in the air. After he had dropped everything, he ran down the hall, trying to find a door that would open, while I continued to shout and throw punches. At last, he found an unlocked door that led to an empty room and an open window. He jumped. I ran to the window and leaned out. The thief had been lucky — there was an overhang just below the sill. I heard his footsteps as he rounded the corner of the building. He was still running hard.

★

During the struggle, I had wrenched the middle finger of my left hand, so the hotel's night manager accompanied me to the Dandong hospital. It took us a while to wake up the doctor who was on duty. He yawned, popped the finger back in place, and took an X-ray of it. The finger looked crooked, so the doctor yanked it out of its socket again, and then put it back in place. This time, the X-ray machine failed to work, and the doctor said that I'd have to return later in the morning, when a technician would be on duty. I went to the police station, where I reported the crime, answered some questions, and filled out some forms. Finally, at 5 A.M., I went back to bed. I didn't sleep well.

A couple of hours later, the hotel owner showed up to escort me back to the hospital. He was a handsome man, who gelled his hair so that it swept, blue-black, across his forehead. He wore a new white button-down shirt and well-pressed slacks. He apologized profusely about the robbery, and introduced himself.

"My name is Li Peng," he said.

"The same name as the former Premier?" I asked.

"Yes," he said. He smiled in a tired way, and I could see that I wasn't the first person to have made this observation. Li Peng strongly advocated the use of force against Beijing students and workers in the protests of 1989, and he is the least popular leader in China. After the Tiananmen Square massacre, a Hong Kong newspaper reported that angry citizens were harassing twenty Beijing residents who happened to be named Li Peng. At least one of them had applied formally for a change of name.

"Do you like Li Peng?" I asked the hotel owner.

"No," he said, using English for emphasis. It was clear that he wanted to talk about something else. He asked me about the robbery.

I had already told the police everything I could recall about the thief: he had black hair, and he was somewhere between the ages of twenty and forty. He was smaller than me. I told the police that I wouldn't recognize him if I saw him again.

This vagueness had bothered them: how could you break your finger on another human being and remember nothing about him? It bothered me as well. I could remember details of the chase with incredible vividness—mostly, I remembered the overwhelming anger I'd felt, a rage that now scared me. The man himself was a blur in my mind. I could see that it also perplexed Li Peng, who wrinkled his brow.

"Was it a child?" he asked.

"No," I said. "It wasn't a child."

"But how did you catch him so easily?"

"I don't know."

"Do you have thieves in your America?"

I told Li Peng that there were thieves in America, but that they carried guns and you didn't run after them.

"Most thieves here in China have knives," he said. "What kind of thief doesn't carry a knife? That's why I think he was a child."

"He wasn't a child. I know that for certain."

"But why didn't he fight back? Why did you catch him so easily?" He sounded almost disappointed.

"I don't know," I said.

The police had followed the same line of questioning, and it was beginning to annoy me. The implication was clear: only a thief of unusual ineptitude would be caught and beaten by a foreigner at two in the morning, and so there must have been something seriously wrong with him. The police offered various excuses. He must have been a drunk. Or a cripple. Or an idiot who was desperately poor. Dandong, the police emphasized, was a modern, orderly city, with a growing tourist industry. It wasn't the sort of place where a foreigner woke up in the middle of the night with a common thief in his room.

Nobody suggested what I suspected — that the man was a North Korean refugee. The police had assured me that there were few refugees along this part of the border, because Sinuiju, the North Korean city across the river, was relatively well-off. People in Sinuiju ate twice a day, according to Dandong residents who had relatives there. But I knew that farther east, where a famine had been particularly severe, an estimated seventy thousand North Koreans were fleeing to China every year. It seemed likely that at least a handful of them had made their way to Dandong. This possibility distressed me. If the locals wanted the thief to have been disabled, I wanted him to be perfectly normal and fit. It disturbed me to think that I'd viciously punched a man who was starving.

Both Li Peng and I were silent for a while, and then he thought of another possibility.

"Probably he was a heroin addict. That would explain why he was so weak."

"Are there a lot of heroin addicts around here?" I asked.

"Oh, no," Li Peng said quickly. "I don't think there are any in Dandong."

★

Apart from the North Korean swimmers, the main tourist attraction in town was the Yalu River Broken Bridge, which had once connected Dandong and Sinuiju. In November, 1950, during the first year of the Korean War, American bombers destroyed most of the bridge when General MacArthur's troops made their push toward China's border. In Chinese, the war is known as "the war of resistance against America and in support of Korea." It is estimated that a million Chinese died in the fighting.

Today, the Chinese half of the Yalu River bridge is still standing. Tourists can walk to the end of it, look at the bombed-out wreckage, and pay one yuan to stare through a telescope at the North Koreans. One morning after the aborted theft, I paid a yuan and looked through the telescope. As usual, the North Koreans were swimming. The worker at the telescope asked me what country I was from. I told him.

"If America and China had a war today, who do you think would win?" he asked.

"I don't think America and China will have a war today."

"But if they did," he said, "who do you think would win?"

"I really don't know," I said. It seemed like a good time to ask him how business was going. He said it was fine, and he added that he had a photography stand where tourists could dress up and have their picture taken with the wreckage of the bridge in the background. They could wear either traditional Korean costume or a full Chinese military uniform, with a helmet and a plastic rifle.

Another vender on the bridge ran a café where tourists could buy "Titanic" ice-cream bars, with pictures of Leonardo DiCaprio and Kate Winslet on the wrappers. The café manager explained that although the bridge was state-owned, private entrepreneurs were allowed to rent space for their telescopes and soft-drink stands. It was an example of "socialism with Chinese characteristics." The ice-cream man paid five hundred yuan a month for his café. On summer nights, he slept on the bridge, where the river breeze was cool.

The bridge was at one end of the Dandong Border Cooperative Economic Zone, which the locals referred to as the Open District. They were very proud of the Open District, because it showed how far Dandong had come during the past ten years, after China's capitalist-style reforms finally started to take hold in this part of the country. People told me that a decade ago the Open District had been nothing but peasant shacks and makeshift docks. Now there were restaurants, coffee shops, ice-cream parlors, and karaoke halls. At the western end of the Open District, a luxury apartment complex, with Western-style villas, was under construction. It was called the European Flower Garden. The eastern end of the Open District featured the bombed-out bridge and the Gateway to the Country Hunting Park. Between the bridge and the luxury apartments there was a twenty-four-hour venereal-disease clinic and the Finland Bathing and Pleasure Center, a massage parlor whose marquee featured a photograph of a topless foreign woman taking a shower.

The Gateway to the Country Hunting Park was one of the recreational options available to Dandong's tourists, a place where they could hunt "wild" quail, pigeons, pheasants, and rabbits. The birds were tethered to the ground, and, for one yuan, tourists could shoot at them with either a .22-calibre rifle or a bow and arrow. For three yuan, they could take a potshot at a rabbit that was also tied to the ground. They were allowed to eat anything they killed. I never saw anybody shoot at the rabbit. It was too expensive.

One day, I watched two tourists from Guangdong hunt the quail. The young couple were in their early twenties, nicely dressed, and the man was very drunk. He missed so badly that the quail didn't even strain at their tethers. They just sat there in the sunshine. They were the most bored-looking quail I've ever seen.

"I'm too drunk," the man from Guang-dong said to his girlfriend. "I want you to shoot instead."

"I don't want to shoot the gun," she said. "It's too loud."

"Here," he said. "You shoot it. I'm too drunk. I can't shoot straight."

"I don't want to."

"Go ahead. It's easy."

The man showed her how she could rest the gun on the fence so that it would be simpler to aim. Usually, customers weren't allowed to do that, but the park keepers were willing to make an exception because the couple had travelled all the way from Guangdong. I was sitting nearby, listening to the conversation and trying to remember which Hemingway story it recalled. In the best stories there were always guns, animals, women, and drunk people bickering. The only difference was that in Hemingway stories the animals were never tied to the ground.

Finally, the man persuaded his girlfriend to pick up the .22 and the keeper helped her prop the gun up on the fence. She shot three bullets, and every time she squealed and covered her ears. She missed badly. The quail appeared to have fallen asleep. It was late afternoon. Later, after it got dark, the Open District was a riot of lights, neon and fluorescence blazing from the restaurants and karaoke bars and the Finland Bathing and Pleasure Center. Meanwhile, across the Yalu, there was complete darkness on the North Korean shore. There was no electricity over there. The North Koreans didn't go swimming at night.

★

I got to know a couple of the local boat pilots, and several times a day they'd drive me along the banks of North Korea. We'd cruise by run-down tourist boats that were empty except for the portraits of Kim Il Sung and Kim Jong Il on the walls, and we'd pass factories that looked abandoned. On the sandy stretches, hundreds of North Koreans were swimming. The children smiled and waved when we went by. Farther upstream, where the river narrowed, it wasn't unusual for adventurous young Chinese to swim across the Yalu, touch the far side, and swim back again. There weren't any North Koreans swimming to China. On the Sinuiju bank, armed soldiers stood stiffly at their posts, watching over the swimmers. They were like lifeguards with guns.

One day, we cruised past a barge where soldiers were unloading bags of grain marked "USA," which had been donated through the United Nations World Food Program. I asked the pilot to draw closer. When we got to within thirty feet of the barge, one of the soldiers glared at me and made an obscene Korean gesture: a fist with his thumb poking out between the fingers. We sped off.

"All that food will go to the soldiers and the cadres," the pilot said. "None of the common people will get it."

He spoke matter-of-factly — the way everybody in Dandong did when I asked about their neighbors. They were quick to say that the North Koreans were poor and that they had bad leadership, but then they'd shrug and say, "Meiyou yisi" — "It's not interesting." They weren't concerned by the North Koreans' poverty or by their isolation; everybody who had lived in China through the sixties and seventies had seen enough of that.

Ordinary Chinese tourists buzzed the Korean shore simply because it was the closest they'd ever get to a foreign country; wealthy tourists, however, could enter North Korea on organized tours. Passports weren't required; the regulations were lax because the Chinese government was pretty sure that no one would want to stay on the other side of the river.

Every morning, tour groups of upper-class Chinese met in front of my hotel before leaving for North Korea, and one day I watched a guide give a briefing. The guide explained that the tourists should be careful to show respect when they visited memorials to the North Korean leaders, and he said that they should avoid taking photographs of people laboring, because the North Koreans might accuse them of focussing on poverty. The North Koreans are proud people, and the Chinese need to be conscious of this, he said. Also, when visiting the thirty-eighth parallel, it was important that the Chinese not shout "Hello!" at any American soldiers on the other side.

"You'll notice that it's not as developed as China," the guide said. "You shouldn't tell the North Koreans that they need to reform and open up, or that they should study the example of our China. And remember that many of their tour guides speak very good Chinese, so be careful what you say."

One day, I met a Chinese veteran of the Korean War. He had been in the Navy and hadn't seen much action during the war, but in 1964 he'd been wounded in a battle off the coast of Taiwan. He was sixty-four years old and had been a member of the Communist Party for four decades. He walked with a limp. The enemy who wounded him had been Taiwanese, but his weapon was American-made. The veteran pointed this out very carefully. As far as he was concerned, everything had gone downhill after Mao died. "Nowadays too many things aren't certain," he said. "Some of the retired people don't get their pensions. And some people are too rich while others are too poor." He disagreed with the views of the younger generation, including those of his twenty-six-year-old son, who had turned down a perfectly good government job to join a private firm. The firm paid more, but there wasn't as much stability. Was this, he asked, how Americans lived? And had his son learned to think this way from the foreign teachers at his college?

I asked the veteran about the situation across the border, and he said that North Korea had a leadership problem. "When Kim Il Sung was alive, he was like Chairman Mao—everybody worshipped him. But Kim Il Sung's son isn't as great as his father. He's too young and he hasn't been hardened by war. If you look at Kim Il Sung's life, he experienced war as a small boy. That's why he became a great man."

★

My hotel room picked up North Korean television, which was one reason that I continued to stay there even after the attempted robbery. The other reason was that Li Peng gave me free food and drinks at the beer garden out in front. I had become a local celebrity — the Foreigner Who Broke His Finger Fighting the Thief.

When it rained, I sat in my hotel room eating cookies and watching North Korean television. North Korean television had everything that fascinated me about Chinese television, but more of it. There were more military variety shows, more patriotic bands, more heroic leaders. The songs were more cloying. The smiles were bigger. The uniforms were more uniform. There were more programs of singing and dancing children wearing heavy makeup.

I got to the point where I could watch North Korean television for nearly an uninterrupted hour. There was the news, which consisted of showing the front page of a newspaper while a commentator read it. There was the great leader, Kim Jong Il, wearing dark glasses and pointing at maps. An Army choir, some violinists and some singers — all dripping with medals. Kim Jong Il visiting a factory. Children in makeup bouncing across a stage. Kim Jong Il in the T'aebaek Mountains. Pyongyang at night. Miners working happily. Children singing. Kim Jong Il.

At night, I dreamed of being robbed. I'd wake up, my heart racing, and I'd lie there trying to recall what the thief had looked like. But mostly I remembered what he had felt like. I remembered his body recoiling from one of the blows, and I remembered hitting him again. I found myself thinking about my anger and his fear — the two emotions shifted uneasily in my mind. What had made me keep punching him, even after he'd dropped my valuables? And why had he not fought back?

★

On my last afternoon in Dandong, the river was full of Chinese wedding boats. At any given moment, there were half a dozen on the water, the couples posing in the prows as they glided past the North Korean shore. The wealthy couples hired big two-tier cruisers; the others rented little motor launches. All of them followed the same route—a scoot out to the ruined bridge; a pause for photographs; a slow cruise along the banks of North Korea. The Chinese brides wore bright dresses of all colors—white and pink and orange and purple—and they stood in the prows of the boats like flowering figureheads. It was a hot afternoon and the North Koreans were swimming again.

I went out with a pilot named Ni Shichao, and we zipped in and out of the flotilla of wedding boats. Ni Shichao explained that it was a very auspicious day on the lunar calendar—the sixth day of the sixth month—which was why there were so many weddings. But on the whole, he said, there were fewer weddings than usual this year.

"People think that years ending in nine are bad luck," he explained. "I don't believe it myself, but many people do. In '89 there was the disturbance"—a euphemism for what happened around Tiananmen Square—"and in '79 there was the trial of the Gang of Four. Sixty-nine was the Cultural Revolution. Fifty-nine was when your America bombed the bridge."

He paused and thought for a moment. "No, that was in 1950," he said, shaking his head. "Anyway, something bad happened in '59."

That had been the climax of the Great Leap Forward, when Mao's mad push for greater industrial production resulted in a famine that killed an estimated thirty million people. But Chinese history books brushed over this disaster. As with many Chinese, Ni Shichao had a shaky grasp of recent history; he had also made a mistake about the Gang of Four trial, which took place in 1980 and 1981.

"What about 1949?" I asked.

"That was when the new China was founded," he said. He

paused again. We were in the shadow of the ruined bridge; the slow-moving Yalu flowed blue beneath us. "That year wasn't the same as the others," he went on. "That was a good year, of course."

★

A week after leaving Dandong, I went east to Tumen, a Chinese city on North Korea's northern border. Tumen was poor; it had none of Dandong's energy and development, but it still drew hordes of refugees from North Korea. The Tumen River was narrow here, and this stretch of the North Korean countryside was reported to have suffered some of the worst effects of the famine that had been devastating the country since 1995. Almost nobody went swimming in the murky Tumen River. The border was heavily guarded on both sides. The Chinese promenade had a few souvenir stands and telescopes, but there weren't many tourists. You couldn't see much across the river.

I walked along the promenade and passed a child sitting in the shade. I approached him from the back, thinking that it was a local boy about seven years old, but then I saw his face, and I stopped. I had never seen so many different ages in a single person. He had the body of a young child, but from his face I could see that he was older, probably fourteen or fifteen. The corners were wrinkled, the skin shrivelled like an old man's, and there was a gray dullness in his gaze that startled me.

I stared at the boy and realized that he was a North Korean who had come here to beg. In that moment, everything I'd glimpsed about this closed-off country — the swimmers and the soldiers and the television programs — slipped away. The boy gazed back. Finally, I fumbled for my wallet and pulled out some money. He accepted it without changing his expression. Neither of us said anything. I felt his eyes on my back as I walked away.

Stowaway

Pete Spurrier

Born in London, Pete Spurrier arrived in Hong Kong in 1993, expecting to stay only a month, but found himself beguiled by the territory's cosmopolitan character, has been based there ever since. He is the author of the "Serious Hiker's Guide to Hong Kong" and "Heritage Hiker's Guide to Hong Kong", both published by FormAsia. Pete is also the founder of Blacksmith Books, an independent publishing house focusing on Asian-themed titles.

THE DISTANCE FROM XINJIANG to Hong Kong was vast – over three thousand miles – from the dead-center of Asia to the edge of the Pacific Ocean. But I had to make the journey somehow.

I was in the ticket hall of Urumqi's railway station: a giant barn filled with a solid mass of people, surging in waves towards a row of barred ticket windows. It took me half an hour to get within shouting distance of a counter, and even when I had my nose up against the glass, people kept trying to push me out of the way from both sides.

"Beijing," I shouted into the mousehole-shaped gap at the bottom of the window, jostling to keep my position.

The ponytailed clerk shouted something incomprehensible back at me.

"What? No – *Beijing!*" I repeated, trying different ways of shouting the name. "Bei...jing!" Maybe they still called it Peking way out here.

The clerk wrote a price down on a piece of paper and held it up. I felt silly.

"Ah..." My stomach fell and I slunk back into the undulating crowd. My funds wouldn't cover the journey.

I was down to little more than the emergency US$50 note I had been hiding in my worn-out shoe for months. China had proved much more expensive than the newly independent Silk Road countries I had come from, and it was here I suddenly found myself insolvent and unable to afford a Trans-Siberian railway ticket home to England.

"Just go to Hong Kong," suggested an Australian backpacker I had shared my woes with in a teahouse earlier in the day. "It's British!" She said these last words with an unveiled excitement that suggested it was the promised land for penniless Europeans adrift in Asia.

A promised land sounded good right now. I had been traveling east from Istanbul over the past three months, the long-distance trains between each stop taking an emotional and physical toll that had pushed me near to breaking point.

In Turkmenistan, the overcrowded trains had looked and smelled like cattle trucks. In Georgia, their windows were smashed and they had no lighting. To leave Tajikistan, which was having a sort of civil war, I'd had to hide between carriages opposite the platform at Dushanbe and then climb onto the wrong side of the evening's only departing train as it rolled in. I got into the corridor through a window but was then instantly buried under hordes of people climbing in from the other side. One man literally sat on top of me, then a woman on top of him; the whole lot of us were then shunted aside as even more people were squeezed in from the far end. Soon, I couldn't move my legs. I began to sweat in silent panic, even though I had found no water to drink that day. It was hard to breathe. "You wanted adventure... well, now you've got it," I cursed myself. After 16 slow hours of creeping through the dark desert – diseased skin pressed against my arms and cheeks, unseen hands probing my pockets – I couldn't take any more. I somehow freed myself, threw my bag out of the window and climbed out after it into the empty night.

Three weeks later, I found myself in Urumqi, the capital city of the Xinjiang region of the People's Republic. My Chinese adventure was just beginning.

★

I pushed against the tide of people to get out of the ticket hall, wondering what to do – was hitch-hiking half the width of Asia an option? Two men in brown leather jackets must have noticed the white guy murmuring to himself, because they came straight over. They had the Turkic features, hazel eyes and bristly stubble of Central Asians, yet they didn't quite look the part. I guessed them to be Uyghurs, the native ethnic group of Xinjiang. They certainly weren't Chinese.

"Friend, change money? Buy ticket?"

"No thanks," I replied, looking away. If there was one thing I had learned from backpacking around North Africa and the Middle East, the words "friend" and "buy" used together in broken English were rarely the beginning of a beautiful friendship.

The Uyghurs didn't give up. "Buy ticket!" This time it sounded like they were telling me, not asking. Were it only that simple, I wanted to say. If I couldn't afford a ticket to Beijing, I certainly couldn't get one to Hong Kong. But I had to move in that direction somehow.

The men pressed on with their offer. I was about to push past them, but then: "Chinese price!" one of them said. Now I was interested, but I had to approach this cautiously. I decided to ask for a ticket only to the next town. For all I knew, I could be thrown off the train for trying to travel on the local price; foreigners were supposed to pay a higher rate. And I didn't have any money that I could afford to lose on dud tickets.

One of the scalpers left straight away and came back with a stubby piece of cardboard. It didn't give me much confidence;

apart from the numbers, I couldn't read anything that was printed on it. But it worked! I flashed my ticket at the turnstile and an indifferent inspector waved me through. I was barely able to suppress my relief as I boarded the train.

Xinjiang is a huge region. It covers the entire northwest quarter of China, but is almost all desert. Mountain ranges poke into it from north and south. Our route ahead lay across flat, scorched land for hundreds of miles, with little evidence of inhabitation; the only scenery an endless line of telegraph poles running parallel to the tracks.

In fact, there was probably more humanity packed inside each carriage of that train than in the whole desert we were passing through. I had bought the cheapest local ticket, a spartan "hard seat" class of carriage with straight-backed wooden benches, and with it came the masses – and their bulky, ancient baggage, stacked up beside the seating and shoehorned into every square inch of luggage rack. Was everyone moving somewhere else?

I didn't know any Mandarin beyond "ni hao" and "xie xie," yet my fellow passengers insisted on speaking to – as opposed to with – me anyway. Mandarin was like no language I'd heard before, sounding alternately disapproving and incredulous but, all the while, melodiously bird-like. I smiled politely and shrugged and nodded and laughed them off, but they carried on regardless, so I passed the time studying their faces, attire and behavior.

The women dressed in utilitarian worker garb with floral patterns, maybe hand-stitched themselves; the men wore black or blue suit jackets, but dusty, torn and faded, as if they had worn them to work in the fields... for their entire lives. The men in little square-cornered white hats were Muslims; their presence on the trains would thin out the further we moved away from Xinjiang.

It seemed like a jovial crowd, everyone looking forward to a mammoth cross-country journey together, all prepared with plastic bags of fruit or paper bags of peanuts and sunflower seeds, which they deshelled deftly with their teeth and spat out onto the floor until a carpet of slimy shells lined the aisles. Each traveler also clutched an old jam jar of green tea leaves, filled with hot water from giant steel boilers at the end of each carriage. But refilling them, or going to the toilets, caused occasional scuffles – every time someone got up, another would not hesitate to grab their place. The entire carriage would then strain their necks to watch the increasingly heated argument between the two passengers, laughing and discussing it all as if it were some form of entertainment for the proletariat trapped on this train together.

But when there were no arguments to watch, everyone in range just stared unblinking at me.

I got off at the first stop, a small station which had no town and no apparent name. The ticket office was not open, and there was nobody else waiting there. I bought a glass bottle of fizzy water from a vendor and sat down on the platform to enjoy some much-needed silence.

On the Silk Road I had been beaten up, robbed, arrested, fined, deported and starved of food or drink for days on end; I'd even been attacked in the street half a dozen times by grievance-ridden Uzbeks and Kazakhs who thought I was Russian. Crossing into China had been more an escape than a conscious desire to visit it, which only enhanced the feeling that I was drifting east without any objective. I had left school, and England, two years earlier for a six-month tour of Europe that had never ended. Why was I still traveling? Was it purely because it was better than turning around and going home, where I would have to make grown-up choices about my future? Or was I waiting to happen across a place that would tell me to stay?

★

A few hours later another train passed through and, owing to the lack of a station attendant, I had to board without a ticket.

I shouldered my way into a crowded hard-seat carriage and sat down on a spare inch of seat as soon as another passenger got up to refill his tea jar. At some point an inspector passed through and stopped at the foreigner with his white face turned to the window.

"Piao," he said, his hand out. I took that to mean "ticket."

"Ni hao!" I replied with an embarrassed smile.

The ticket collector didn't smile back. "Piao!" he demanded again in a sharper tone that denied any chance of reasoning, which of course didn't matter as I was linguistically impaired. I tried using sign language to explain that I did not have a ticket, and that the office at the previous station had been closed.

He then said something else. He said a lot of things, in fact, none of which I could reply to, and then he started talking out loud to everyone in the carriage; maybe he was asking if anyone could explain the basic rules of rail travel to this crazy foreigner. The passengers laughed and jostled to get as near as possible to the scene of the crime. The ticket inspector at last threw his hands up in frustration and moved on, leaving me free to sit there on my tiny corner of hard seat. This was great; it was suddenly the most comfortable wooden bench I had ever sat on.

Thus I fell upon the strategy which was to get me most of the way across China: I would walk through the length of each train until I saw a ticket inspector, then all I'd have to do was turn right around and walk all the way back again, or duck into the latrine, alighting only if it looked like I would be challenged.

This leg of the journey took 26 hours. Drowsy from sitting upright and staring out of the window all day, I considered bedding down beneath the seats. But the floor of this particular carriage was vile with phlegm and other fluids, so I surrendered my seat and relocated to the drafty gap between the carriages. It was bitterly cold, as it always is in the desert at night. My reed mat didn't provide much insulation from the metal surface but at least it kept my sleeping bag off the filth. I curled up inside my bag, listening to the footsteps of people passing by and the rhythmic clatter of the train couplings beneath me until exhaustion took its course.

I awoke in Gansu province. The purple peaks of the Tibetan plateau had appeared on the southern horizon. The day was burning hot and the sky an unreal blue. Gansu has an odd, elongated shape on the map; a narrow strip of low land which runs for several hundred miles between the plateau and the barren hills to the north. Geography made it the natural entrance into China from the Silk Road. Arab and Persian trading caravans had followed the route of this railway for thousands of years. Gold, jade, saffron, myrrh, pistachios and sandalwood were carried into China; prized silk and porcelain traveled the other way.

As I paced the length of the train, avoiding the ticket inspector, I met an American who was traveling with his family in a private compartment.

"Come on in," he said, as pleased to see a fellow round-eye as I was. His cabin was a world away from the hard seat carriages. Instead of spittle and hard benches, it had upholstered beds, a lace cloth around a little table, and even net curtains across the window.

He was studying the Uyghurs, and over tea and walnut biscuits he explained some of their story: "They thought they had something right after the Chinese Civil War ended," he said. "A bunch of them declared independence. For a short while Xinjiang was called East Turkestan. But the Chinese moved back in pretty quickly. Now it's a bit like Tibet – there are so many Han coming in all the time, the Uyghurs are becoming an ethnic minority in their own homeland."

The next ticket inspector I encountered was not very happy about the stowaway foreigner on his train, and it didn't help my situation that he knew some English. "Okay-le, you get off here!" he snapped angrily as we pulled into another station.

"Here" was Jiayuguan, a neat little town with few motor vehicles on the roads but hundreds of bicycles. The Chinese pocket atlas I had bought with my spare change in Urumqi seemed to indicate that the western end of the Great Wall of China was in the vicinity. I thought I should see at least one famous sight of this historic country while I could, and walked some way out of town to find it. A Chinese-style fort with upturned eaves marked the wall's end. The architects didn't need to build any further: from here the mountains took over and formed a natural barrier to any raiding barbarians from the north or west. Standing at the fort, I saw stretches of the wall snaking across the hills towards the eastern horizon, looking strangely unnecessary and forgotten in this uninhabited landscape.

It was getting close to sundown and I decided to camp out next to the wall. A roving policeman on a motorbike with sidecar didn't approve. Shaking his head, he motioned for me to go back to the town. "Okay-le," I assured him, using the Chinglish I had picked up from the last angry authority I'd encountered. I nodded my head obediently, put on a stupid grin and waved him goodbye until he finally left me on my own, then I quickly doubled back around the fort and found a gully to sleep in. The night was cold and windy, and I awoke frequently to the sound of animal howls coming from over the hills.

The following 33-hour train journey was made quite enjoyable by big bottles of local beer at only two yuan a pop, which I shared over a box lunch with a Japanese student. He was seeing a bit of China in between terms at uni.

"So, do you also use these things in Japan?" I asked, surprised to see that he was so good with chopsticks

"Um, yes, of course," he said, giving me an odd look. I really knew nothing about Asia at all.

The Great Wall was now far behind us, the desert and mountains a memory as we entered the verdant, watery landscape of China proper. Every square mile of land in these parts was used for growing crops, terraces carved into the side of nearly every hill surrounding sparsely populated villages.

It was midday when a young man started shouting at and

slapping his wife or girlfriend, which naturally drew a crowd of close-quarters spectators who watched intently but never intervened. It was almost like a cockfight had been put on to enliven their journey, I thought; I half expected the onlookers to start placing bets. And yet I too failed to speak out for the woman, partly from an uncertainty about their customs but also from a reluctance to draw attention to myself and get thrown off yet another train.

At night I continued to sleep cocooned in my sleeping bag on the carriage floors, protected from flying seeds and peanut shells. And then, one morning, we crossed the legendary Yellow River. The whole train fell silent as the passengers pressed themselves up against the windows in awe of this winding, silty river that is seen as the cradle of Chinese civilization. The river was so wide and misty that I couldn't see the far bank. We crossed it on a long, narrow bridge, momentarily lost in the fog.

★

The city of Xian has some claim to being the eastern terminus of the Silk Road – the opposite number to Istanbul. As Chang'an, it was the capital of China during the Tang dynasty, and its ancient pagodas and thick city walls that still surround it are signs of its former importance. I should have been jubilant that I had followed the ancient trade route from end to end, and had witnessed people's features gradually changing as I journeyed east. Every different eye color and facial shape told the story of an empire or an army that had come and gone. Instead, I was shaking with anxiety about my shrinking wad of banknotes and my 10-day entry visa. Both were steadily nearing zero.

What would happen if my visa expired while I was still in the country? I didn't know, but I had been caught without a visa in Uzbekistan, thrown in the cells, fined and then deported to Kirgizstan next door. Such experiences made for good story-telling as I passed the time on trains with the occasional backpacker over beers, but it didn't mean I wanted to repeat them. Especially not in China, which I'd heard could be something of a brutal police state when it wanted to.

Xian's railway station was filled to capacity with prospective passengers, and no wonder; the city is at the center of the country's rail network. A line of ticket windows were marked with the Chinese characters for destinations. I was standing there with my mini-atlas open, trying to decipher which window to push towards, when a hand landed on my shoulder. I turned around to see an unusually tall man in green uniform.

"Don't worry!" he declared. "I am a soldier of the People's Liberation Army!"

I started to worry.

"Where do you go?" he asked.

"Well, Beijing, but..." I started to say, but he was already off, swimming through the sea of the crowd. I watched his head and shoulders rise and fall amid the waves of people struggling to reach the counters. Eventually he came back, red-cheeked, and handed me a ticket for Beijing – and wouldn't accept any payment for it. I felt totally disarmed. I had been anxious not to do anything that would bring me into contact with representatives of this reportedly brutal regime, but here a PLA recruit had taken it upon himself to help a stranded visitor.

Soldier Cheng was going to Beijing himself to join his unit, so I treated him to some roadside noodles and then we waited together for a few hours in the square outside the station. His brother had come to see him off, and the three of us had a group picture taken by a photographer who had set up a stall there.

"Your brother?" I asked. I had thought there were no brothers or sisters in one-child China, but what did I know.

"Yes, brother," he exclaimed, grinning and throwing his arm around him.

Compared with Central Asia, rail travel in China was well organized – especially where food was concerned. Besides the dining car – off-limits to normal hard-seat passengers but, because foreigners *usually* traveled in higher-paying classes, open to an incomprehensible barbarian like me – trolleys of food and drink were pushed through the carriages day and night. As we rolled into each station on our 20-hour route, a row of women in white caps and uniforms stood to attention next to carts laden with steaming-hot food. People rushed onto the platform to order pancake-like breads cooked with spring onions, noodles with sliced beef, kebabs on sticks, pungent fried tofu, strange pickled vegetables, lunch boxes full of all sorts of animal parts on rice…

I went to buy lunch boxes for Soldier Cheng and I with FEC, the parallel Chinese currency which foreigners were supposed to use instead of Renminbi, but he laughed when he saw the banknotes. "You can't use your English money in China!" he said. The soldier had never seen FEC before and naturally thought it was foreign currency.

★

In Beijing I went straight to the police office that dealt with visa extensions. I had only one day left on my visa and there was no way I could get to China's southern coast in that time. I thought it was better to go and surrender myself before I was found out.

I took a grimy, clapped-out bus across town to get there. The vehicle drove along the side of a vast open space sprinkled with monuments. A large group of people was gathered around a flagpole. I suddenly recognized it as Tiananmen Square – it had been in the news at home just a few years earlier, when the tragic incident of June 1989 took place.

The police were closing up their office. "Come back on Monday," the officer said without looking at me, as he put away his assortment of stamps.

"But, can I please just…"

"Monday," he repeated, a bit more gruffly.

"Please, I can't," I sputtered. "My visa will expire tomorrow!"

If I waited until Monday, I would be staying in the country illegally, which meant either a fine or a cell.

"Okay-le," he sighed, sitting down again and picking up a folder. "Passport please."

I was overwhelmed with gratitude, but tried to remain composed.

"You are British," he remarked, stating the obvious as he leafed through the pages.

"Yes," I said, smiling and trying not to look like an imperialist or an opium smuggler.

"We can give you four more days, but the fee for British passports is higher."

"Ah... I don't have enough money." It was a half-truth; I did, but only just.

He looked up at me. My mind turned like the wheels of a locomotive.

"I also have a New Zealand passport at home," I blurted. Now I was just flat-out lying. "Is it possible to charge me the New Zealand price?"

He looked pained. This policeman just wanted to go home. I envisioned him kicking off his shoes and hanging his epaulettes on a hook while his child greeted him over homework and his wife fried dumplings in the kitchen. With this vision, I was suddenly jealous that he had a warm home to go to. He relented and stamped an extension into my passport before pulling down the shutters with a resounding finality.

Relieved as I was, even the lower fee had taken most of my remaining cash. Parting with it had not been easy – it was food for the journey onwards. I would have to set off for Hong Kong on the first train out.

That night in Beijing I was caught in a ferocious thunderstorm. There was little street lighting, and buses and bicycles were careering everywhere. Looking for shelter, I found the bike sheds of a Soviet-style apartment block and bedded down for the night. The concrete was cold and I was worried I would be discovered, so my sleep was fitful. I was up before sunrise. I walked along tree-lined roads towards the central railway station, watching the city's elderly performing graceful tai chi moves in the early morning light. Soothed by this, I took a deep breath of the coal-scented Beijing air and forged onward.

★

I followed the same disgraceful procedure as before: I bought a ticket to the first small town outside a city, then alighted and boarded the next train without a ticket. It worked every time. Being unable to speak Chinese actually helped – ticket collectors would simply wave me away, exasperated.

After the frequent food trolleys had passed through the carriages, attendants followed with giant rattan brooms and swept all the beer bottles, lunch boxes, orange peels and various shells into the corridor. A door on the side of the train was flung open, all the rubbish was sent flying into the countryside, and then the door was closed. Once, we rolled over a level crossing where members of a rural family were patiently waiting for the train to pass by. A flying lunch box hit one of the farmers' shoulders and burst open, scattering rice and diced chicken all over his shirt. He didn't even flinch. An illustration of urban China's disregard for the peasants who feed it, perhaps, but in my insecure mind also an analogy for China's efficiency in rejecting all unwanted flotsam from its borders – especially stowaway foreigners.

Shenzhen, a border town developed as a special economic zone, was my final port of call. There was certainly wealth here – the first Mercedes I'd seen in China pulled away from the curb and honked at me as I crossed the road – yet a beggar with twisted legs was sitting on the pavement. Development had come for some but not all.

As I left the railway station, I found myself looking at a line of jade-green hills. The Union Jack was flying from a lookout post on one of them. This was the border I had been scrambling for all this time. What a strange sight it was, and what strange feelings of discovery and relief I had. The familiar flag had a new brightness to it: it seemed to promise stability and order. It was like coming home to somewhere I'd never been.

I crossed the bridge into British territory. "Welcome, sir," said the immigration officer, and asked no questions. After journeying through an entire continent that seemed to only ask questions but give no answers, this was unexpected and gratifying.

I took the local train to the city center, changed my lonely £20 traveler's cheque into Hong Kong dollars and scouted around for a rooftop to sleep on. While traveling in Europe I had made a habit of sleeping on the rooftops of apartment buildings; it was relatively safe and quiet, and provided I was up and away early enough, no residents knew about it. Here in the Tsim Sha Tsui district, the bustling heart of Kowloon, I found a tatty 16-storey building with a flat roof that was accessible by a staircase. If I climbed over the perimeter wall onto a wide ledge, I could have a rest without being seen by anyone.

My perch looked down on the thundering artery of Nathan Road, and also across at the curtained windows of the Hyatt Regency and Holiday Inn hotels. What a difference in lifestyle the width of a street could make. Across the rooftops, and across the harbor, I could see the taller buildings-and-mountain backdrop of Hong Kong Island.

I was in Hong Kong to find work, yes, but I wasn't quite ready for it. I needed some time to get my head together. Crossing the breadth of China had been a frantic race which hadn't given me time to decompress from Central Asia.

A few days later, it happened to be my 21st birthday. I used my final handful of coins to buy a can of Guinness and celebrated alone on a bench in Kowloon Park. This patch of green in the middle of Tsim Sha Tsui was well used by the locals. Their loud Cantonese sounded coarse and earthy, very different to the melodic Mandarin I had grown accustomed to on the trains of Mainland China.

With the final sips of that beer I was officially money-free. I wondered how I would obtain a job with my beard, long hair and unkempt clothes. I hadn't bathed for weeks. At some point very soon I would also have to make a reverse-charge phone call to my family and explain where the hell I was.

"Pete?" a voice suddenly rang out. "Pete! What are you doing here?"

I looked up. It was the Australian girl I had met in that teahouse in Urumqi. The coincidence was so bizarre it wasn't even worth mentioning.

I spent a few seconds trying to find an answer. "I don't know," I said.

Hands of Stone

Jeff Fuchs

Based in Asia, Jeff Fuchs' works have centered on indigenous mountain cultures, oral histories and tea. He is an "ambassador" for the North Face clothing company, and has consulted with *National Geographic*. Fuchs' most recent book, "The Ancient Tea Horse Road", documents his seven and a half-month journey along the 3,000-mile Ancient Tea Horse Road. He currently lives in Yunnan province in China.

WIND IS RUMBLING THROUGH every surface and the black tent around us flaps and shudders under its force, yet remains resilient. The yak-wool tent, one of six dwellings in Arong Dhotok, is an icon speaking to a timeless faith in local knowhow. Time tested over centuries, the tent symbolizes a lifestyle wholly revolving around geography and untouched by the modern world and its intrusions. A local saying sums up the powers that rule the Tibetan Plateau:

"It is the mountains' winds and snows which dictate all."

I am riveted by our host, an old man wrapped in primordial furs hunched in the corner of the tent. His every gesture and word is mesmerizing and intense. Sun-scarred, hollow-cheeked and ancient, Yeshi and his long body remain as formidable as the elements outside – and as resolute as the tent that withstands them.

Yeshi is one of the last remaining muleteers to have made repeated journeys ushering tea, salt and other goods across the trade highway spanning three thousand miles from Yunnan to

Lhasa known as Cha ma Gu dao, the Ancient Tea Horse Road. Famed for his ability to safely arrive with cargo intact in even the most brutal blizzards, it is evident that the elder muleteer is still regarded as royalty within his clan, even though only memories of his successes remain.

The team I have been trekking with for over a month are tucked close and immediate around a dung-fueled fire within the tent. Wafts of acrid smoke and pungent yak butter are immediately sucked out of a flap in the roof into the harsh, five-thousand meter atmosphere. Our hardened faces hint at the struggles encountered along this route. Worn down and withered by the bludgeoning sun and relentless winds, we are modern day voyageurs along this highway in the sky.

Our journey to re-trace the Tea Horse Road has pummeled into us a sense of what traveling this route once required by the likes of Yeshi. But that is the very reason we travel as we do, to feel the physical dimension of a journey that some say was once the most dangerous route upon the planet…and to access these ancients who gave lifeblood – and often their lives – to the route.

Sonam, our team's indestructible, reed-thin guide, is sitting closest to Yeshi and is attempting to translate every word being offered up before the ancient's low, rumbling voice is swiftly swallowed up by the roar of wind. As Yeshi harkens to the old days of trade, his massive hands seem to uncoil and tense and uncoil again, as though touching every bend and pass in his mind's eye.

"There were many ways to die on the route. You could freeze, starve, or simply wander disoriented in a blizzard until you fell exhausted…sometimes the thieves would get you too."

His words are delivered without any colorful language; it is a tale that doesn't need any embellishment, but it is spoken with a voice that has weathered elements that are scarcely conceivable. There is a hint of a smile upon his wide mouth when he recounts the dangers of travel, as though the memories simultaneously stir in him both melancholy and joy.

Beside me, the short powerful frame of Norbu, the youngest member of our team, bends forward to catch the words. Nomè, our patient and vital cook, sits cross-legged, slurping the yellow, frothy butter tea being served by a wool-encased woman whisking around the tent.

I ask Yeshi about tea and its vital role along the route. Those massive hands of his lift palms-up, and he tells us, "Tea was wealth. It was the most important currency for us muleteers. If one had tea one could trade for anything. We were often paid in tea."

We've heard ja, tea, referred to with this kind of veneration by hardened muleteers and nomads before. It astonishes at times how much a simple desiccated green leaf could inspire such awe amongst a people known for their resiliency, as if this stimulant leaf from leagues away was a panacea of sorts.

Yeshi's mere presence and desire to speak of his time upon the trade route is as nourishing to us as the tea itself. In doing rough calculations of his various journeys, we come up with a rough number of more than 18,000 miles traveled *by foot* across the Himalayas. Yet, as remarkable as this elder is, there is not a smudge of arrogance about his incredible feats. Yeshi has the rough grace of a being who has tread through Mother Nature's every mood. Though his manner is quiet and his movements sparse, his green-tinged Tibetan eyes burn with the knowledge of what he was part of, and of what he survived.

In Tibetan, the word for muleteer speaks to what is required to travel along the daunting length of the journey. La'do is made up of two words: la, meaning hand or hands, and do, meaning stone. Having "hands of stone" was a requisite along the Tea Horse Road.

Norbu respectfully observes that this man must have been quite resilient to survive so many decades of travel, but Yeshi waves away the compliment with those ancient hands of stone.

"We had no choice," he says in his wind-rumbling voice, "and when you have no choice, you simply do."

★

Arong Dhotok (Stone Roof) rests in the belly of the grand and secretive Nyenchen Tanghla Range, where needs are measured upon a far different scale than that in the lowlands. In the words of a nomad we had encountered here, the local version of a luxury was an extra bowl of tea, or an hour with friends around a fire.

This nomad camp is its own little empire; to every edge we are walled in by gray spires of stone. Up far above the tight, little valley are the black dots of yak grazing upon the sheer slopes. Less than 8 miles to the east, a 7,355-foot monster of stone pierces the sky.

This miracle of a community exists until the snows begin in September, when the entire clan will move to less formidable altitudes and better grazing for their precious yak. The annual migration route of the community has remained unchanged for as long as any can remember. Every member of the community is somehow related, and our own arrival the day previous, with two mules and four wind-shorn bodies, was remarkably well-received.

Our welcoming to the community was issued in the words of an age-old question by a thickset elder wrapped in furs and giving us a smile, "From where have you come?" Tea was prepared for us, our bags unloaded by competent hands, and only then, when we nestled into a tent with fire at our side, were we questioned about our destination and purpose.

This tea-fed, mountain-bound route spanning the Tibetan Plateau had obsessed my years of wandering and wondering within and upon the Himalayas. Crucially for me, the Gya'lam ('wide road' in Tibetan) brought two of the earth's most divine elements together: tea and mountains.

Long a spiritual, and perhaps physical, addiction of mine, tea had been one of the few constants in my own life, and I found the likewise ageless addiction of the Tibetans fascinating; that a rawboned, fierce people living so close to Mother Nature's every mood needed, above all else, a stimulant green leaf.

And so a four-year obsession led to my assembling a team of both capable and curious mountain men to trace the route, by foot, for as long as legs, lungs and resolve would last. It brought us to this point in the very tangible heart of here and now. As vital as it was to travel, suffer, and take in the geographies and elements, it was also necessary for us to engage with as many of the route's survivors as possible, and to rekindle, even if briefly, their memories of tea and survival.

Generations had manned the Arong Dhotok community, one of the more desolate gonkar, camps, along the ancient trade route, and now it hosted us with the same passed-on skills and warmth as in the past. Following our conversation with Yeshi, dinner is prepared for us by the entire community, which in typical Tibetan tradition is an affair of the hands. Boiled yak meat is torn, ripped, and peeled off the bones. A soupy butter concoction that stimulates the sweat glands is served up and sprinkled with barley powder.

Sated, I rest by the fire's comforting crackle, but Sonam allows himself to let loose and is in full spirits, singing to the fire, to the sky, to everyone. Calm as always, Nomè shares stories about our plights along the route with some children who seem to prefer his sane and soft tones to Sonam's vocals. The young nomadic children are mini-versions of their handsome parents. Callused hands, indestructible bodies, and gleaming smiles, they are forcefully impetuous and relentlessly curious.

And yet, as the sole occidental, it is comforting to be given no more special attention than my companions. To these good people I am just another gaunt traveler with a belly to feed and questions to answer. Here up high, all are foreign, but all are welcome...as long as who come, come in peace. Though there has been incredulity at our journey at certain stops behind us, at Arong Dhotok there is a sense of pride that *their* route is being revisited, and sincere concern if we can physically continue.

Old Yeshi had conveyed no surprise at all that the route was, in his words "getting its due." He reminded us that the Gya'lam received "all peoples and all lands."

★

Mornings at three miles in the sky are something similar to a blunt force instrument hitting the entire being. Nor have we slept well due to the nighttime ramblings of a local species of rodent, the avra, who run rampant throughout the camp at night not unlike nocturnal royalty. As they scuttled over our sleeping bags with abandon, I struggled with sanity. I need tea in a ferocious way. Its potency is the perfect antidote to slow-starting mornings, and will hopefully banish my murderous feelings towards the rodents of Arong Dhotok.

"Not all made it over Nup Gong La," Tenzin, a camp elder, says forebodingly, nodding his head toward the impending 5,470-meter pass we are to cross this day. With a braided coil of hair hanging to his ribs, and scars ranging across his face, Tenzin looks as if he of anyone knows the lands of which he speaks. If one is to survive in Tibet, one listens to the locals, their intuition holding far greater weight than any technology. Here, the elements of wind, sun, and snow are still spoken of as if they were living, breathing things.

Butter is wrapped in paper as a caloric gift for our upcoming trek, and dried yak meat is shoved into our packs. The clan waves us on without any fanfare. They have work to do, and in the Himalayas, where the summer months are ever so brief, time is more crucial than elsewhere.

Rounding a ragged ridge of stone, we realize the trail we are to take is covered in an ever-deepening layer of snow. Our horseman informs us that he cannot risk his horse in such conditions. We have been warned – and fallen victim to this condition – before. Mules' and horses' hooves are at risk from perilous rocks and chasms, invisible under the snow. One wrong step and a hoof would snap. The locals won't risk one of their dear mountain partners for any amount of profit. All beings are precious in this high altitude world, and each are dependant upon one another. In short: cooperate or perish.

We undertake to reconfigure our gear, unpacking the horse and splitting up the extra weight onto our packs. The winds hound us, relentlessly ripping at all loose items. The skies dim slightly as though the scene is setting for another phase of mountain travel. Our horseman, bidding us farewell, touches each of our forearms in a gesture, the kaleo (a departing wish to "go well"), common among travelers and friends in the mountains. He then starts his slow journey home. The four of us are alone once again, with all of our necessities upon our backs. There is a kind of simple comfort in this fact; that whatever may come we have what we need…I hope.

Norbu's raw, flaking face grimaces as he looks at our icy route ahead. Soft outlines of feet remain as reminder that there are no roads across the pass. With his now-bulging pack, Norbu makes his way ahead, his legs simply disappearing hip-deep into the ever-thickening snow. The sun suddenly breaks above us, sending down bolts of warm sunlight as I too plunge forward into the grand abyss of white.

THE PARTITIONED POT

Audra Ang

Audra Ang was a Beijing-based correspondent for The Associated Press from 2002 through 2009. In between meals of "saliva chicken" and "fragrant and spicy potato shreds," she covered topics ranging from disasters, disease and dissent. She also reported from North Korea, Mongolia, Pakistan and Afghanistan for the AP. Her book, "To the People, Food is Heaven", about her experiences reporting and eating in China, was published in 2012.

A LIGHT SNOW WAS falling the first time we arrived in Xiahe, two weeks after ferocious anti-government rioting in Lhasa triggered ripples of similar protests in surrounding Tibetan enclaves in western China. The violence, which had erupted on March 14, 2008 after peaceful demonstrations by monks were blockaded by police, was the largest and most mutinous challenge to Beijing in almost 20 years. The root of the turmoil was festering, diurnal – the desire for independence from decades of Chinese controls which Tibetans lamented was suffocating their unique Buddhist culture and religion, the equivalent of destroying their way of life.

I was traveling with Mr. Di, a driver I had hired in Lanzhou, the provincial capital of Gansu, where Xiahe was located, and my colleague Han Guan, a soft-spoken but dogged photographer. Together we had covered a gamut of stories, from deadly gas explosions to beauty pageants, and had teamed up on assignments in Mongolia and North Korea. Like me, Han was from Singapore, and like me, he loved food. When possible, we made sampling the local cuisine a priority while in the field. It was a ritual I enjoyed not only because it gave me a window into understanding the people and the country I was reporting about, but also because it often comforted and rejuvenated my spirit in difficult situations.

On this morning, we asked Driver Di to take us for beef noodle soup, Lanzhou's signature dish that was popular nationwide. The place we ended up in was tiny and grimy but the broth was clear and savory, and the noodles were freshly pulled. The thin slices of meat were almost an afterthought but added surprising heft to the meal. We spooned chopped spring onions and a dangerous looking chili sauce into our bowls. Like all the other customers, we hunched over on plastic stools and slurped everything up in noisy silence; breakfast in China was for fortifying, not socializing.

★

Only a week before Han and I set out for Xiahe, colleagues trying to report from affected areas had been detained or turned back at checkpoints that had sprung up overnight, the result of authorities unleashing legions of troops to quell the unrest – and prevent news about the sensitive and potentially embarrassing situation from spreading. Helmeted and armed with batons and riot shields, soldiers jammed into convoys of trucks that rumbled through streets already crawling with police cars. They lined up along major intersections, staring down ordinary citizens who passed them, or performed drills in packs, shouting rhythmically to keep pace.

Xiahe was now recovering from two days of revolt. Crowds of monks and lay Tibetans had marched through town holding pictures of the Dalai Lama – the Tibetan spiritual leader Beijing openly reviles – smashed windows of government buildings and, according to one witness, ripped a photo of then President Hu Jintao from its frame and burned it. They also incinerated Chinese flags and displayed the snow lion pennant of independent Tibet, labeled a "reactionary flag" by China's communist regime.

For such a politically charged region, the landscape for most of our 150-mile journey from Lanzhou was arid, mountainous, desolate – and miraculously clear of blockades. Along the way, we stopped at monasteries where monks stared at us but were reluctant to speak. Despite his wooden manner, one smiled and said things were "fine." Slowly, cautiously, a few others eventually told us of great anger and sadness in their hearts, and of how their actions were monitored by plainclothes minders. The situation was both complicated and complex, they said, their words wrapped in nuance.

To speak out was dangerous; to remain silent was unbearable.

I had written before about the religious and social controls imposed by Beijing since Chinese troops invaded Tibet in 1950, including limitations on the number of monks in lamaseries, and mandatory political and patriotic classes in which they were forced to denounce the Dalai Lama. And now, in the shadows of the prayer halls, where candles flickered and the smell of yak butter hung heavily in the air, I got a small taste of their bitter burden.

★

After making the final turn into Xiahe, we immediately spotted what looked like a checkpoint, wooden barriers blocking the way. Not wanting to stare out the window, I couldn't tell if anyone was manning the post. Han and I sank a little deeper into the backseat.

My clothes – austere cuts in dark, monochromatic hues – often set me apart from other modern Chinese women, and my Mandarin accent, a hybrid of a sibilant southern one peppered with the guttural "er" sounds of Beijing's northern dialect, marked me as a "non-local" wherever I went. But being ethnically Chinese was still a gift of conformity while covering sensitive stories. My skin color had helped me blend into a crowd many times as authorities, anxious to deter and detain foreign journalists, zeroed in on Western faces. At a road-block, however, the only thing that mattered was identification papers. The journalist visa in my bright orange-red Singapore passport was a guaranteed trip to a police station or government office.

I held my breath and stared fixedly ahead, praying that we wouldn't be stopped; not now, not when we were so close. The car kept moving. "No one's there," Driver Di finally said, and I nearly whooped with relief.

Unfolding before us was a modest, narrow strip of a frontier town with the glass-and-tile architecture of the Han Chinese – the country's ethnic majority – on one end, and more rustic Tibetan housing and shops on the other. Driver Di drove slowly so we could take in the considerable military and police presence. Han shot a few frames as we passed government offices with guards standing at attention at the entrances. Windows pockmarked with holes from rocks thrown by protesters sat unrepaired and many shops were shuttered. Even so, residents bundled in winter coats went about their normal routine, buying and selling medicine, cosmetics and clothes. Around them, grim-faced uniformed officers patrolled the sidewalks and police cars were parked every few feet.

The street ended at Labrang, an eighteenth-century monastery that is one of the most revered centers of Tibetan Buddhism outside of Tibet. It comprised a sprawling maze of ornate temples and white-walled residences where the monks lived. To our relief, not a policeman was in sight.

I zipped up my jacket against the cold and felt tiny snowflakes melt as they landed on my face. A few monks walked by in pairs or small groups, their robes of crimson, fuchsia and scarlet bright in the weak afternoon sunshine. The ones I tried interviewing shook their heads and hurried away. Was it because of my ethnicity, or my profession? Minutes later, I heard strains of prayer chants as I passed some temples, punctuated by the echoing, staccato shouts of troops performing their drills in the town square. Those clashing sounds seemed to sum up the story we had been sent to cover.

That afternoon, I talked to a 13-year-old Chinese girl with wide eyes and braids who had watched from home as the demonstrators began gathering. The crowd, she said, had swelled in numbers, and anger, as it smashed its way through Xiahe.

"Glass was everywhere. Thick glass was broken to bits this big," she said, pointing to the tip of her pinkie. "I was scared. My mother's hands were shaking so badly she couldn't pick up her chopsticks for the rest of the day."

I also interviewed a young Tibetan shopkeeper whose voice trembled with unshed tears as she talked about hiding for hours with her mother and sister in the crammed second-story space in which they lived and ran a little eatery out of. They had covered their ears to muffle the shouts and thumps.

"Not many people come in anymore. They are too scared to leave their homes much," she said, apologizing moments later for not have much food on hand to prepare for us. The five-table space was empty except for two men eating soup noodles. The dish was one of the few things readily available on the menu that, like many businesses in town, reflected the area's mix of Chinese, Tibetan and Muslim Hui residents. In the tiny kitchen, her mother was steaming momo, Tibetan dumplings usually filled with beef, yak meat or vegetables.

In a larger restaurant a few doors down, we had tea with a young monk who Han had met earlier while walking around Labrang. I enjoyed a grassy green leaf while the other two sipped a traditional Tibetan concoction called boeja, black tea fortified with yak butter and salt. The monk had a dimpled chin, a soft voice and an awkward laugh. In halting Mandarin, he said his friends had asked him to march with them, but he had refused, afraid of the consequences. About four or five monks had been taken away from Labrang in the aftermath and an 8:30 p.m. curfew had been imposed, he said with an expression I could not read.

"I don't know," he said looking down into his cup when I pressed for more details. "We can't talk about this."

★

The sky was darkening and it had started snowing again. I was tense from skulking around and unsettled by the stories I had heard. I hadn't realized I was hungry until my stomach growled as we drove down the main drag, weighing our options for dinner. We finally settled on Little Sheep, a popular Chinese chain serving hot pot ("fire pot" if literally translated), an Asian-style fondue said to be a legacy of nomadic Mongolian horsemen who gathered around fires and immersed fresh beef and lamb in a communal vat of bubbling stock.

Little Sheep was the biggest restaurant on a block of mom-and-pop operations and had a direct view of the town square where soldiers were powering through evening drills. We asked for a private room on the second floor, a freezing, fluorescent-lit space with a round table big enough for a family of 10. As we walked in, I noticed that the door to the adjoining room was open; my heart skipped a beat as I caught sight of a table full of military-types. Luckily, they seemed jolly with alcohol and food and didn't look our way. Politics rarely get in the way of a good meal.

Like many modern hot pot restaurants, Little Sheep used partitioned pots, which meant we could cook the food in more than one kind of broth, opening up all kinds of flavor pairings.

In my years in China, I had tried soup bases distilled from a number of ingredients – from mushrooms to medicinal herbs to curry powder – but usually stuck with a combination of a robust bone stock with Chongqing's shockingly fiery yet pleasantly numbing concoction boosted with dried chilies, ginger and Sichuan peppercorns.

During Beijing's frigid winters, my friends and I would huddle together at our favorite hot pot hot spots as the savory aromas curled and deepened around us. Plates heaped with pyramids of paper-thin slices of raw beef or lamb, bunches of pungent greens called haozigang, bricks of tofu, nests of noodles, and rows of shrimp dumplings ringed the pot, set deep into the center of the table. After plopping in the lot, we would impatiently count down the minutes before plunging our chopsticks into the roiling stock to pluck out the precious morsels of food and dunk them into sauces redolent with sesame paste and chili oil.

Encouraged by those happy memories, I hungrily thumbed through Little Sheep's menu, which had more than 150 items, and ordered portions of lamb and beef, leafy greens, cuttlefish, lotus root, enoki mushrooms, fried tofu, tripe and clear vermicelli noodles.

Driver Di, who had been nervous all day about heading into a potentially sensitive situation with foreign reporters, finally looked happy when the waitresses filled the pot with the two broths, turned on the heat and began piling dishes on our table.

"Chi ba, chi ba," "Eat, eat," he urged us, picking up his chopsticks as the stock came to a brisk boil. We slid batches of raw food into both sections of the pot and watched them dance in the bubbling soup. The tofu, tripe and cuttlefish went in first, followed by the delicate shavings of meat, which had to be closely watched so they didn't overcook and disappear. The vegetables were last to ensure they retained their crunch. Noodles didn't go in until everything else had been cooked, a nod to the old Chinese custom of eating starches last to fill up.

The tender curls of meat and cuttlefish were perfect vehicles for my pungent dipping sauce of mashed garlic and sesame oil. I bit into a piece of lotus root savoring its crisp earthiness, and drank bowl after bowl of soup sweetened with everything we had cooked in it, grateful for the heat in my belly, finally.

At first, we ate in silence. Then we talked about the riots and what had happened since. Driver Di began looking uncomfortable again so Han and I switched topics, telling him about the Singaporean version of hot pot we had grown up eating. Called "steamboat," it had a simple chicken broth and was accompanied with a garlicky chili sauce and finished off with a fresh egg or two beaten into the soup for extra richness. Di laughed at our enthusiasm for the dish.

But hot pot seemed oddly appropriate for the tense and complex situation we were in – a variety of ingredients and distinctive flavors, separate yet simmering together, reflecting not only China's myriad regions and tastes but also capturing immutable cultural partitions and the slow, albeit forceful, discontent percolating within its people. In my world, the essence of the dish was distilled into something much simpler: the perfect antidote to a day of difficult work, the sort of shared comfort food that rekindles smiles and resurrects childhood pleasures. Already my heart felt a little lighter.

With hot pot, it was easy to forget the reason we were in Xiahe. The little girl, the frightened woman in her tiny restaurant, and the self-censoring monk seemed to live in a different place, away from the drunken laughter coming from the room next door, from the abundance of food before us. The town's disconsolate, resigned air was lost in the tropical steaminess of the room.

All it took, though, was one glance at the window from where Han had been shooting photos and seeing the scar of tape that covered a large crack from where a rock had hit a pane to jar me back to reality. There was a lot more ahead in a situation where things were likely to go from bad to worse as the crackdown widened and deepened. And just like the hot pot in front of us, tensions, always brewing, seemed ready to boil over again.

Our plates were now empty and the soup was cooling. We paid up and walked back out into the cold, dark street. Everything had been shuttered for the night save for a small shop selling cigarettes and bottled drinks. The soldiers were finally silent.

WHERE THERE ARE CROWDS

Susan Conley

Susan Conley's memoir, "The Foremost Good Fortune" (Knopf 2011), was excerpted in *The New York Times Magazine* and the *Daily Beast* and was an Oprah Magazine Top Ten Pick of the Month, a finalist for the Goodreads Choice Award, and won the Maine Literary Award for Memoir. Other of her writings have appeared in The Paris Review, The Huffington Post and elsewhere. She founded The Telling Room, a nonprofit creative writing lab in Portland, Maine. Her debut novel, "Paris Was the Place", is due to be published in 2013.

OUR BEIJING APARTMENT SAT on the edge of downtown in a dizzying grid of concrete high-rises, all recently landed on the wind-scoured Gobi Desert from outer space.

We lived in Tower Four of an enormous complex called Park Avenue. Grand Central Park and Park Place were our closest neighbors, and I won't say the surreal names of the compounds didn't make me long for home in those early days. One bank of our windows faced a packed, five-lane highway that snaked its way around the capital city. We could stand in our living room in our pajamas and count the fleets of shiny new Audis and older V.W. Santanas. Always black. Always sedans. The other side of our apartment faced a hutong – an old-school warren of grey-brick barrack-like buildings and narrow alleys and blind turns. The highway spoke of New China. Of progress and pollution, of snarled traffic and the unwillingness of Beijingren to ever use their blinkers when turning. The hutong out back, however, was about Old China. Of families and traditions and culture and history.

And more than anything we came to learn, the hutong was also about *food*.

During our first wobbly weeks in Beijing, my husband, Tony, and our two small boys would stare down at the hutong. Packs of laughing kids roamed the streets kicking balls and wrestling. Grannies sat talking in their doorways. Solitary men stood in an open patch of land next the outhouses doing tai chi. We were so close to the hutong we could see floral designs on the enameled chamber pots they emptied into the squatter toilets every morning.

In the afternoons a loudspeaker played warbly public service announcements describing recent changes in local laws, followed by screechy cat-in-heat erhu music. Every day the voice of Chinese Reason intoned over the speaker, and every day Aidan and Thorne would ask me when we were going back home to the States.

It wasn't that the boys didn't like China. There were lots of things they thought were pretty terrific: the 1972-era roller coaster in Chaoyang Park. The Great Wall at Mutianyu and the metal toboggan they got to fly down from it on. Plus the epidemic of soft drink consumption was a clear bonus: my boys had never had such unfettered access to Coke and Sprite.

But they hadn't wrapped their heads around expatriatism yet. Why would our parents leave the coast of Maine to make a home in a foreign country where we didn't speak the language and didn't have one friend? They thought China was a great place…for a vacation.

★

On one of those first days in Beijing when our refrigerator was still too empty, we headed into the hutong to find something to eat. We took a left out of Tower Four and saluted the teenage security guard who stood at attention in his oversized, gold-buttoned, blue uniform. We never shook off the military feel of Park Avenue. It crawled with security guards, all of whom had a penchant for saluting, when they weren't dozing. We took another left through a high, back-end iron gate and found ourselves in a rutted lane. The driver of a speeding pedicart carrying Hami melons screamed something I didn't understand, probably to get out of his way. We jumped back.

"Here we are in China!" is what Thorne said then. He was six-years-old and earnest. When he wasn't singing the odd patriotic American song as part of some kind of private nostalgia trip, he kept repeating those words: *Here we are in China*. The words were his coping technique; a way to help himself get through what his kind first-grade teacher said was his relocation "spillover stress." It made him feel good to state the obvious – a tendency that, as we came to learn, allowed him to fit in very well in China.

"Two?" The security guard standing by the road asked Tony in Mandarin and smiled. In a country that enforces its one-child policy more vigorously than most of its other many laws, he was incredulous at the idea of a duo of male heirs. "You have *two* boys?"

"Shi de," Tony said. He was the elected Mandarin speaker of our family. The only one who knew any Chinese verbs. In fact, he knew a lot of them. He was what I hoped would be our ace in the hole in Beijing; a way to get through the bureaucracy faster. He lived in China for years in the 1980s and could handle the four, inscrutable Mandarin inflection tones almost as if he'd spoken the language all his life. Tony was why we were now in China. It was his consulting office. His grasp of the endless Mandarin idioms. His sweet memories of hitchhiking his way across China's closed border regions. It was entirely Tony's gig.

"Two boys," Tony repeated, a testament to the obvious.

Here we are in China, Thorne repeated. He was trying hard to process things. Maybe it would become our theme song, because I liked hearing Thorne's words that afternoon, standing next to a dozen blue flatbed cement trucks while the motorbikes and throngs of shoppers fanned out around us. We all needed to state the obvious sometimes in China. It was a way to get some footing. Things were moving so fast in the capital. Even there on that dirt lane next to the hutong I could feel the winds of progress. There were mounds of dirt for sale and bags of sand and so many dove-grey cinderblocks. The storefronts hummed with men in black sports-coats smoking cigarettes and making side-deals. We could smell the industry.

But Aidan, our four-year-old, wasn't interested. He was starving by now and close to tears. He whined, "You promised something to eat. You promised I was going to like China." He was struggling to embrace the People's Republic. *Here we are in China* wasn't quite having the same palliative affect on him that it was having on Thorne. Aidan knew where he was; he was in China, and it was suspect. None of the food we'd found him so far had been quite as good as we'd promised him it would be.

It takes time to suss out the best dumpling dives in Beijing. As we came to learn, they don't often go by a name. You have to ask around. You have to look at what people are eating when you pass by. You can even sometimes poke your head in the kitchen.

We hustled the hungry boys past the cement shops and through the high stone gate that marked the hutong's official entrance. The red and blue painted dragons had faded, but the stonework still spoke of some former glory. We walked three more blocks and ended up at a makeshift food stall next to a used electronics store. There was no door to the stall; it was an open-air canteen, with pastel-colored pre-schooler stools resting too close to the edge of the buzzing street. A woman in tight jeans and shiny black pumps tended to vats of water on two propane burners. A small crowd gathered around her.

Where there are crowds in China, there is usually good food. So we found a spot to sit. At the table next to us a group of men in their early twenties slurped bowls of noodles and yelled into flip phones. They had a palpable energy, hunched over their bowls, laughing, eating, and taking calls. Four older, red-faced Chinese businessmen sat closer to the kitchen, wearing short-sleeved dress shirts and black polyester slacks. They smoked Chinese cigarettes with ferocity while they waited for their food, six bottles of Yangjin beer on the table between them.

"This is going to be good, Aidan," Tony said. "You're going to love this place." The air smelled of cooking oil and garlic and tobacco smoke. Thorne harbored a thing for cigarettes: they made him crazy-mad. He'd even weep sometimes when people smoked around him. Other times he'd just storm off. This afternoon he sat stone-faced and stared at the smokers, trying to shame them. This is what happens when you've raised your American kid to think of cigarettes as something akin to heroin.

Tony called out to the waitress. I hadn't gotten used to this yet: the part where everyone in Chinese restaurants yelled at one another. The patrons yelled and waved their eyes at the staff, and the staff yelled back at the patrons. It was just how it worked – a tough love that no one except me seemed to mind. "Fuwuyuan!" Tony yelled again. "Waitress!"

The woman in pumps came to our table, unsmiling. She only said, "Ai?" Then she and Tony did the thing they do in China where they talked about the food. There was no menu. There often isn't a menu. Together the two of them decided on way too many dishes.

"Tripe?" Tony asked me, reverting back to English. Tony was as into Chinese street food as he was into Chinese hitchhiking.

"No tripe," I frowned. "Can we just keep this simple please? Don't they have dumplings?"

Slowly the waitress warmed to Tony's Mandarin and brought each of us clear glasses of sweet ginger tea. It was the best tea maybe we'd ever had and we all drank it down. When Tony asked her where she was from she said Zhengzhou. Then she smiled shyly and all her toughness evaporated. When she slid the plastic plates of jiaozi on to our table, she called out each one by name: "Jiucai jiaozi! Shucai zhengjiao! Xianxia jiaozi!"

The skins were pale and hot and glistening. These were not your doughy, American pot stickers. They were light and succulent: first a trace of garlic, then the shaved ginger and last the fresh, minced shrimp. The boys were transported. Their favorites were pork and chive. Aidan ate and ate and smiled his biggest grin in weeks. Then he dipped the next round in the little saucer of soy and chili paste and vinegar and ate again.

These were the dumplings that became our road map to Beijing. The dumplings and noodle soup and baozi and the plum sauce we spread on the roasted duck...these were how we were able to translate China.

★

I got busy taking Mandarin classes with a hip, 22-year-old graduate from Beijing University who'd given herself the Western name Sophia. Every day Sophia and I enacted skits in Mandarin in which I bought vegetables from her until, finally, she decreed that I was ready to go out on my own to the hutong market.

The sky was a rare, piercing blue that day. Strong desert winds had pushed the pollution out and over the low ring of mountains to the west, and I took this as a good sign. The fruit and vegetables had been arranged so carefully, so lovingly, on the wooden tables in the alley that they almost looked like candy. The strawberries were immaculate and incredibly red. I wondered what kind of dye had been injected into them. The apples were a disarming color of lime. Could they really be that bright? But I liked the look of the long, serpentine green beans, and the shiny, purple eggplant. There were small mountains of yellow potatoes and dark orange yams. Tight flowers of bok choy and heaps of various green leafy vegetables I never learned the names of.

One of the Chinese housewives near me called out to the vendors for some green beans. The two middle-aged women behind the table were short and stocky. One wore a flecked brown wool blazer over dark baggy pants, a look I'd begun to recognize as utilitarian country-farmer garb. The other woman tried more for urban chic in a v-neck purple sweater with swaths of black beading across the chest. Maybe she had dreams beyond the market. They both had the weathered skin of women who'd spent a great deal of time in the sun, deep smile lines creasing their faces.

The one in the blazer put a handful of beans in a plastic bag and asked Housewife if this was enough. I could see a gold-capped front tooth. "More," Housewife said. "Give me more." Her rapid-fire Mandarin sounded almost like barking. So blunt and fast. "More," she said again until the plastic bag was almost full.

Then the vendor barked back a price, something about "ten kuai," or was it 100? I was madly trying to do the Chinese math in my head. I didn't want to get it wrong when it was my turn. But Housewife didn't like the price. She scoffed. Then she said, "No," and something else that had to be along the lines of 'are you kidding me?' I got really nervous then. How was I going to pull this off? All I wanted was a few onions and maybe some carrots. My boys loved carrots.

Finally the two women arrived at a price. Both seemed peeved now. Was this just an act? Could someone really get this worked up over the difference of what sounded like about 90 cents? And who knew that you could barter over beans in China? Who knew that you could barter over just about anything here?

The crowd thinned until it was clearly my turn to go next. I tried to drift away; I decided I'd walk down the road a bit further. Maybe there was another stand with a nicer vendor? And what were those hand-held scales for sitting next to the eggplant? Was I supposed to actually use one of those to weigh my vegetables before I bought them? Because I couldn't. If I tried, Gold-capped Tooth would get mad at me, but I wouldn't be able to understand her and that would only make it worse.

I turned to go. "Yao bu yao?" she barked. "You want or you don't want?" At least I think that's what she said. Her face was stern and impatient.

"Yao," I said, grateful I knew the simple word for want. My heart was in my throat. I wasn't from here. Everyone at the market knew that. But I still needed to be able to ask for potatoes. It felt like a test. There was no English in this back alley. I pointed at an onion and said, "Yang cong." Gold-capped Tooth grabbed one and plopped it in the plastic bag and shot me another look. Then she smiled, turning on her charm, gold glinting in the sun. It was a much better way to win my beating heart.

"Did I want another?" she asked in machine-gun Mandarin.

"Liang ge." I was now counting in Chinese at the vegetable market. It was going to be okay for my family in China.

But then I had to pay. This was the part I'd been dreading. I knew my kuai and yuan and reminbi, though why there were three names for the same Chinese currency baffled me. It was just that I didn't always recognize the numbers when they got yelled at me. Gold-capped Tooth barked a figure. I had no idea what she said. But I possessed a wad of red 100 yuan notes in my back pocket and I knew I needed to make a gut decision: two onions, a bunch of carrots and four potatoes couldn't be worth more than 100 yuan.

I carefully pulled one of the bills from my pocket. A small crowd had formed around me. This would happen so frequently during the following years we lived in China that it became natural, something expected. The Chinese were eager for drama; some healthy distraction. They were more than willing to stop and take in the silly foreigner as she struggled to find words for what she owed.

"Yi bai," I finally managed to say. And that was enough. I even got some change back and maybe the hint of another gold-flecked smile. Had I just been ripped off? Action over, the crowd quickly dispersed. The woman handed me my plastic bags, and I hung them off my wrists proudly like all the other Chinese women I saw did, and I made my way back towards Tower Four.

★

It turned out that three-block radius around Park Avenue sold almost every major food group a family would ever need to survive. And it was this street food that got us closer to the city and more attached to the streets: local vanilla yogurt that we drank with straws from small clay pots. Congyoubing, a kind of delicious scallion pancake that became Thorne's favorite. Small Chinese crabapples glazed with caramelized sugar that Aidan became obsessed with, to the point that we'd have to pull over in our taxi, jump out and buy him some. It was the pure joy on his face when he ate those candied apples that proved how far China was winding and wending its way into his heart.

All four of us grew to crave shaobing, an oily pancake served with a salty egg and a red pepper and soy paste. There was a woman who cooked them by the side of the road on a giant, flat skillet. She had dark hair cut short over her ears like a young boy, and she never stopped talking while she ladled batter down into long rectangles. When the edges of the pancake were golden and crispy, Shaobing Lady would sprinkle in the green onions, roll it up and slice it with her cleaver. Sometimes there was a line for her shaobing in the morning. This never fazed her. She'd knead the dough and chat and laugh with whoever would listen and keep three shaobing going on her griddle at once. During the cold Beijing mornings, when the inversion effect tamped so much smog over the city that it looked like a big Northeast fog had rolled in, Shaobing Lady's hands couldn't move fast enough to feed her swelling line.

The meat market was housed in a falling-down, grey stone hall with holes in the tiled roof. On Saturdays Tony and I would buy our veggies from the two women in the alley, then stop in here for the meat. This was an otherworldly place. It smelled of history and old blood and pigeon (flocks of them lived in the wooden rafters). There was turtle for sale too, and whole claustrophobic aisles of chickens. Some were free-range and paced the aisles worrying, but most watched intently from their wooden cages. The butchers were thick-armed men with buzz cuts and blood-spattered clothes who suffered no expat fools. They hung the bigger pieces of meat on wires. The display cases were for the smaller cuts of pork and beef, plus the brains and lungs and livers and hooves… all the working parts of the animals laid out like a small banquet. It was the dead ducks, hanging by their necks, that always got the boys. They'd stand under the birds and stare up, creeped out by their limp heads.

In mango season we could walk out of the meat market and buy bags of the soft yellow fruit from wooden carts parked out front. And when there were mangoes, there were *so* many mangoes. It became gluttonous. We ate them for breakfast and lunch and dinner. Then, suddenly, the mangoes were gone, and we'd wait for the miniature tangerines. These were tart and sweet and addictive. You could peel the loose rinds in seconds and pop the entire fruit into your mouth whole. Aidan and Thorne would eat dozens in one sitting.

If you walked past the Mango Man and the Tangerine Lady there was almost always a Banana Vendor closer to the main street. He often sat under a willow tree and snoozed or read the newspaper upright on the torn seat of his bike, his cart stacked with hundreds of bunches. His bananas cost 10 yuan but they had to ripen at home. Further towards the highway was the Sweet-Potato Man. He had a small metal stove on the back of his rickshaw that he fed with chunks of coal. The sweet potatoes he sold were bigger than my hand. Aidan and Thorne would get off the school bus in the afternoon and buy one giant potato to share between them.

The whole time we lived in China, we were trying to figure out how we belonged and *if* we belonged and if we even had the right to want to belong. But Thorne and Aidan weren't interested in the psychology of expat life or how we did or didn't fit in.

To them we were, quite simply, Americans living on the edge of what was a poor but thriving hutong. They'd sit on the stone wall that ran the length of Park Avenue and split open that sweet potato and talk about their new friends from Shanghai and Seoul and Harbin and talk about how their Chinese teacher liked to sing opera in class, and about why their schoolbus driver didn't stop at red lights.

Thorne no longer needed to say "Here we are in China." He was too busy learning Mandarin adverbs and eating congyoubing. Because in the world of small boys, wherever you go there you are. They could hardly remember a time they *hadn't* lived in Beijing. It was their home now. They just wanted to know if they could buy another sweet potato.

Point of Attack

Derek Sandhaus

Derek Sandhaus is an American author, editor and blogger. He is
the author of "Tales of Old Peking" and "Tales of Old Hong Kong"
and the editor of several books including Edmund Backhouse's
"Décadence Mandchoue." He currently lives in Chengdu, the
heart of China's baijiu country, where he writes about Chinese
alcohol and drinking culture.

FIVE CHINESE AND FIVE foreigners walk into a Chengdu hot pot joint
with two bottles of baijiu. If this is the beginning of a joke, it
is a joke to be made at my expense. There is a price to be paid
for overconfidence. I had walked into the Sichuanese sweat
lodge with a prideful heart and been humbled. But I went down
swinging – swigging, rather – and didn't fall alone.

A word of explanation. Baijiu, white liquor, is the Chinese
word for the nation's gullet-searing traditional grain alcohol.
Baijiu is at once sweet and fiery. It shares common ingredients
with rose essence and paint thinner. Most baijius are made with
sorghum, a type of millet found in parts of Asia and Africa,
though they can also be made with rice, wheat and even peas.
Anything with starch will do, taste is subordinate to strength.
And it's strong enough to derail a freight train – topping
150-proof at the high end.

Baijiu is the drink of the people, beloved by Chinese
commoners since ancient times, who drain it in excess of two
billion gallons and rising per annum. It's also the drink of the
People, with a government liquor tab as great as the national

defense budget. Foreigners, to put it in polite terms, are less enthusiastic, though I had managed to develop a taste for it.

The modus operandi for drinking baijiu in Sichuan, the hard-drinking southwestern province in which I live, revolves around repeated ganbei, dry the glass, toasts. Every cup becomes a shot glass and bottles are consumed in quick succession. Refusing a toast, or refusing to return a toast in kind, is a breach of etiquette impolite in the extreme. The end result is that everyone, in order to be respectful to the others, ends up drinking more than anyone wants to, or should. Drinking in this environment becomes a battle of wills. This is not stepping out with a casual drink with friends; it is distance running in a hurricane.

★

On the evening in question, the contest was held in a private room at a large, well-lit restaurant in Chengdu. There's a saying in China, 'You can't set the table without alcohol.' All major holidays and life events must be celebrated with baijiu. This evening I had brought two bottles. The first was an inexpensive local baijiu weighing in at 52 percent alcohol by volume. The second was a low-alcohol baijiu I'd been gifted from America with the improbable name Confucius Wisdom. Above a picture of the Great Sage on the label was a quote: "Spirits may wane. Wisdom prevails."

An American baijiu is odd, and one invoking the name of Confucius odder still. Confucius is famous in Chinese history as a voice of moderation and boring restraint. His attitudes toward alcohol were clear: drinking should only be practiced in a ceremonial context. It was respectable, even desirable, to drink while performing a religious rite or dispensing with the formalities of hospitality. Alcohol was not to be indulged to excess by oneself, but always in the company of others and always with a greater purpose in mind. So rigid were Confucian proscriptions on alcohol that for much of Chinese history the imperial court had an official Drinks Master who instructed everyone when to drink and when not to drink. The official cut-off point was three cups of wine, and not a drop more.

For the first step in the delicate ballet of Chinese festal etiquette, the seating must be arranged. Unlike Western table settings, the Chinese banquet table is almost always round or square – there's no obvious head of the table. This leads the uninitiated to the mistaken belief that this engenders a sense of egalitarian camaraderie. Not so. At the Chinese table, the seat of honor is that with the best line of sight to the door, with the lesser mortals fanning out from him in order of descending importance.

In our merry band, Laoban, the eldest and presumably the wealthiest (the most important status determinants in China), was ensconced at the table's "head." A local businessman and the boss of Alex's girlfriend Grace, I'd need to keep an eye on him. Alex and I, who had conceived of the evening's festivities, took seats to his left flank.

Dry beginnings to such meals are always awkward. No one is sure with which language to lead off; the natural linguistic segregation having yet to set in. While small talk is made in halting Chinese and English, the waitstaff encircles you removing chopstick holsters and covering jackets to protect them from the ensuing carnage. They set a still pot of oily crimson broth in the center, lukewarm and placid.

"So you work with Grace?" I asked Laoban.

"Correct."

Feeling him out, I said, "You must drink a lot of baijiu."

"Not tonight, I have to drive. I'm sticking with beer."

It seemed that he wasn't going to be the primary threat; time to crack open the Confucius Wisdom and find out who was.

Whatever wisdom Confucius had in regard to alcohol, it should be noted, endures merely as an empty husk of protocol. Save for a general notion of giving and receiving face, the meaning behind the actions have been lost. There is slight variation from one region to the next, but the basic program is the same wherever you go: if you can still hold up a glass, you're expected to keep drinking. As for the once ironclad three-drink Confucian threshold, it is now the "penalty" for arriving late to the party.

One's jiuliang, alcohol tolerance, is his calling card in contemporary Chinese machismo. If you want to succeed in business, politics or society, you must be able to drink deep and often. Failure to keep pace with other drinkers would indicate weakness or, worse, disrespect.

I rose to make the first toast of the evening. Everyone standing, we raised our glasses of Confucius while I spoke. I gave a generic welcome and thanked them for participating in my social experiment. To Laoban, I added a brief though less detailed Chinese addendum. With a "ganbei," we leaned in, clinked glasses and drained their contents.

"A little on the weak side," the bossman noted of the 78-proof baijiu. I agreed, filling his glass with the second, 104-proof local variety. He moved the glass to a table behind him. "I can't," he explained. One down.

Grace, a dangerously thin young woman who always seems to be suffering some ailment, was already flushed. "I don't think I can drink any more tonight," she said. "I think I'm having an allergic reaction to some bad fish from lunch." The nearest body of water was about a thousand miles from Chengdu. If she was making this up, no one could call her on it; she was thus appointed de facto ordering mistress. She began reading us our options.

"Tripe?" Yes. "Tofu skin?" Absolutely. "Quail eggs?" A must. "Pig brain?" Pass.

Turning to Alex, a seasoned baijiu tippler and now the primary target of my offensive, I rose and toasted his health.

Individual toasting is when things get dangerous. One can target anyone one likes, but the damage is reciprocal. For each glass you make someone drink, you too must drink. The toastee must also keep a running tab throughout the evening, as propriety demands that every toast given must be returned.

This is particularly dicey territory when some drinkers abstain from baijiu and toast with beer, as in Laoban's case, resulting in a roughly 10-to-1 alcohol imbalance per toast.

Laoban may already have been sidelined, but he was calling in reinforcements. "I'm drinking with a bunch of foreigners," he shouted into his cell phone. "You gotta get over here."

★

By the time the dishes began to arrive, our pot was at a slow, gurgling boil. All manner of vegetables, flesh and innards were plopped into the vat. Still no toasts from other contenders at the table. Sensing weakness, I started picking them off one at a time. Pointing at Lex, another American guest, I said, "Get up and drink." He downed it with a grimace. Another challenger out of contention with little resistance. Everything was going according to plan.

Laoban's friends blew into the room like a pack of furies. Leading the charge was Abo, a bald, chubby and bespectacled middle-aged Chinese man wearing a shirt so loud that one would have to shout to be heard over it. He was happy to oblige on that account, introducing himself to each of us in turn with a grab bag of stock English phrases.

"Hellllllloooooo," he said, shaking my hand. To Alex: "Niiiiiice to meet yooooouuu." "Welcome to Chengdu." Stopping at Carmen, a Spaniard, he pantomimed bull fighting for a moment before climbing atop a chair to dance flamenco. With every step he took, the room's center of gravity shifted toward him.

Also just arrived were a heavy-set middle-aged woman of unclear affiliation, possibly Laoban's girlfriend, and Yang Yang, an attractive young woman in a tight, neon-yellow "Just Do It" shirt from another era.

"Yang Yang is my girlfriend," Abo explained. "No, she's my sister." He let out a burst of high-pitched tittering laughter. "No, Yang Yang is my mother."

"I'm his mother," agreed the younger woman.

Abo produced a flask of dark liquid and poured everyone a glass. It was a homemade paojiu, baijiu infused with who knows what kind of medicinal herbs, spices and animal parts. Abo clinked glasses and then whipped his glass around his head in a quick blur, ending in an underhanded pour into his mouth. This was the kind of move you had to practice in front of a mirror – I was up against a professional.

Pot at a rapid boil, chopsticks and molten oil flew in every direction. Every time I attempted to pour baijiu from the stronger of the two bottles, the woman who had not introduced herself, dubbed The Referee, slapped my hand and handed me the Confucius sauce.

"You're a bad person," she said.

Assuring her that my intentions were honorable, I told her that I was celebrating the proud tradition of Sichuanese baijiu. She didn't take the bait, repeating the accusation: "You're a *very* bad person."

Yang Yang, on the other hand, played the part of enabler, toasting every man in turn. For most of China's history, the role of a drinking hostess – pouring glasses and encouraging the menfolk to drink – was the only function permitted to women at the alcohol table. Yet today women are among the most formidable drinking combatants.

I asked the women present why they liked to drink, and the Ref explained that it was that very breaking from tradition that appeals. "When I drink I can speak my mind," she said. "When you drink you can say the things you wouldn't want, or dare, to say."

Women may use alcohol to break out of well-defined roles, but they still play by a different set of rules. Grace and the Ref, for example, were not drinking nor were they compelled to drink by others. Yang Yang dispatched her first 10 to 20 shots with beer and *then* switched to baijiu – a most unequal warfare considering that the latecomers were a half dozen shots behind the rest of us.

By this point the toasts had started flying at random and things were getting sloppy. Alex toasted Lex from across the table, but Lex spat out the contents the second they entered his mouth. "What the hell was that?" he said, face contorted into a grimace. He'd poured his beer into a full glass of baijiu. Rookie mistake.

Abo sidled up next to Carmen, almost sitting on her lap, and began rambling away in breakneck-speed Chinese, which she may or many not have understood. Behind her forced smile, she looked at the rest of us with a pleading expression. Nobody threw her a lifeline.

I meanwhile was attempting, without success, to learn the Byzantine rules of a drinking game that involved throwing fingers while shouting an incoherent chant.

"Shuo cai, yao cai," "Speak of fortune and you shall receive it," the chant began, but that's all I got.

"It doesn't matter what you say in the second verse," said Yang Yang. "Just say a number and throw out a random number of fingers."

The only other rule seemed to be that, no matter what was said or how many fingers were collectively thrown – Two! Five! Eight! – the result was invariably (for me) "Drink!"

The hotpot now sat neglected at the center of the table, a bubbling cauldron slowly evaporating down into a concentrated liquid fire. Bits of hard, overcooked pig resurfaced for an instant and sunk back into the depths.

Not a minute too soon, our Costa Rican delegate Donnely arrived to breathe fresh life into the party. Abo rushed from his chair, opened his arms wide and yelled, "Hey!" Donnely returned the gesture and the two men, complete strangers, were now embracing. (Though none were as pleased by his arrival as much as Carmen, I suspect.)

Within minutes the mania had spread. Everyone was up and dancing with Abo in the now empty restaurant. The dumbstruck waitstaff took a break from mopping and formed a rough semicircle near the threshold of our private room.

There was more drinking, much more drinking. How much drinking, I can't say with any certainty. I have a distinct memory of talking to the Ref and smoking slims – I haven't smoked cigarettes in years, but these things happen.

"Why don't we do this every Tuesday night?" I asked the table, to a general murmur of agreement. The real answer would not be long in coming.

★

The next thing I knew, I was lying in my bed next to a serene and lightly snoring dog. A ray of morning light crept in through a crack in the blinds. Peace.

I looked over my shoulder to survey the damage. My clothes were in a neat pile on the floor. A full glass of water rested off-kilter on the nightstand. I rolled over to grasp it and found myself atop a soggy pile of vomit.

In my hubris I believed I could drink my way to the top of the heap, but instead found the bottom of the table. The problem was not that I entered the contest with a losing strategy, but that I had deluded myself into thinking that there is such a thing as a winning strategy where baijiu is concerned. There are only varying degrees of defeat.

How I had gotten from the table to my apartment was a mystery. Reconstructing the night's conclusion based on photographic record and eyewitness testimony, I appear to have made a second attempt to learn the finger thrusting drinking game with Abo. Neither of us left the contest unscathed. In my favorite image of the night, Abo and I have our arms around each other in an overblown but genuine gesture of camaraderie, heads flung back and howling with laughter.

It's the bonds forged over baijiu, more than anything else, that keep me coming back for another ganbei despite the hiccups, figurative and literal. You can learn more about someone after three shots of baijiu than in years of sober tea sipping. And a friend made over sweet sorghum hooch is a friend for life. Chinese social intercourse is lubricated with baijiu, and if you want to see the more intimate side of China, you must drink. There is a physical price to be paid for such excess, but much to be gained.

Confucius may have had the right idea by instituting limits to alcohol consumption, however impracticable they seem today. But implicit in his strict delineation of when and how much you may drink lies an even greater truth: there are certain circumstances in which you *should* drink. That's real wisdom.

Diplomacy On Ice

Rudy Kong

Canadian Rudy Kong moved to China in 1998 where he raised two children and started a traveling ice hockey team. His 2010 book, "Dragons, Donkeys, and Dust: Memoirs from a decade in China", details his experience with life and death during his 12 years in China.

IN RETROSPECT, IT MAY have all started to go wrong with the poem.

I was up in Dong Bei, North-East China, in a little town of eight million people. Encircled by Mongolia, North Korea, and Siberia, this region was the head of The Cock, as the Chinese like to refer to their country, chicken-like on a map. There was something familiar about Dong Bei. It was not the rickety bicycles precariously pedaling down ice-covered roads with a child, or a duck, perched on the rat trap. And certainly not the constant whiff of burning coal, or the dog carcass for sale on the sidewalk, steam rising from the skinless beast like a final, pitiful woof. No, it was the crispness of the winter air, the kind that rushes up your nose and gives you brain-freeze the instant you step outside.

"Same as Russia," the cabbie says, pointing through a small patch of defrosted glass at a curiously out-of-place onion-domed church. I am reminded of the churches the Russians and Ukrainians sprinkled across every town in the Canadian West.

"Same as Saskatchewan," I stutter, half to myself, realizing too late that I don't know how to say Saskatchewan in Mandarin.

"You Russian?" the driver asks. This is refreshing; farther south in China I am usually assumed to be American. Up here, you also just might be called "old hairy" (lao maozi), the name the locals had given the Russians back in the day, instead of the usual "laowai," old outsider.

"No, Canadian."

"Same thing," the driver suggests as he deftly weaves through the world of chaos that is Chinese traffic. Like the Russians, Canadians are seen as "old friends" of China. The cabbie, like nearly every single cabbie I have ridden with in China, cites Dr. Norman Bethune, who died in China serving the communist cause. I nod in agreement that he was a great man.

Russians left another mark, too. Here in Dong Bei, when you put your hockey stick in the taxi, the driver *knows* it's a hockey stick – not a golf club, like they think elsewhere.

"Dao le," he grunts, indicating our arrival at the ice rink.

★

In my first year of teaching at a Canadian curriculum school in Dalian, on the southern tip of Manchuria, I was given a teaching load that included several Physical Education classes. The school didn't have a gym and winter got much colder than I had expected. Beach volleyball wasn't much fun in January, so when I noticed the frozen ponds around the school I decided that I would introduce ice skating and hockey to the students. I ransacked thrift stores in Canada during my summer holiday, liberating them of old skates to bring back to China.

And then I met Wonger. A Dong Bei native, Wonger told me he played hockey and that a vanishing hockey subculture still existed in North-East China, introduced by the Soviets after they drove the Japanese from Manchuria in the 1940s.

This was like walking through a Narnian wardrobe and discovering a magical, wintery world where inexplicably strange people played hockey. It became my mission to create a *real* hockey team in Dalian. Hounding the locals like a pre-Boxer Rebellion missionary, I engaged in sinister and self-serving efforts to coerce and convince my colleagues – many of whom had never played hockey before and could not even skate – that they were excellent prospects for the Dalian Bing Long, the Dalian Ice Dragons.

This is how I found myself that day in a murky, cold locker room reeking of urine and mold with a ragtag group of Canadian teachers and Chinese friends suiting up for The Big Game.

Yes, this was a big game. If there ever is a time when Canadians understand the Chinese concept of face, it's when playing hockey – especially against our arch rivals, the Russians. We had seen Chinese teams before and knew them to be the offspring of Soviet-style hockey. Invited up here to represent Canadian hockey, we would damn well show them how this game is played properly.

The problem was: we were hardly a hockey team. 12 of us were preppy teachers at a school that taught Canadian curriculum classes to Chinese teenagers from elite families. The remaining four of our members were just regular Chinese guys who skated on frozen ponds in the winter for fun. None of them knew what the blue line on the ice meant. One of them was perpetually drunk on baijiu.

If it's possible for hockey players to look like rag dolls, we did. Dressed in whatever gear we could scrape together, many of us protected our heads with ancient SPAPS helmets, which we jokingly decided stood for Soviet Produced Advanced Protection System. But the laughter and banter in the dressing room did little to suppress the anxiety I was feeling about the game: I had a horrible feeling we were going to be embarrassed.

Our oldest player, well into his 50s, was an English teacher named Al. A cagey veteran-type who apparently had a soft spot for literature, Al startled the team by suggesting he read us a poem prior to the game. Athletes who play team sports are accustomed to a group huddle and a cheer. Sometimes the cheer could be aggressive in tone. Think Rugby. Think All Blacks and their Haka; scary stuff that pumps up our boys and scares the shit out of theirs. But a poem?

Impressively, 90 percent of Al's poem met the criteria of most good poetry: alliteration, a healthy mix of free verse, and some rhymes. I can't rightly recall any of the poem's stanzas other than the last, but that last line sure packed a punch.

"Fuck 'em in the death rattle!"

My teammates and I cast confused glances at each other. "Shenme? What?" some of our Chinese guys muttered. Yet we rallied. We got into it. We laughed for a second, and then caught the spirit. Fuck 'em in the death rattle! *Fuck 'em in the death rattle!*

Our new battle cry, I confess, barely masked the underlying fear that we would not represent our country, and our beloved past-time, very well. But we continued the chant in unison as we charged out of the dressing room and onto the ice.

Fuck 'em in the death rattle. I still don't know what that means.

★

On the other side of the ice, the Chinese team warmed up, impressively making crisp passes, looking a much more reasonable facsimile of the Red Army team than we did of Team Canada. Each of their players donned an identical, Canadian-made helmet, matching hockey sticks from Finland, and bright-yellow jerseys emblazoned with their sponsor's name and logo. Doubtless the spoils of New China's burgeoning economy. And these were not slightly built, effeminate Chinese from our Western stereotypes; no, they were large, solid Manchurian men.

"They're police officers," Wonger whispered with a look that said we might as well not even try. Pointing to their team captain, he said, "That one there is the Chief of Police."

And therein revealed the unspoken rule of today's game: that even if we were good enough to beat this team, we wouldn't. We were obligated to give them face in their home town, *especially* because they were police officers.

Face is a perplexing aspect of Chinese society for Westerners, although it sounds simple enough at first: give face to others and don't force them into situations where they will lose face. Yet our values and our national pride as Canadians obligated us to try our hardest to give this team a good battle. The not-so-subtle irony is that hockey games start with a Face-Off.

In fact, we really only had one "good" player, Ian, who had once played university-level hockey. Ian is normally the nicest, calmest guy you would ever come across. But on that night he was different. He had an edge. On that night he was going to fuck 'em in the death rattle. As the game began, Ian, playing center, said to hell with face and skated through the opposition with power and confidence. In return, he was hacked, held and tripped up.

When Ian responded angrily to these cheap shots, tempers began to flare on the Chinese team. The referee, sensing things were swiftly getting ugly, called us together and reminded us that this was friendly hockey and there was to be no body checking. He dropped the puck, and on the next play our defense, Blake, threw a hip check at one of their guys. A couple of minor scuffles ensued. Again, I blame the poem.

The police got their revenge. I'm not sure if I was run over by a train or kicked in the head by Jet Li, but when I got up off the ice I had instinctively thrown my gloves off and was charging around looking for the guy who had hit me. Disoriented, it took a few seconds before I realized the play had continued on and I was in a hockey game, not a fight to the death game of survival. A premonition, I suppose.

Their players started chirping at our Chinese teammates, but our goalie refused to respond to them – mostly because, despite his Asian features, he was Canadian and didn't have a clue what they were saying. One thing *everyone* understood, however, was that when they sprayed him with snow during a stoppage in play and he responded by throwing his blocker up into one of their guys' nose, he meant business. To be fair, he was not the first foreigner in China to lash out when frustrated by this culture.

It's always good to know PSB officers in China. Great guys. Ethics be damned, they will bend the law any which way to help their friends. Which is why I don't recommend punching a Chinese cop in the face with a goalie blocker. Especially if he is the guy who organized the hockey tournament you were invited to. That's not how you give face in China; that's how you destroy it.

If you've ever watched a hockey game, you know what happens after somebody messes with your goalie. A scrum breaks out. There is pushing and shoving, heated words, and a gloved punch or two. In exceptional cases you might thrust your gloved hand into someone's mouth, just to humiliate them.

But you never, never, ever hit someone with your stick.

Needless to say, just as the Chinese learn different musical scales, different eating utensils, and a different language from us, they also learned different hockey etiquette. Sticks began swinging immediately and, at once, their whole team left their bench to help. Decked out in yellow jerseys, they swarmed our goalie like nasty, killer hornets; one could almost hear a buzzing sound. Yellow peril indeed.

I've almost never seen in China what Westerners would consider a fair fight. Somebody always pulls out a meat cleaver or picks up a brick to smash your head in. Or they simply gang up on you, like the cops were presently doing to our teammates. Our instinct was to help, but it would only escalate things if we all joined the fracas. Besides, it goes against our Canadian sensibilities to fight as a gang. From the safety of the bench we watched in horror as the five-on-five fight quickly turned into fifteen-on-five. Brownie, another one of our defensemen, had been knocked down and was being kicked. With skates!

The rink now filled with shrieks and screams as a veritable Sino-Canadian War was declared, the whole dream unraveled before my eyes. All that work to convince the Canadian teachers to haul their hockey gear to China. All the phone calls and guanxi to arrange this weekend of games. All of it being ruined by a bench-clearing brawl that *our* goalie started. We would never play hockey in China again.

Fear and anguish consumed me. I went into full diplomatic mode, deftly weaving through the apocalyptic scene like a Chinese taxi driver through traffic, approaching each Chinese player and blurting out in broken Mandarin, "We are bing qiu pengyou, we are hockey friends." I shook as many gloved hands as I could. I could see it working too. The anger began to leave their eyes when they saw that we were not all foreign devils.

As I skated towards center ice, I reached out my hand to a man with a bloodied face. "Hao pengyou," I called out to him with a smile. But he glided determinedly past me and straight to our bench where our goalie, now safely off the ice, had just removed his helmet and face mask. The blood drenched Chinese warrior lifted his stick and speared our goalie just below his throat. Gengis Khan hadn't trained his men to be this savage. An inch or two higher and our goalie could have been severely injured, if not killed.

My on-ice diplomacy vanished. No longer was I Trudeau or Kissinger skating around looking for Zhou En Lai on skates. I morphed into General MacArthur, exploding in an atomic rage. My head filled with demonic poetry: Fuck 'em in the death rattle!

I mauled Gengis from behind, clawing him down onto the ice and began pummeling his head with my bare fist. I delivered six massive blows. In this moment of temporary insanity I heard and felt nothing.

Whack! The first bingqiu pengyou raised his stick skyward and brought it down over the top of my helmet-less head like a butcher at the local wet market.

Crack! The second pengyou drove the butt-end of his stick into the back of my head, just above my neck. Darkness.

★

As the fighting died down and we staggered off the ice battered and bloodied, the mostly-Chinese audience of several hundred jeered and booed us in a Dong Bei dialect I presently was thankful I did not fully grasp. A shrill voice yelled "go home!" in accented English. We dressed hurriedly, and with anxious tones wondered in all seriousness if we were going to be attacked by the crazed cops outside the dressing room. Someone said they saw one of them wielding a knife blade on the bench, and I believed it.

We walked as a pack through the darkness to the hotel a few blocks from the rink. Some of the cops, piled in a Santana, drove by slowly and glared. I had on many occasions witnessed PSB officers and their chengguan, henchmen, beating people excessively on the streets. Would we be the first foreign drive-by shooting victims in China?

Adrenalin still coursing through my veins, I went to bed feeling quite sick. I knew for certain we would never be welcomed back to play hockey. And given the pull that the authorities here have, I doubted we would ever set foot in an ice rink anywhere in the head of The Cock.

But in China anything is possible. There is always a banfa, a way. Even when the Chinese say mei banfa, there's no way, there's a banfa. Like an elder statesman, Wonger went to work on repairing relations with our hosts. Our perpetually drunk defenseman, Lao Fu, went along as reinforcement, pockets bulging with bottles of Wuliangye and a carton of Chung.

When they returned mid-morning to the hotel, they delivered the news. We were kicked out of the tournament, yes, but we had been invited to have lunch...with the cops.

We entered their clubhouse with trepidation. The chalky walls were adorned with posters of Soviet-era hockey players. The CCCP on their red jerseys matched the large Chinese flag that hung beyond round banquet tables overflowing with Dong Bei cuisine. Several plastic crates of Harbin sat against a wall.

Awkward is the only way to describe how the lunch started. How could we face the very people who literally tried to murder us the night before? How could we break bread, or baozi, as it were, with these savage North China cops? PSB officers are notorious for being above the law, and their behavior the night before certainly did not help negate this stigma.

Alas, like all Chinese banquets, this one started with a speech and moved right to drinking, that great unifier of nations. At each table we met a different group of their players who each said something complimentary about our play, apologized, declared friendship, and knocked back a glass of light-amber beer. And another. And another. With each glass we gave face, and it was given in return.

Only the referee still seemed resentful, blowing an imaginary whistle and yelling in mangled Chinglish "tooo minuss!" Two minutes, he meant to say, as in a two-minute minor penalty. Even in the midst of the make-up party the referee was dishing out penalties.

But as the 3.3 percent beer flowed, we began to see another side of Chinese police. Gone were the stern-faced goons who spend their days collecting bribes and looking the other way. In their place were flush-faced comrades who had forgiven us just as quickly as they had nearly exterminated us. The Chief climbed atop a chair and gave a concise albeit slurred speech in broken English before placing his official police cap on Ian's head, effectively forgiving him. Let's drink to that, ganbei!

Splash! The first bing qiu pengyou raised his glass skyward and poured his beer over my head. Ian was now handcuffed to the Chief.

Thump! The second pengyou wrapped his arm around my head, just above my neck. Bedlam ensued as little love-fests erupted throughout the clubhouse.

In my inebriated and elated state I pondered how Westerners in China routinely get pushed beyond our limits, and how we react in ways much more aggressive and intolerant than we do at home. We then justify our embarrassing behavior with an air of superiority. I smiled to myself thinking about how strange and uncivilized foreigners must seem to the Chinese – and the remarkable forgiveness and leniency they give us. Despite their own air of superiority, the cops not only wanted but *needed* to have this weekend end with the foreigners as their friends.

★

Following our diplomatic piss-up, which concluded with the Chief of Police performing fellatio on a 620-millileter beer bottle, the Dong Bei hockey ambassadors gathered up our gear and loaded it for us onto the bus. Red and blue lights flashing, we arrived at the local train station by police escort, the Chief driving (not a little swervingly) ahead of the police van in a shiny new Geely with no license plates; a super-sized red envelope by one of his less scrupulous constituents, perhaps?

The Chief gave us a quick farewell speech and ushered us on the train, showing respect by helping hoist our bags up into the carriage. As we struggled down the train's narrow corridor with our hockey bags and sticks, I saw the Chief and Wonger shaking hands, the Chief whispering into Wonger's ear.

On the overnight train home our little lao maozi party continued, each retelling of the insane weekend more embellished than the last. At five in the morning we were startled from our drunken slumber by a nasty attendant shrieking at us to prepare to alight at Jinzhou station.

"Has anyone seen my stick?" one of our teammates called out over the din of disembarking. "It has DANIHER written on it."

"Where's my helmet?" someone else asked.

Various pieces of equipment were apparently missing, but before I had a chance to help find them, Wonger instructed me to collect everyone's used train tickets and to give them to him.

"To send to the Chief," he explained.

The way he told it, the Chief would submit the tickets for reimbursement. 15 x 250 RMB; I calculated that would more than cover the banquet. In China, even forgiveness comes at a cost.

The next time I saw the Chief was a year and a half later,

in, of all places, a shopping mall in Kowloon, Hong Kong. A roller coaster roared over our heads as we skated through the subtropical humidity at the World 5s, a four-on-four hockey tournament in a mini-rink.

Elated to see an old friend, I waved at the Chief and walked clumsily in my skates over to shake his hand. In his left hand he held a red Jofa stick. Faint but visible was a handwritten name: DANIHER.

Bu Keyi!

Deborah Fallows

Deborah Fallows has written extensively on language, education, families and work, China and travel for publications including *The Atlantic, National Geographic and The New York Times*. Her latest book, "Dreaming in Chinese: Mandarin lessons in Life, Love, and Language," is based on her 3-year experience living and working in China. She now lives in Washington DC with her husband, writer James Fallows.

THE DAY WAS WARM, the air was surprisingly clear, and the sun promised to hang in the sky over Beijing well into the evening. It was June 3, 2009, the eve of the 20th anniversary of the events at Tiananmen Square. Foreigners like me who were living in China had been talking about this day for quite a while; we wondered if it would be acknowledged in any way. Many Chinese people knew little about the events of 1989. At the time, the news had not been widely known throughout China. Since then, any reference to Tiananmen Square or what happened there in 1989 had been routinely blocked from China's internet and left unmentioned in schoolbooks. The younger generation was particularly oblivious. Curious about what might be going on that evening, my husband and I decided to head to the Square to find out.

Tiananmen was a few miles west of our Beijing apartment, five stops away on the Line 1 subway. During our past three years in China, my husband and I had probably ridden the subways in Beijing and Shanghai a thousand times. As usual, most of the Line 1 riders on this day were young, and they predictably disembarked at Wangfujing, a bustling shopping area catering to China's burgeoning consumer class.

By the time we reached Tiananmen Square East station, the train was quiet and there were only a few passengers left on board – a rare blessing, but on this day slightly ominous. We climbed up the steps to street level, where broad Chang'an Avenue runs along the south entrance to the Forbidden City. It is a scene of infinite photo opportunities, with the massive portrait of Chairman Mao as iconic an image as the Eiffel Tower or the Statue of Liberty or the Sphinx.

There are always plenty of people along the streets of Beijing, but on that evening the composition of the crowd was unusual. Far outnumbering the laobaixing, the ordinary people, were flanks of young paramilitary in their drab olive-green uniforms, as well as regular police officers in their blue uniforms, plainclothes officers conspicuously dressed down in shorts and Hawaiian shirts (which I recognized as current stock from the knock-off goods markets in Beijing and Shanghai), and, of course, the "cool guys": buff, young, undercover government operatives dressed all in black, wearing sunglasses and looking a notch more menacing than anyone else.

We walked south toward the National Museum. Tiananmen Square to our west was blocked off to pedestrians. "Bu keyi!" snapped the guards when we approached the metal crowd barriers standing between us and the Square across the wide boulevard.

Bu keyi, Cannot. It was one of the first Mandarin phrases I learned, and it is the phrase of choice for all things forbidden, out of bounds, not possible, or otherwise not allowed. I had also learned over my years of living in China that there are great cultural keys hidden inside that phrase. Its meaning seems to vacillate with circumstances: sometimes bu keyi means no, sometimes it suggests maybe, and sometimes it even hints at yes.

On June 3, the meaning was quite clear: No!

★

Trying to sort out when the meaning was vague, and when bu keyi might even mean its opposite, keyi, can, had become an obsession with me. For example, on red lights in China, cars often turned right, but they also went straight ahead, and just as often turned left; every man for himself. Powerless traffic assistants flailed their arms and blew their whistles, but really they were just more background noise amidst the unruly street life at China's intersections.

I tried to be a good visitor in the country and follow all of China's numerous warnings of bu keyi. I was often far more observant than the locals, who shamelessly skirted rules and laws. When Beijing installed new security scanners inside the subway stations in preparation for the 2008 Olympics, I would dutifully wait in long lines to place my bag on the belt. Then I began to notice that many ordinary Beijingers would dodge the scanner and walk straight through the turnstiles, bags in hand. One day, pushing against my instincts (and the crowds) I decided to skip past the scanners. None of the gatekeepers even glanced my way.

Soon I was on a roll and began to finesse my responses whenever bu keyi stood in my way. I talked my way into the Cultural Palace of the Minorities with my apartment key card instead of the passport that was supposedly required. I threw my support behind a throng of Chinese housewives as we bullied a young guard in his size-too-big uniform, who was blocking our shortcut to the highway overpass; he could cost us a good half-mile hike to the corner. "Bu keyi," he droned until we finally, collectively, shamed him like the child he was into stepping aside. I even forced my imported, triangular Toblerone chocolate past the guards at the entrance to the Olympic grounds, who were religiously confiscating all drinks and food.

"Bu shi tang! Zhe shi wo de yao," "It's not candy! It's my medicine," I cried, taking a bite.

June 3, however, was different; on this day there would be no softening the phalanxes of formidable Tiananmen guards. It was all and only bu keyi. Aside from a handful of Chinese tourists who looked to be in from the countryside, few people were out strolling. The atmosphere was stern but calm...until we heard a scuffle near us and turned to see a man being strong-armed by some of the security. He was calling for help, first in his native Chinese and then in English, maybe for our benefit. We slowed and looked, interested and then a little alarmed as they walked him in the direction of a mobile police station.

"This does not concern you," said one of the casually dressed toughs in practiced English before he warned us to move along. His words were not ambiguous.

We ambled ahead a few dozen yards, feigning lack of interest at the small yet ongoing commotion behind us. Then, in an unthinking, or simply foolish, moment, my husband turned to take a photo.

"What is he doing!" I panicked inwardly. "This is so unlike him. We don't need that photo." In an instant, that same security operative was at our elbows.

"Did you take a picture?" he asked.

"Yes," answered my husband truthfully.

More undercover police convened, yet they didn't seem to know quite what to do with us. So they asked us for our passports; we didn't have them.

"Ah, here it comes," I thought, recollecting what one of my Chinese tutors had explained to me: China had laws for so many things – just in case someone needed to enforce them. Indeed, there *is* a law requiring foreigners to carry their passports "at all times." But it was a law few of us actually observed, reasoning that the risk of being pick-pocketed was greater than the risk of authorities demanding that we produce our passports. (My husband had been a victim of pick-pocketing just the previous week; maybe that explained his recalcitrant behavior.)

The security detail carefully, almost gently, deleted all the photos in our camera, but they seemed reluctant to let us go at that. They pulled walkie-talkies out of pockets, to discuss our situation with their command, we presumed. Then they made a decision:

"You will write a confession," said the security man. "You will write that you are sorry for interfering with the police. And you will write that you broke the Chinese law by not carrying your passport."

My husband demurred. On the one hand, this seemed a little silly and hyperbolic; a clear throwback to the public struggle sessions of the Cultural Revolution. On the other hand, the guard was dead serious.

Out came paper and pen, and my husband began scribbling about the police and the Chinese law.

★

Chinese law. There were so many Chinese laws; new ones kept popping up and old ones were in constant flux. Many of my Chinese friends admitted that even they had a hard time keeping all the sundry bu keyi straight. I would scour the newspapers for references and clarifications: Only one pet dog per household; no remodeling your domicile if you intended to sell it; stand-in-line day on the eleventh of every month (this, as part of the national etiquette campaign before the Olympics).

Not even historically freewheeling Shanghai was impervious to their government's totalitarian bu keyi. A recent controversial regulation decreed that no pajamas may be worn as street attire. When we lived in Shanghai, I would watch women emerge purposefully from their houses in the mornings, a shopping bag slung over an arm but wearing just a flimsy nightgown and sturdy walking shoes. In the evenings, old men strolled the streets of the French Concession in their boxers and t-shirts, or, as the weather cooled, in flannel jammies patterned with wooly sheep or Scottish plaids. I was puzzled, until my Chinese friends explained to me that Shanghainese considered the streets as extensions of their small cramped houses – so why bother to dress up when you headed outside? Shanghai authorities lately decided that this custom reflected poorly on their city's new cosmopolitan image. Hence, the bu keyi.

Along with these rather bizarre rules, there were serious ones: the fine points of the hukou residence registration, which tied social benefits to the place of birth; the one-child policy and its fluctuating exceptions, which came with fines or worse; the USD $50,000 limit that Chinese were allowed to take out of the country each year.

With years of attuning to all the rules, I was surprised how quickly we got ourselves into hot, or at least lukewarm, water at Tiananmen that pleasant day in June: we went on an outing; we took a picture; we broke the law; we were writing a confession.

This was a moment when my husband's decades as a professional writer and editor – in English – paid off. He deftly finessed the language between what he was told to write and what he actually wrote; no native speaker could ever misinterpret his words as an intentional "confession," but the Chinese could accept his prose with its critical vocabulary.

> *"I am sorry that the police felt I interfered with them, and that I broke the Chinese law that said I should carry my passport, because I was afraid of having it stolen after my wallet was taken last week."*

30 minutes later, the police agreed that the confession was good enough. "You should go home now," they advised us. Indeed, we thought, and retraced our steps as fast as we could back to the Line 1 subway.

★

We were a little shaken from the whole affair, but overnight I planned and schemed. On the morning of June 4, I pulled back my hair, put on lots of lipstick and a pair of big sunglasses, wore a different dress, carried a different bag, and headed, by myself, back to Tiananmen. My disguise, such as it was, made me more relaxed, but was probably unnecessary; after all, to the Chinese one blonde non-Asian looks pretty much like the next.

Security guards were letting people cross over to the Square, albeit in small numbers, before funneling us into orderly groups inside a tent to face scrutiny from more guards. A young, uniformed woman scrounged through my bag, examining my money, my phone, my hairbrush, even my lipstick. True to Chinese culture, she seemed more nosey than security-minded. She asked for my passport, and I showed her the photocopies of the name page and the visa page, having researched the rules overnight and discovered this was a legal substitute for the real thing. Finally, grudgingly, she conceded there was no reason to further delay me.

I emerged from the tent and joined thousands of people already in the Square. Tiananmen had been transformed overnight! The mood was festive, and yet it felt somehow odd, like a stage set. The normal crowd movement that I had come to expect in China, with its Brownian-motion quality, where people bump into you, brush against you, or cut in front of you, was wholly absent. Instead, everyone milled about stiffly, as though in assigned spaces.

This crowd, I soon determined, was deliberate and planted, and the casual-seeming afternoon at Tiananmen was as orchestrated as the opening ceremonies of the Olympic Games. Here, a cluster of people in matching yellow shirts, there, all in pink shirts, over there, the purple shirts, and there, the turquoise shirts.

"Controlled crowd-building," I reasoned. There were formations of guards marching in uniform ranks, police trucks patrolling slowly around the edges, and an occasional official car easing briskly through the crowd. The undercover police were just as conspicuous as they were the previous evening: many wore black, others their own street clothes but with telltale pins of a Chinese flag surrounded in gold. I watched these men skirt around the side of the security tent and into the Square, a dead giveaway that they were "official people."

A few hours later, satisfied the veneer on Tiananmen Square would remain "harmonious," I headed back to the subway. Spirited young Chinese nudging their way through the masses of Wangufjing boarded the train, laden with shopping bags and parcels but free of any weight from the anniversary of the events of June 4, 1989.

I was still feeling my way through the nuances of the Chinese language, and through the tangles of rules and regulations and endless bu keyi that characterized this society. The more I learned from the thousands of moments like these that I had experienced in China, the more I also knew remained locked away somewhere in its long history, just waiting for me to discover.

LIVESTOCK

Jonathan Campbell

Jonathan Campbell worked in various capacities in Beijing's local-music scene between 2000 and 2010. He's played in bands, taken international artists on China tours, helped bring Chinese bands to the West and written for a range of media outlets. He is the author of "Red Rock: The Long, Strange March of Chinese Rock & Roll", and he continues to promote Chinese rock.

YES, ON SOME LEVEL, you do know that goats are not your ideal audience. You probably didn't need nine years in China's rock scene, or even nine seconds in the vicinity of farm animals, to figure that out. But as you bash your drums it occurs to you that the four-legged creatures for whom you are playing actually might be preferable to the people in attendance. After all, you can see the confusion on the faces of most of the human observers.

It's pretty obvious, isn't it, that the concertgoers didn't realise that they'd be confronted with your band's particular form of music. You've played too many shows for confused audiences to think that you're going to win these folks over.

Not that you don't try.

Because when you're playing rock and roll to a mostly-barren field still recovering from the first two days of the Wulong Fairy Mountain Music Festival and, suddenly, the number of eyes watching the stage increases exponentially when the field's fencing is breeched by a pack of mountain goats, what else is there to do?

You try, damn it. And you rock. And, sure, you laugh.

★

Livestock, as the festival came to be known, seemed like a good idea at the time. When you were approached to perform – as always, by people several steps removed from the actual organisation behind the festival, but people you knew and trusted – you would have to admit, wouldn't you, that you were excited at the prospect: a trip out of town, and festival gigs for both of your bands. Some cash, too.

And this offer couldn't have come at a better time, could it have? Your one band had, after all, just been yanked from a different festival because it was on a list of groups that the local Ministry of Culture said "must come off the festival line-up," for reasons made no clearer beyond those six words. So, ok, not a tough sell. Plus the so-often-promised-but-so-rarely-received cash deposit you were actually given in advance. It all seemed so…what's the word…? Professional.

It's funny how many times in China you can get zapped, and yet, it seems like every time you walk near an electrical outlet, you still believe that sticking a fork inside will be a great idea. And what better outlet in which to stick your proverbial fork than a national park in the wilds outside Chongqing?

You were, nonetheless, careful when you agreed to the gig. Or, if not careful, you were, at least, sceptical. "I'll believe it when it happens," is how you put it to your bandmates. And suddenly, you had a couple thousand RMB in your pocket, and perhaps some of the mountain's pixie dust took effect, because you weren't as on your guard as you had been in the past. But that was how you planned it. For one of the first times in your rock and roll career, you decided to be at peace with being told where to go and what to do; just, you'd add, like a real rock star.

The plan this time was to sit back and let the Wulong Fairy Mountain Music Festival take you and your bands where it may, like some Chinese Tinker Bell, who was, in your mind, the Mountain's eponymous maiden. Yes, the fairies of Wulong would lead the way, and you were fully prepared to take them by the hand and fly off to Neverland.

And so, when the plane landed at Chongqing's sleek, newish airport, you allowed yourself to be herded – oblivious to any foreshadowing, metaphorical or otherwise, that might represent – onto a bus without a sense of how long you might be trapped therein, confident in the knowledge that, at some point, you'd end up in a national park somewhere a couple hundred miles from where you started.

When the bus seemed to repeatedly circle the grey, dank, eternally-filthy-but-yet-moist-enough-that-its-foliage-often-literally-jumped-out-at-you-in-an-explosion-of-deep-green city, you kept your frustrations in check, preferring to chuckle to yourself at the smacked lips of your fellow passengers, who were expressing, as only the Chinese seem capable, that most passive of passive-aggressiveness.

Of course your bus was also charged with picking up the more famous musicians already ensconced at the better hotels of Chongqing, since an hours-long meander through the megalopolis of 35 million was perfectly on the way to the mountains. And besides, when the trip went into and beyond its third hour, and the fog and darkness descended, shielding you from the mortal danger awaiting over the hidden cliffs just at the edge of the mountain roads not built for a vehicle of your bus' size, there was a camaraderie among the passengers, all of whom, save the big names and their bands, had been trapped in this mass coffin of a vehicle for the better part of a day.

Pulling into what can only be described as a post-apocalyptic holiday village, you were certainly concerned over the prospect of the accommodations that awaited. And when you found your "villa" to indeed be three-storied and balconied, with beds aplenty for all members of both of your bands, you were kind of psyched. The excitement soon dwindled upon the discovery that the effort at recreating the private karaoke rooms of a third-tier Chinese city in the villa's living room did not (until, on reflection, it depressed you further to realise that it *did*) extend into the bathrooms, toilet-seat-less all. Used to be, squat toilets would be an excuse to flaunt your adventurous spirit. That day was long passed, and you winced at the digestive calculations you automatically began to make.

★

The next day, in the grey, misty afternoon that seemed the only kind of weather this part of the country ever saw, your first band headed into the festival shuttle for the several-mile journey to the backstage area, the final leg of which featured a road more sludge than trail, a road you weren't convinced the blimp of a bus you were on could get through without an airlift. But something, Wulong's fairies perhaps, pushed that bus through the muck, and there you were, deposited in front of a growing crowd at the festival's massive stage.

If you chose to interpret as a bad sign the fact that the power generator for the entire festival, a massive orange box with a tangle of wires bursting forth, was also helping to boil a kettle of water plugged directly into its socket, then you'd have to see a yin-yang-like balance in the backstage makeshift Offering to the Gods the crew had fashioned out of a soggy cardboard box filled with muck, incense sticks, candles and, yes, a whole chicken.

You were treated like stars – as much as is possible in a backstage area that featured jerry-rigged tents slapped upon a perpetually-damp landscape. It was an ecosystem you'd seen, and would continue to see, at festivals across this developing nation, defined by muck and the by-products of a civilisation advanced enough to create a setting, far outside of any urban center, for the playing and enjoyment of live music, but not yet at a point where it can control the piles of refuse that result, which threaten, always, to overtake the backstage area.

Empty bottles of local water, countless pairs of chopsticks and a million styrofoam boxes scattered around the backstage area were the only evidence that the artists and crew were not completely forgotten; they'd been fed with an item so low on the food chain that its container defines its nature: hefan, box meal, that instrument of torture constructed of bio-undegradable space-age material designed to host equal parts unidentifiable bits of an equally unidentifiable animal, vegetable matter, and rice.

Your minimal soundcheck was delayed by a Taiwanese pop star's inability to keep his soundcheck under two hours, but that's okay, because, for one, you're going the zen route and two, you knew that the idea of a quick level/line check is not something that has made it into Chinese rock's DNA and your band prided itself on the ability to get a better sound with less prep time than anyone else. You know that, just like Charlie Watts said, rock and roll is mostly waiting around. But Charlie was only in China for a quick gig; you've been here for years.

Yaogun, the Chinese breed and form of rock and roll, in your experience, is more than just waiting. It seems to you that, elsewhere, one generally knows what it is that one awaits. In China, though, it's not just waiting. It's waiting, to be sure, but it's waiting with the dread, stress and fear about what, exactly, is coming. But when it's time for your set, you have a growing crowd of not-disinterested folks, which, you later learn, swelled from the maybe-couple-thousand you initially predicted to several thousands, and so this time, you revel in the small victory of a set played for a crowd that eats it all up. Because you know how easily things can go the other way.

Which is why your disappointment, on the cusp of your second band's gig the following day, weighs so heavily. It's not so much that there's nobody there to watch you. It's that nobody told the festival crew that the festival hadn't ended yet. They are literally packing up the stage as you and the other bands slated for the festival's final day arrive onsite, and they are not convinced by your presence, protestations or pleas that there is, in fact, a third day of performances. Phone calls are made, and they concede, finally, that the stage cannot yet be packed up.

And: cue the mountain goats. And don't forget the shepherd running full-tilt after them.

★

What still runs through your mind at moments like these, even all these years into your China time, is "how can I possibly explain this to the folks back home?" Here's the other thing that you have to explain to them: things like this keep happening. That if you can group the experience of playing to an empty-but-for-goats field into a series of related events, well, things have gone so pear-shaped that it occurs to you to worry about whether you'll ever find 'normal' again.

Sure, this is the first time you've played to animals, but still. You have to admit that you don't actually find that fact as strange as perhaps you should. And that, too, takes explaining. Context has become your new mantra; fitting things into an overall picture your new obsession. And you have a clear sense that it's not going to be easy to draw that picture in a way that's understandable back home.

How to contextualise a time and place where massive stages are erected and enormous festivals hosted in the wilds of a country still figuring out what, exactly, a music festival is? How to describe where you, a musician, sure, but a musician of a different – foreign – type, fit in all that? How to contextualise your China life and your yaogun life, filled with the amazing feelings that come from playing upon those massive stages but threatening to be overshadowed by the gauntlet often more literal than proverbial that is the path – ditto on the literal/proverbial tip – to the stage?

But, most pressingly in this case, how to properly portray that only-in-China mixture of disgust, frustration, confusion and bliss that has seen this several-day journey end atop a stage playing for a rapidly dwindling audience of perhaps several dozen, comprised of those either paid to be there, those looking for a way the hell out, or those who are members of the bovine family?

This is one of those times when you reflect back to your fresh-off-the-boat days, when every gig was awesome, and the festivals were glorious messes but it didn't matter because you were doing it – playing rock and roll in China! Who does that? You resist the urge to retreat into believing that your time served should be taken into account; that you should be treated specially; that You. Deserve. Better. than an audience of goats and sheep-people.

You realise, in a moment of serenity and, sure, near-grace, that what you're doing is pretty awesome. Even though the (human) audience for whom you currently play would be equally bemused by the onstage action if the goats were the main attraction and *you* busted through the fence.

Rock and roll lives in China in a way that is impossible to imagine anywhere else in the world. It exist against all of the odds: a world that can't process the fact it exists; a government that alternates between caring too much and not enough; a populace that, for the most part, could care less. And a metaphor for the whole thing has materialised in the field in front of you, walking on two legs away from the speakers, running toward them on four (and scattered behind and astride the stage trying to pack it all up), in the shadow of the mighty Wulong Fairy Mountains.

But there it is, in all its glory. And there you are, right up in it.

THE STATUE

Mark Kitto

Mark Kitto built a well-known network of China's English language city magazines, *That's Shanghai*, *That's Beijing* and *That's Guangzhou*. He was described by *The Financial Times* as "a mini media mogul." After losing the business in 2004, he retreated to Moganshan to write his memoir "China Cuckoo: How I lost a fortune and found a life in China." For many years, he wrote a column for UK's *Prospect Magazine*. He now also runs a coffee shop.

"THAT MAN OUTSIDE WANTS to make your statue," my wife said. "I told him to piss off and not be ridiculous."

My wife is Cantonese and doesn't mince words. I had no doubt she'd said precisely those ones to the man in a tweed jacket, with large glasses and an unruly mop of hair, who was sitting outside in the sunshine, drinking coffee with a teaspoon.

"My statue?"

"The local government want to put up a memorial to the first foreigner who came here," she said – we live in a village built by missionaries in the late 1800s – "and they don't know what he looked like. No photographs. You're the only foreigner around, so they want *you* to be the model."

Even if it doesn't have his name on it, what man would turn down the chance of having his statue put up? I tried to stem the flood of vanity surging like adrenalin through my veins. My heart was racing.

"I agree it's damn lazy of them not to look harder for a

photograph," I said, struggling to keep my voice calm, "but imagine a statue of me in the village. Wouldn't that be fantastic for our grandchildren?"

My wife ignored me. She busied herself behind the bar of our coffee shop.

"I'll go and talk to him anyway," I said, and headed out the door.

"Do what you like, but I still think it's stupid." (Hari Kunzru created a crazy Cantonese mamasan character based on my wife for a short story. I am borrowing her back for this one.)

★

The man whose photograph the government couldn't find was an American reverend called J.W. Farnham. In the late nineteenth century he was the director of the Chinese Religious Tract Society and a board member of the Foreign Missions of the Presbyterian Church, USA, Central China Mission. In the summer months Farnham and his missionary friends used to rent farmhouses on the upper slopes of the mountain near Shanghai known as Moganshan. They wanted to escape the heat of the East China Plain and the deadly seasonal diseases that often killed their children.

One day in 1896 Farnham climbed the summit of Moganshan and found a neglected tea plantation, some scraggly fir trees and a jumble of rocks. He also stumbled on fresh water springs. He made enquiries with the local magistrate and, after testing negotiations, purchased the whole place for 50 Mexican dollars (they contained the most reliable silver content.) He and his friends divided the mountaintop into lots and sold them on, keeping the best for themselves. They built summerhouses, and if they didn't use them rented them to other China-based foreigners. Hence the old joke:

The missionaries came to China to do good, and they did very well.

By the 1920s Moganshan was a thriving summer resort, with

300 well-appointed villas, some modest, many grand, inhabited through July and August by missionaries, opium dealers, British customs and municipal council officials, and the people they referred to – without a trace of irony or hypocrisy – as "the better class of Chinese," including Shanghai's biggest gangsters.

When I came to live here, almost a hundred years later, Moganshan was a ghost town. It wasn't a shadow of its former self. It was a ruin of it.

The grandest villas were reduced to four walls supporting rusted iron roofs over rotten beams and hole-punched floors. Weeds, creepers and full-grown trees had overtaken gardens and tennis courts. Swimming pools were cracked and empty, often used as concrete chicken coops. Hilltops that once commanded sweeping views were walled in by the feathery bamboo that spreads, underground, across the hillside like a secret army.

The only signs of human habitation were the vegetable patches outside Soviet-style "country" apartment blocks, slow ticking electricity meters outside apparently abandoned houses, and the soggy, bedraggled chickens that pecked the pathways for stranded insects. Once or twice a day a coach swept along the narrow village high street, blasting its air horn, to disgorge a cargo of baseball-capped, pennant-waving tourists of a certain age who mobbed the local sites: the Sword Pond, the Mao Villa, the Chiang Kai Shek Villa, and then vanished long before dusk, terrified of the dark...and the ghosts.

In the evenings, ageing locals sat on stone walls with sunset views and chatted about their day, the same as hundreds before it. They still spoke of the time Mrs. Zhang died of a heart attack when she was dealt a perfect hand at ma jiang. That was years ago, almost a decade. They complained about the price of vegetables, their stiff joints and smoking stoves in their ramshackle homes. There were 50 of them at the most. Every year the number fell. Today there's barely a handful left.

But today there is new life coming back to the village. Moganshan has reprised its role as a summer getaway for

Eastern China, Shanghai in particular. Foreign families flock up the mountain in people carriers stuffed with cool boxes, prams, and Philippine maids. Today's "better class" of Chinese, with better cars, jam the roads behind and in front of them.

During major holidays the hilltop is overrun like the last outpost in a war movie. On the path to our home, which is a long walk from the road, I have nailed a sign to a tree. *Please don't take the snakes* it says in Chinese characters. It works for the moment. We have managed to keep our island of calm in the torrent of tourism. We had to expand the coffee shop.

Well-meaning neighbors, hotel managers and local officials tell me I am partly responsible for this resurgence, the invasion. They are "patting my horse's arse," as the Chinese expression has it. I say I simply saw it coming and set up an appropriate business at the right time.

I remember the argument I had with our landlord, Mr. Wang:

"I want to rent that disused wing in your hotel please, to set up a coffee shop."

"No you don't."

"Why not?"

"No one drinks coffee in Moganshan."

Now they do. The foreign visitors, that is. And the Chinese with better cars.

For all the naysaying (Mr. Wang wasn't the only one) I put up with and the obstruction I had to fight through, maybe I *do* deserve a statue, with Farnham's name on it of course.

★

The sculptor took my photograph: face front and profile, both sides, like a police mug shot. He thanked me for agreeing to be the model and returned to the Hangzhou Art Academy. He was a nice man. Over time I forgot about the project.

The local government seemed to as well. It was never mentioned when I dropped into their offices to ask permission to cut a tree down near our house ("If it's dead, do what you like"), plead for help with a visa for a foreign member of our staff ("We can't have foreigners living here with official approval, though *you're* okay"), or try to rent and restore an abandoned house for staff accommodation ("It is forbidden to rent houses, they all belong to the government, but, if you can find someone who can come to a private arrangement...").

If the government chief, also called Wang, heard I was in the building he would drag me into his private office, sit me down and ask my opinion of his latest scheme.

"We're going to restore the church," for example. "So that people can have weddings and take photographs."

He pulled out the plans for a shopping mall to be built along the short village high street, Shady Mountain Street. "It will be just like Xintiandi in Shanghai. Did you know there is one in Hangzhou too?"

He asked me which direction I thought the one-way traffic system should go, when it is finally implemented. It has been talked about for years and never happened. I said anti-clockwise, just for the hell of it.

My own ideas and suggestions for the benefit of Moganshan – surely, if there's going to be a statue of me I should contribute to the place – are quietly ignored or bluntly dismissed.

My regular question for some time was to ask Chief Wang if he wants the village to be a tourist resort or a bamboo farm. One or the other? The 40-foot high feathery bamboo doesn't just block in the viewpoints, it obliterates the view from just about everywhere, and there are many spots, and houses, that could have stunning vistas. In the old days they did.

"Both," was Chief Wang's response.

There is much money in bamboo, especially for the government. They dictate when the locals can harvest their smallholdings. The date is always a few days after the government's significant crop has been sold on the market.

My favorite annoying question was: "Chief Wang, why don't

you let foreigners and Chinese individuals lease villas here on reasonable terms, and allow the village to become again what it once was, the Chamonix for China? Then you might even have customers for your shopping mall." Chief Wang can't answer. Mind you, he is not really in charge. As the locals who run small businesses on the mountain put it, Chief Wang is a concierge for the senior officials who stay in state guesthouses for a night or two of mountain peace and quiet, bamboo shoots and wild boar washed down with yangmei jiu, and KTV.

His deputy did once answer my question, straight. He is a local man, a civil servant, who knows what is going on behind the scenes. "To have foreigners return to Moganshan," he said, speaking to a foreigner who has returned to Moganshan, "would be like going backwards. It will never happen."

Modern China has an awkward relationship with history. We know.

★

One day I had a serious question for Chief Wang. We needed to renew the lease for our coffee shop. Before we could do that however, our landlord, Mr. Wang, had to renew his lease on his hotel. His landlord is the government. He asked me to accompany him to see Chief Wang. He said my presence, since the government seemed to appreciate what I had done for Moganshan, would help him get a fair deal.

Mr. Wang is from the leading local family in the village. His grandfather came from Anhui to work for the foreigners, as did most of the local families. He built an icehouse and made a fortune from the American missionaries. They lost everything in '49, and were hit even harder in the Cultural Revolution. Mr. Wang's father supported his family by digging up the stumps of harvested bamboo to sell as brushes to clean woks. When he died a couple of years ago, the entire village attended his funeral. If anyone deserved a statue on the mountain, it was one of the

Moganshan Wangs.

Chief Wang's deputy ushered Mr. Wang and me into his office. We accepted paper cups of local tea and sank into enormous pleather armchairs. Chief Wang began, as usual, by patting my horse's arse. Business must be good, he said. More and more foreigners were coming to the mountain. The New York Times had written about Moganshan; he assumed that was my doing.

While he spoke I glanced around his office. Apart from some bookshelves and a shanshui painting there wasn't much to admire, until my eye fell on the windowsill. There was a head on it, a life-size bust, made of clay and painted gold. It looked familiar. I stared harder. I think I might have let out a gasp of astonishment.

It was me.

"Ah, yes, your statue," Chief Wang said. "That's its head. What do you think?"

I think I wanted it. "So the statue going up at last?" I asked, once again trying to fight off the vanity attack.

Chief Wang looked me straight in the face. His expression gave nothing away. He remained silent for a painful pause and then said: "Now, you're here for a lease, aren't you?" He did not want to talk about the statue.

"Actually, Chief Wang," I said, slowly. "It is not my lease but my partner and landlord's here." I indicated Mr. Wang beside me, who had not said a word. Nor had Chief Wang looked at him.

He jerked his head from one pleather armchair to the next, quite a distance when you factor in their size, even though they were right against each other.

"I'm sorry," he said, to a scion of the most distinguished Chinese family on the mountain, respected by all…except for the Americans missionaries who complained how his grandfather charged according to weight as the ice left his icehouse, not when it arrived at their homes after a long hot journey in an open wicker basket, "and who are you?"

I smiled at Mr. Wang like a child with his hand stuck fast in the sweet jar. He grinned back. He knew I was embarrassed, he knew why, and he didn't mind. I swear he glanced at my head on the windowsill and winked at it.

Chief Wang promised to do his best to renew Mr. Wang's lease with decent terms, and a fair price but, he said, it was out of his hands. Government leases were drawn up by the vice-chief in charge of village properties. The meeting was over.

As Mr. Wang and I went to leave I hung back. "Chief Wang," I said. "If you have no need for it, I would very much like that," I pointed at my head, "please."

Chief Wang looked at me for a moment. "Of course," he said. "Do take it."

There is no statue of me (or Farnham) in Moganshan. There never will be. My wife is happy. Nor is there, or will there ever be, a statue of Mr. Wang's grandfather. But I do have a fine hat stand on the top of my bookshelves in my study. It looks just like me.

RED COUPLETS

Jocelyn Eikenburg

Jocelyn Eikenburg writes Speaking of China, a blog focused on love, family and relationships in China inspired by her marriage to her Chinese husband. She has resided in the cities of Zhengzhou, Hangzhou and Shanghai. A native of Cleveland, Ohio, Jocelyn is currently working on her memoir.

JUN LOOKED ASHEN WHEN he burst through the door that September evening. His face made me tremble, because a pale complexion meant something was wrong. My intuition was, unfortunately, correct.

"My professor asked where I live."

"Are...are you in trouble?" My heart pounded and I could feel my palms starting to sweat. It might seem an extreme to react this way to such a simple question. But living together with my Chinese boyfriend, still a graduate student at his university in Shanghai, was anything but simple.

"I told him I moved from the dormitories into an off-campus apartment with some other students." He laughed and then smiled, two things the Chinese usually did to cover their anxiety. Because I understood this, my heart only beat faster.

"Did...did he believe it?" I continued to stutter.

"I don't know. He said he was 'just curious' since he found out I wasn't living in the dormitories anymore."

"But how did he even know?"

Jun shrugged. "People talk."

A nagging tension at the words "people talk" lingered over

me the rest of the night. It reminded me that gossip in China comes less from what people say than from what people see and then infer. Even if Jun and I weren't touching or holding hands in public, anyone who merely saw us together might soon spread the word that we were dating.

Would that mean it would only be a matter of time before his professor really knew where he – we – lived? And if so, would it mean the end of his graduate school career in China?

★

According to a 2003 notice on the U.S. Embassy's Beijing website, we had good reason to worry:

Chinese students generally are permitted to marry if all the requirements are met, but they can expect to be expelled from school as soon as they do. American citizens wishing to marry Chinese students should bear this in mind. It also should be noted that at least one school in Beijing has required Chinese students to reimburse the school for hitherto uncharged tuition and other expenses upon withdrawal from school to marry foreigners.

Jun and I weren't married, but we were nonetheless quite concerned about what his school would think of one of their graduate students living with a foreigner. So Jun had little choice but to lie constantly about his residence in Shanghai to professors, administrators, and even fellow students. His campus became Off Limits for our relationship; I never dared to visit him at the university, nor accompany him over on a trip.

But that still didn't mean we were somehow safe.

I remember one Saturday afternoon that summer when we hopped the Shanghai Metro to visit a department store on Huaihai Road. We had already spent months together in this city of then 10 million and growing – shopping, taking walks and dining out – and never ran into anyone from his school. So I laced my fingers with his as we rushed up the stairs toward the store's main entrance. The fact that the crowds of people who exited the metro at the South Shaanxi Road Station engulfed us somehow made me feel even safer and hidden away. As we emerged from the exit, Jun suddenly dropped my hand, something he never did.

"What's wrong?" I asked, swallowing thickly.

Jun's face was flushed with worry. "I think I saw my shixiong," he said, using the Chinese for his elder male classmate.

My heart rapped at my chest, and to me, it sounded as loud as the perpetual jack-hammering one hears across New China. I instinctively shrank into a corner. "Did he see us?"

Jun arched his neck and surveyed the square, bustling with crowds that flowed in and out of the space like waves on the East China Sea. My stomach tensed with every second that passed without an answer from him.

"He just crossed the street," my beau finally smiled, while I exhaled with relief. But I kept my hands to myself for the rest of the afternoon – a lesson I also learned earlier that year during Spring Festival, when Jun brought me to his family home in rural Zhejiang province to meet his parents for the first time.

The moment we walked through the weather-faded red couplets hanging beside the open doors of his family home, Jun hid his feelings for me, the way we hid our own bodies beneath layer upon layer of clothing to survive the winters in central-heating-less Shanghai. No kisses, no holding hands, no touching, not even a single flirtatious look or glance. He was as cold as Shanghai's concrete-block buildings. He seemed nothing like the Jun in my bedroom, a man who could make me shiver with delight when he traced my curves under the covers, and that realization only made me more anxious about what happened when Jun first mentioned me to his parents.

After he told them we were dating, which came out more like a Cultural Revolution confession than a family heart-to-heart, his father said flatly, "You can be *friends* with a foreign woman, but not date her."

By then I'd already heard variations on this theme from other men in China: "my parents could not accept a foreign girlfriend"..."I must marry a Chinese girl..." I imagined these parents thought I threatened the "harmony" of the family; that Western women were just loose seductresses who couldn't be trusted in relationships, and who, unschooled in Chinese culture and family expectations, wouldn't raise the next generation with the proper values, etc., etc.

For Jun's family, it was just easier if we looked like friends, instead of boyfriend and girlfriend. Of course, Jun's parents didn't even hint that they themselves were married – at least, according to *my* standard of what married couples did. They didn't hug and kiss, nor touch hands and swap smiles, nor even link arms while walking around, like my own mom and dad used to. No, Jun's parents seemed more like a couple of friends running a family business; two people who just happened to share the same bed and also have kids together.

Maybe hiding a relationship was a part of Jun's cultural genetics. Still, that realization didn't calm my nerves. At a time when I most needed the reassurance of Jun's embrace, he and I would sleep in separate beds and behave as if we had separate lives too.

★

From the first time I started to love a Chinese man, hiding became a part of my life.

"Whenever I arrive at the airport in America, the first thing I notice is our men, how handsome and how tall they are," one of my white female colleagues mentioned over lunch just weeks into my first job in China teaching college English. "I'll just stare at them for hours, as if *I* was Chinese and had never seen a foreign man before in my life."

She smirked, while the other Caucasian women sitting around

our table smiled knowingly as they reached for another helping of rice or fish-fragrant eggplant that the school's chef had just prepared for us.

And as I watched them chatting and eating, my face burned with embarrassment at the thought of the Zhengzhou native I had just developed a crush on. My burgeoning infatuation had made me self-conscious because I wondered if it had more to do with the loneliness and culture shock I suffered, instead of a genuine connection with the Chinese.

At least that woman wasn't as blunt as another colleague, who used to bicycle with me through the streets of Zhengzhou. As we stopped on the corner of a side street and watched the mostly-male populous pedaling past us through the intersection, she grimaced.

"Chinese men don't really seem that attractive."

"How can you say that?" I retorted in a slightly insulted tone.

"I don't know…they just *aren't*." She sounded too casual for a woman who just dismissed the entire male population in China.

How could someone brand all Chinese men as undatable? Yet, in a way, hadn't I done the same during my university days back home, where I never entertained the thought of sharing anything beyond a polite conversation and a cup of green tea with the handful of Asian men I encountered on campus. But here in China, my crush on that Zhengzhou native made me aware that something changed inside of me – something I learned to keep to myself.

When I moved to Hangzhou, where I met Jun, and later to Shanghai, I never realized just how invisible I would feel whenever I held his hand in the street. I ran into couples of Chinese women and Western men on an almost hourly basis. Meanwhile, in the three years I had already lived in China, I could count on one hand the times I actually spotted a Chinese man and Western woman together in public.

While visiting the Shanghai Museum with Jun one afternoon, I spied a couple just like us, wearing jeans and the bright smiles of two people deeply in love. My heart fluttered with excitement at the sight of them. They literally twirled around in each other's arms for a few seconds, as if such an audacious public display of affection could somehow compensate for the overwhelming absence of couples like us in China. I hurried downstairs to introduce myself, but when I reached the floor of the lobby, they had already disappeared. Had I become so hidden that even my own supposed community didn't notice me in public?

Sometimes I thought about the woman I was before I made the last-minute, serendipitous decision to move to China: a science graduate with a penchant for Spanish and bird watching and a blind contempt for pop music. But by the time Jun and I began seeing each other, that woman of the past seemed to fade like the Pudong skyline on a smoggy Shanghai day. I now worked not as an environmental biologist but as a writer; I spoke Mandarin Chinese far more fluently than Spanish; I spent most weekends inhabiting the restaurants, shopping centers and side-streets along Huaihai Road and had yet to intentionally watch birds in China other than those caged song-birds kept by old people in the parks. The hipster music snobs I used to know would have shuddered upon learning that these days I listened mostly to Mandopop, watched Taiwanese idol dramas and even sang their theme songs at karaoke joints.

Was there some kind of immutable law of identity change inherent in my experience? That the closer you get to a foreign country through dating and even marriage, the more you find parts of your former personality becoming hidden in the process, leaving room for new and unexpected things to replace them? It startled me to imagine that the woman I had become in China might not even recognize the woman she left behind.

And what about Jun? How had being with me changed *him*? And had I unwittingly brought him as much hardship and rejection as love and affection?

"They refused me, they said I was too young," Jun announced

that September at the result of his U.S. visa interview. I had hoped to finally introduce him to my parents in Ohio, but now it looked like I would have to spend my vacation there alone.

"Oh," I said, the only response I could squeak out.

We were sitting at the Taiwanese cafe across the street from my office building for lunch. Before our fried rice even arrived, we had already chewed on that helping of sadness the news brought to our table. By then, I couldn't blame my wet face on the rain outside. I also watched Jun's face tremble with tears, the first time I ever saw him cry. It scared me to see him like that; the more his own tears fell, the more I willed mine to stop.

"I'm so sorry I put you through this. I was stupid to think we could get a visa," I said. Admittedly, the only evidence I had armed him with for his visa interview were two letters, one from me and one from my parents, extolling the love between Jun and I. But how can you really prove to anyone, let alone an unfeeling government bureaucracy, that love, something hidden deep in your own heart, exists?

Yet, sometimes, the things that are never seen and never said matter much more. Jun never told me "I love you," and years would pass before he finally put into words exactly why he fell in love with me. Yet he moved in with me only days after our first kiss, without any of the typical debate about the merits of living together or how it might affect our relationship; pasting up a fresh pair of bright-red couplets around our door, my apartment immediately turned into "our" apartment. He never spoke when we made love, yet I felt the promises in the way he touched me and the way he embraced me, promises as sure as words or a diamond engagement ring.

Even though at times it seemed quite surreal that I, a woman from the Midwestern American suburbs, could find myself in the arms of a man from rural China, I felt surer about Jun than anyone else in my life.

★

"I finally told my professor about us," Jun said to me later that winter over dinner in our apartment.

My stomach wrenched, and I felt the warmth draining from my face. "How-h-how could you?"

"Don't worry, he won't tell the administrators."

I wanted to ask him how he could be so sure? But then again, someone could easily ask me the same thing: how was I so sure that someday *I* would marry *him*? And the answer is, some things, like having faith in others, aren't seen, but simply known through your intuition.

"So, what did he say?" I asked, too stunned to continue eating.

Jun laughed, but not in a way that Chinese way that seemed anxious or embarrassed. "He said he thought I really had character to date a foreign woman."

A sense of relief poured over me, and I didn't keep it to myself. Of all the consequences I imagined that would befall us if the professor finally knew about me, admiration was the one I never saw.

You Buy Me Drink?

Nury Vittachi

Nury Vittachi is a Sri Lanka-born author living in Hong Kong. He writes several columns a week, which appear in publications throughout Asia and on his website, Mr Jam. His latest work, "The Curious Diary of Mr Jam: Official humorist for repressive regimes," analyzes the Asian sense of humor. He is currently working on volume five of "The Magic Mirror", a Scholastic series animating true stories from Chinese history.

NOT AGAIN. BEING CAPTURED by murderous Beijing gangsters is *such* a bore.

The odd thing about the guy facing me was that he was tiny for a strutting super-villain: a short, thick, chubby man in his early 40s. If he'd been a superhero, he'd be Gangstergnome. But his size wasn't an issue, since anyone can beat me up, including little old ladies, as I am phobic about even the thought of pain, which triggers waves of whimpering and self-pity. Torturers would never have to get their pliers out. A quizzical glance in my direction would have me screaming secret formulas into their ears.

But then Gangstergnome's helpers strolled through the door. They were large and clearly made entirely of boulders, including between their ears. Evidently Gangstergnome was the brains and the others were the brawn, forming a single organism, like bees in a beehive, but probably with a smaller cubic volume of brain matter. Gangstergnome reminded me of Peking Man, who was of course discovered right here in Beijing. They were probably related: maybe he was a direct descendant. Peking Man had been a shorty too.

As I waited, the villain explained in faultless broken English that I owed an enormous debt to his organization and was required to hand over all my money and credit cards. He held out his hand. I placed my wallet into it. It contained nothing but old business cards and a forgotten receipt or two. This was going to be bad.

★

How did I get myself into this situation? A better question would be: Would I ever stop getting myself into these situations? I was a trouble magnet at that period. But I was getting tired of it. In my younger days as a reporter, I had a very simple method for finding things to write about. On arrival in any new city, I would get out a map and a pen and ask my host:

"I'm planning to wander around town – can you tell me which parts of the city I should avoid?"

He or she would peer at the map and mark several streets. "Well, I wouldn't go down there, especially since it's getting dark…"

"Thanks," I'd grin, hailing a cab as soon as I could politely take my leave. I would then hand the map to the cab driver, saying: "Here's the address."

Wasn't I afraid of danger? Naaaah. I started my writing career as a 20-something male. At that age, the brain is a minor subsidiary organ of the testosterone gland. The brain stem helps guys maintain automatic functions such as breathing, but that's all. The testosterone gland does all the actual reasoning, which should be obvious when you see what young men get up to. Journalists always start their careers as courageous shiners of light into dark corners, before their idealism disappears and they start writing press releases for arms manufacturers. Usually this takes seven to 10 years, although it still hasn't happened to me.

I'm a slow learner.

Another thing: I'd actually had quite a lot of experience in "dangerous areas" thanks to an accident of history. I was born on the Island of Serendipity, but have spent much of my life outside that glorious land, now known more prosaically as Sri Lanka. Whenever I mentioned to friends that I was visiting relatives in Sri Lanka, they'd say:

"Doesn't it scare you, the war and all that?"

I didn't want to tell them that I spent my evenings sipping pressed mango juice on the verandah of my uncle's house, so I'd just say: "I can't really talk about it."

★

That's why I used to go straight for the dark side of town whenever I visited a place. I don't do this now – from about the age of 45, the room service menu became sufficient excitement. So what would I actually do when I was dropped off in the badlands of Beijing or Shanghai or Shenzhen? Just go into a bar and order a Sprite.

In movies, when a man goes into a bar, a sophisticated, sexy blonde immediately strolls in and takes the next seat. In reality, an emaciated, tired-looking woman wearing too much makeup will approach you saying:

"It my birt'day. You buy me drink?" (As in most of China's metropolises, the bar girls in Beijing are all invariably from out of town, and thus speak in a variety of accents, Chinese and English.)

You reply: "Hmm...I was here two months ago. It was your birthday then as well."

She is unfazed. Lie Number One having crashed and burned, she smoothly sails to Lie Number Two. "You very handsome, big boy."

What happens next? Well, in books, people looking for information go into sleazy bars, chat to the women, and then, after they get the data but before they actually do anything that could be construed as immoral, they tell us: "I made my excuses and left." Don't believe it.

Many of the women who work in bars are highly intelligent. They don't spill secrets. Secrets are their income. Their biggest skillset – okay, maybe second biggest skillset – is saying the right thing at the right time. This means that they are pretty much worthless as journalistic sources: everything they say is untrue.

Consider the typical bar-room conversational gambits: *It my birt'day...You so handsome...Sure, I remember you...You buy me drink we have good time...Drink very cheap...Wow you plenty big boy...*

Sorry, guys, none of the above statements are true.

In contrast, everything spoken by the *men* you meet in Chinese bars is painfully, bitterly true: *I drank too much...I was so nervous I couldn't do anything...She overcharged me like crazy...I'm a disgusting piece of low life...The chick in the corner with the boobs is a guy...I hate myself...*

So the trick is to talk to everyone and buy everyone drinks, which is do-able if you sternly insist that the barman charges you the local price, not the tourist price. You start off collecting stories from the fellas. Once you have managed to switch the conversation from superficial lies to bitter truths, the women join in. Honesty is infectious. The result: lots of funny, embarrassing tales, and an easy way for a columnist to gather stories to fill his pages for weeks.

★

But of course there are times when it all goes horribly wrong. Like this time in Beijing. I'd been out enjoying the evening, just aimlessly strolling around town, marveling at the huge, bizarre constructions going up (apparently Beijing architects are all trained by Dr. Seuss). I was grateful that I could actually see through the air. Beijing had just suffered a huge dust storm, which had dumped 50,000 tons of particulates onto the city. Even on ordinary days, the capital's atmosphere is often so thick that you have to chew before inhaling, though I suppose you could argue that it's good that you can see what you're eating.

Despite the pollution, I still loved the place, even though it often appeared to be run by madmen. Party officials had announced recently that they had decided to control the weather. There was an actual bureau which would organize when it would be rainy and when it would be sunny. A few years earlier, they had even organized battalions of guns to shoot at the clouds.

"Take that. And that! Now will you give up your rainwater? Or do we have to shoot you again?"

Oh, Beijing.

A little old lady caught my eye. She was begging on the street, or so I thought. But closer inspection revealed that she was just sitting there, smiling at people passing by. She had a tin plate for coins, but it was tucked almost out of sight. You could see that she was just a regular, intelligent old person who had fallen onto hard times. Not having any other recourse, she was sitting on the street, brightening people's lives with a sincere smile – something you rarely see in any big Chinese city these days. But out in the provinces, there are a million like her for every heartless member of the nation's elite.

Just as I was about to cross the road to go to her, someone grabbed my arm. It was a tout; a young fellow, maybe a student, hired to patrol the streets and promote bars to passing foreigners.

"Drink, only twenty yuan, very cheap, very nice bar, pretty girls," he sang in practiced English.

I glanced over at him for a moment too long and he instantly knew that I was a free agent, heading nowhere in particular. "Come I show you," the tout said, pulling at me. He dragged me round a corner and to a staircase leading down into a basement dive.

From then on, everything went wrong. First, it wasn't a bar. It was a network of separate rooms. Second, there were no drinkers. Just thin, hard-faced girls in glittery costumes, two of whom grabbed me and pulled me into one of the rooms. An intelligent person would have turned around and walked out. My testosterone gland urged me to stay and see if this would provide a new tale to tell.

"What you drink?" the young women asked in stereo, like a transpacific phone call with a slight echo problem. They dragged me to a sofa. "Beer? Blandy?" they suggested in sync.

I always ask for a Sprite, which I don't touch. Bar managers can get away with overcharging outrageously for alcohol, but it's hard to do the same for soft drinks. The girls conveyed my order to a waitress.

The room was large and there was a karaoke set in one corner. They pulled me over to it and encouraged me to go through the lists of songs. Behind me, I was dimly aware of a waitress entering the room with a tray. My Sprite? I turned back to the sofa to find that 11 drinks had appeared on the coffee table: 10 huge balloon goblets of an amber liquid and one fizzy drink. While puzzling over this, the waitress returned with the – or *a* – bill:

10,000 元

Of course I declined to pay…for the simple reason that I couldn't. That's when it all became rather predictable, with Gangstergnome entering, flanked by his heavies, and relieving me of my wallet.

★

The villain of this story made a cursory inspection and found my wallet had nothing of interest in it, on account of I had deliberately left my credit cards and passport in my hotel bedroom. My jacket and trouser pockets were equally disappointing to him. This caused a problem for the villains, since there was no obvious way for them to extract a large amount of cash from me. It caused a problem for me, too, since there was no obvious way to avoid being beaten to death and deposited in the nearest dumpster.

Beijing wouldn't be a bad place to die, I thought as Gangstergnome and his goons loomed over me. When you see images of the city, you always see these big grand places – the Forbidden City, the Great Hall of the People, Tiananmen Square – large and stately vistas, with wide avenues and buildings on an enormous scale. But that's such a tiny part of the city. The rest of the place is a warren of small streets and buildings. Many of the buildings are ugly, but time has rescued a few, lending a patina of worthwhile historicity to what are really just crumbly streets of small dwellings. Then there are a few which have real charm: old hutong lined with trees, small homes, and a feeling of timelessness.

The old generation in China does what old people do everywhere – and I guess what *all* people did everywhere before the curse of TV blighted our lives. They take their chairs to their front doors and sit outside. Their television is the street, their program is the people passing along it. Their fellow viewers are the neighbors on either side. Together they watch the world go by and make random comments.

I loved to wander into Beijing's old siheyuans, which are basically clusters of courtyard houses, and swap smiles with the families, often three generations of them, who sit outside their homes playing mahjong at all hours. But every time I visited, more of these would be boarded off, replaced by massive billboards for forthcoming shopping malls. Pretty soon, Beijing citizens will have a shopping mall each. This will be good for the consumerists among them.

★

Speaking of whom, there was an uncomfortable silence in the Extortion Bar when we all ran out of conversation. Humans are funny creatures. No direct threats of pain or death had been made, so I was coping well. But just sitting there without being able to think of any small talk to make…well, that was intolerable.

"So what do we do now?" I asked, pressing for some sort of denouement to take place.

"We go back your hotel room, you give us ATM card," was Gangstergnome's decisive solution after conferring with his goons.

Then I remembered! In addition to the pitiful amounts of Renminbi in my pockets, I had some foreign currency in a secret inner jacket pocket, having been in Europe on a book tour recently. I reached into the garment took out a note.

"I have Euros!"

The bar boss's expression changed slightly. It was what poker players call a "tell." There was a slight widening of the eyes, a slowing down of the rate of movement of his thick neck, and a barely perceptible head tilt to one side. I had said a Holy Word.

Now let me tell you about elite Beijingers and money. The city *is* deeply religious, but it is not religion as we know it, Jim. Actual religion, which is always rooted in a desire for social justice, has long been banned in China. Modern Chinese society has been carefully shaped by education and relentless state-sponsored propaganda media into being ultra-rationalist in a way that destroys not only religion, but also creativity and the imagination.

This has created a problem. Humans are not rational creatures, either on an individual or a group basis, nor is it a good thing to try to force them to be. They fixate on things. They worship things. They need heroes. They need good books which remind them to be nice to each other. They're built like this…or at least have evolved to be like this. Most humans need something to believe in, someone to believe in, some timeless advice to follow: they are vital parts of our make-up. I know many people who have given up their parents' religion and replaced it with new age beliefs or evangelical atheism or the watery "I'm spiritual but not religious" mantra; and they fail to see that it is the same thing, but stripped of magical ritual and the poetic wisdom of the ancients.

Beijing banned religion in 1949, replacing it with Communism. At first, this filled the bill pretty well, as my father, a former Trotskyite whom visited the Mainland before it opened to the world, can attest – we had the unifying big principles, we had altruism, we had bonding, we had a sense of sharing, we had leaders who were revered for expressing grand and worthy principles, we had regular meetings where virtue was studied, we had idealism, and we even had a book to carry around.

What happened? Communism is perfect in theory, and perfect in practice, but it doesn't bloody work. It has been quietly abandoned at almost all levels. Yet what has been provided to fill the space? Nothing.

So people in China are looking for something – anything – to fill that gap. Despite their outlaw status, there are probably more practicing Christians in China now than in all of Europe, including all the Catholics in Italy. Others have rediscovered theosophies from China's own past. Feng Shui, too, is quietly thriving. But the folk who haven't rediscovered any form of traditional spiritual values have found their gaze drifting towards money.

Yes, materialism has become the biggest religion of China, and foreign banknotes are the scriptures.

★

Gangstergnome was obviously a passionate disciple of the New Materialism, and as such was deeply interested in what I had to offer. Beijingers basically think in terms of two currencies: yuan and dollars. The first is their familiar daily tool for buying a steaming youtiao on the way to work. The second is the "big" currency – each unit of U.S. dollars being six or seven times the worth of the first currency. People don't realize it, but Beijing has long been a big financial center, with more Fortune Global 500 companies than in London or New York.

The U.S. dollar was familiar, even passé. But the Euro was fresh and intriguing; it was one of the very small number of important global currencies which was worth more, unit for unit, than the greenback. When you've been brought up to think of Big Money as a $100 bill, the notion that there can exist a piece of paper worth *more* than that is mind-blowing. Gangstergnome had heard of Euros but had never seen one.

"Show me," he demanded.

I handed over a 100 euro note. He reverently held it in both hands. He turned it over. He turned it back again. Euros feel different to other banknotes. They are printed on pure cotton fibre and feel expensive. They are also large. A 100 Euro note is 147x82mm, considerably bigger than either Chinese or American banknotes.

Gangstergnome fell in love. He turned to his henchman and explained in erhua-accented Mandarin that this was a Euro banknote. This single piece of paper was worth more than 100 American dollars, he explained. They should have gasped or looked awestruck or something – that's was clearly what was required of them at that moment by their boss – but their prehensile brains were unable to respond in such a sophisticated way. They just blinked at him. Perhaps they really were the direct descendants of Peking Man.

Our villain immediately lost interest in the foreigner cornered in his bar. He wanted to run to the phone, and call *his* boss (everything in China is run by networks of networks of networks) and tell them that he was in possession of a 100 Euro note. Then he would drive his black Santana over and show him.

"I keep this, you go," he instructed.

I nodded, smiled at the two young women and the two early hominins, and took my leave, climbing the stairs two at a time before stepping into the cool night air. The dust had gone and stars shone overhead. How nice to be alive and entirely unpulped!

Crossing the road, I reached the little old lady, who smiled directly at me. You drift through life and occasionally you connect with people, good and bad. What I would have given to know her life story.

From my *secret* secret inner jacket pocket (I have two) I drew out some RMB banknotes and put them in her tin. But she didn't look down at them. I like to think that our exchange of smiles was the more important part of the transaction for both of us.

ONE OF THE PEOPLE

Bruce Humes

Bruce Humes first arrived in Asia via Taipei and Hong Kong, and has since lived in Shanghai, Kunming and Shenzhen. He has translated two Chinese novels, Chi Zijian's "Last Quarter of the Moon," and best-selling "Shanghai Baby" by Wei Hui, as well as coffee table books "Chinese Dress & Adornment through the Ages" and "The China Tea Book." He hosts Ethnic ChinaLit, a site devoted to documenting writing in China by and about non-Han peoples.

"YOU'LL HAVE TO EXCUSE us, Bruce. We've always looked after you as a guest," said longtime friend Liu Jie, pausing delicately. "But yesterday we treated you like one of our own."

Indeed. My reception the previous night at the emergency room of this People's Hospital in Shenzhen, just north of Hong Kong, was probably typical for many citizens across the country: I had been summarily treated, hastily diagnosed and then sidelined, proving that there is at least one bastion in China where a foreigner needn't worry about receiving "special" treatment.

My evening had begun with a cheap imported Mexican beer and a live Filipino cover band in a bar on Shangbu Road. At half past 10 I exited with my date, said goodnight to her, and began my homeward stroll alone. I got a call, put the mobile to my right ear and kept walking. Near the intersection of Shangbu and Shenzhen South Roads, a lively juncture just a stone's throw from the seat of the city government, I got the ugliest surprise of my life.

First came a violent tug at my hand with the handset, and

then a searing pain ripped across the right side of my head. Bizarrely, I could hear a man nearby grunting like he was being kicked, again and again, in the ribs.

Don't ever resist! is Shenzhen's proverbial advice to the naïve victims – and there were hundreds every month in the early years of the 21st century – confronting a determined thief. Yet there I was doing just that. I grabbed at something shiny, seized it in my palm, and held on for dear life.

The grunting stopped suddenly and I opened my eyes. Against the deep blue sky, the stars twinkled above the heads of onlookers drawn to the sight of a bleeding Westerner curled up in a fetal position on the still-warm summer concrete.

★

Doctors stitched up my skull to stop the bleeding, then parked me, unconscious, in the hospital's hallway, along with the rest of the proletariat. At four in the morning I came round and began to scream. Just a few inches away from my eyes, I noticed that my right hand, virtually severed in two at the palm, lay untreated and uncovered.

"We can't operate," said a medic who eventually responded to my howling. "You'll never be able to use your hand again."

"We'd better amputate right now," piped up another. "Otherwise, if it gets infected and the gangrene moves up toward the shoulder, we'll have to saw your whole arm off."

"Forget that!" I shot back in fluent Mandarin. "I want you to stitch my hand back together. Ma shang! Right now!"

They hesitated. I was a foreigner with no identification, no next of kin to contact, and – crucially – no cash to pay upfront for what could be a challenging and costly procedure. They recommended waiting a few hours until they could contact my consulate.

"Let's get this straight: I have plenty of money in the bank. I'm laowai, for chrissakes!" I argued forcefully. "As for responsibility,

I don't intend to sue you. I'll sign whatever you want saying I know the risks. Just give me the *tamade* papers!"

Maybe it was my swearing in Chinese that did the trick, suggesting that I was lucid and not a new arrival to the Middle Kingdom. Soon after, they wheeled me into the operating room, put me under anesthesia, and I was lost to the world.

★

In fact, I had next to no money in the bank and no medical insurance, so I was alarmed when I awoke in the Intensive Care Unit. I'd read in the local press that many hospitals in China charge patients according to their nationality, which meant I'd be paying the same fee as for a day's stay in a New York City hospital.

But that wasn't the only factor that made me want to escape the unit. In order to fight against infection and save my hand, over the course of a day the nurses pumped at least eight large containers of antibiotics into me via the omnipresent Chinese Drip. That's a lot of liquid, and what went in had to come out.

Curiously, as also happened during an earlier hospital stay in Hong Kong, I found that female Chinese nurses were, well, let's say disturbed by the sight of my manhood. Admittedly it's not a domestic model.

But the unfortunate reality was that, as a result of all those drugs being poured into me, I had to pee several times an hour. I was too weak to go to the loo, so at first I had little choice but to lie in bed and relieve myself into a urine bottle. Even the mere sight of that receptacle irritated the nurses, and they eventually stored it under my bed, out of my reach. At one point I was relieving myself almost every 10 minutes, and having to ask repeatedly for the bottle angered me.

I finally managed to stand up on my own and perform the task vertically, which was a real relief. But a few seconds later I lost my balance and fell over, smashing a few glass containers on my way down. The very idea that I was paying through the nose for this "intensive care" enraged me, so I warned them: transfer me to a standard hospital room the next day, or I'd walk out on my own.

I was in a bad state with a nasty head wound, three broken ribs, a punctured lung and a hand that might still have to be severed, they cautioned, so I was in no state to go anywhere.

Nine o'clock rolled around the next day with no sign of a move. I stood up very awkwardly and painfully, and somehow managed to wobble out the door. The staff couldn't believe their eyes. In the end they relented, and I was moved to what they labeled a "cadre room," ostensibly reserved for officials. But as far as I could tell, it was simply a room for a single patient equipped with a TV.

★

"Could you change my bed sheets?" I asked the nurse the next morning.

"What for?"

"Well…if my hand gets infected, they'll have to amputate it, understand? So I want to make sure my sheets are clean."

"Mr. Xu," she said using the Chinese family name I've used ever since I arrived in Taipei in 1978, "we change the sheets once a week. If your sheet gets dirty, we'll change it."

"But you can't 'see' germs," I retorted.

The following day the Head Nurse made her rounds. "Good morning, *Mr. Xu*," she announced, accentuating my Chinese surname as if to imply I wasn't qualified to use it. "I understand you requested that we change your bedding. Is everything fine now?"

"Yes, thank you. I appreciate it."

The Head Nurse walked out the door, a queue of interns in tow. "Who does he think he is?" I overheard her say. "Expecting us to change his sheets daily!"

★

"Am I ever going to see a doctor?" I asked anxiously on the third day of my stay.

"Of course," said the nurse. "The surgeon who operated on you will come by this afternoon."

The day dragged on. Every few hours a nurse came in to hang a new bag of transparent glop on my IV pole. In between drifting in and out of consciousness I had learned to take the contraption along on frequent trips to my very own private toilet. At three o'clock in came a no-nonsense member of the staff who sat me up, took a firm hold of my injured hand and proceeded to unwind the bandage at a frightening speed.

"Wei!" I shouted, "What are you doing?" It felt like she was slashing my palm all over again.

"Shush! I'm just changing your dressing," she said. "Don't be a baby."

Just when I was preparing to call for help to save me from this hellish orderly, she completed her task and marched out without a word.

My nurse came back in. I hurt so bad I was almost speechless. "Isn't my doctor coming today?" I whimpered.

"Don't be silly. The one who changed your bandage just now – *that's* your doctor."

It must have been past midnight when the door flew open, the ceiling light lit up, and someone jacked up the mattress behind my head. The mystery woman spread a newspaper on the sheet over my thighs, and plopped three styrofoam boxes on it. The scent of hot chilies permeated the room.

"Heard you like spicy Sichuan food. Eat up!"

She handed me a pair of chopsticks and then I saw her face clearly: the brutal bandage-changer. My doctor!

"You've been in our hospital four days and still haven't eaten a thing. How's your hand ever going to heal like that?"

Granted, I hadn't ingested anything. But then, who eats the

rubbish they dish up in hospitals anywhere? This, however, was *food*. I dug in with delight.

As we chatted in Mandarin, I got some insight into her earlier cool behavior. My boss, the publisher of a magazine under the Communist Party Propaganda Department of Shenzhen, had kindly visited me the morning after my emergency operation and had brought along the head of the hospital. The hospital honcho then met with my doctor's superior, who in turn instructed my doctor to "take extra special care of that laowai."

My doctor, who happened to be one of the nation's rare examples of an authentic Lei Feng – a semi-mythical PLA soldier and do-gooder vaunted by the state press as a model for all citizens – was deeply offended by this order to treat me preferentially. At the time, she had already transferred one patient out of her ward just to free up a bed for me. But these instructions from above, combined with my lodging in a "cadre room" reserved for the elite, and the fuss I made over having my dressing changed, had persuaded her that I wasn't worthy of her 24/7 care.

Happily for me, our chat that night broke the ice. She revealed one reason why some emergency medical care in China is delayed. When the patient or relatives can't pay upfront, the staff have to decide whether to go ahead on their own; if the patient is later unable to cough up the cash, the fee for the operation will be deducted...from the salaries of the doctors and nurses who perform it.

★

As consultant to the publisher who dealt mainly with the man himself, I had never really gotten to know the editorial staff at the Chinese business magazine where I worked. But that changed almost overnight thanks to my 12-day stay in the People's Sickhouse. My boss made it known that staff should take turns at my bedside, deliver meals, and, once I was out of danger, visit me daily to keep my spirits up. This turned out to be a royal pain in the butt.

Day after day my colleagues did their dutiful best to ensure I was never lonely. They often arrived in pairs at noon toting two or three boxes of take-away. They'd spread the meal out on a table and encourage me to eat with a forceful "chi ba!" But I didn't have much of an appetite, and I couldn't handle chopsticks with my clumsy left hand.

"Why don't you sit down and take lunch with me?" I asked as they hovered over me during a round of force-feeding.

"No need. We've already eaten."

Very, uh, hospitable.

As the days went by, oranges piled up on a table near my bed. It was apparently obligatory to bring a gift of oranges to convalescing Mr. Xu, despite the fact that he never touched them. Other well-intentioned but less familiar colleagues also showed up in my hospital room and, perhaps feeling uncomfortable due to my ghastly demeanor and disinclination to make small talk, they turned on the TV for my presumed entertainment.

Now, I despise television – haven't watched it for 30 years – but my aversion was even greater then because the cacophony gave me a throbbing headache. After 10 days or so, I snapped when yet another well-wisher turned the boob-tube on.

"Let's make a deal," I proposed through gritted teeth. "Why don't you go home, sit down, turn the TV on, and make yourself comfortable," I suggested amicably. "Then call me on the phone and we can chat."

Over the years, aspects of Chinese hospitality had occasionally proved difficult to handle. In the hospital, however, I was a captive guest, virtually unable to decline unwanted attentions. This eventually became a source of real irritation. But then Jack Yang called.

A native of Southwest China where Mandarin isn't widely spoken, much of what Jack pronounced in editorial meetings sounded like babble to me. I suppose this made me question his mental capacities, and as such we were never on the best of terms.

"I'm going to visit you tonight," he announced out of the blue. "What should I bring?"

The thought of yet more citrus fruit to add to my pile didn't appeal. I knew he had the key to my apartment, so I let fly: four pairs of my own underwear, three bottles of fruit juice with no added sugar, two English novels and a few other items that would require trips to several stores.

Jack came through with flying colors. I had many visitors at that Shenzhen hospital, but he was the only one who seemed truly mindful of what this hospitalized laowai really needed.

★

"Won't you be leaving soon, Mr. Xu?" my boss's personal assistant, a mechanical personality and "Model Party Member" incarnate, asked during the last stretch of my hospital stay.

"For where?" I queried. By that time, I hadn't washed my hair for more than a week (the doctor wouldn't allow it) and it was piled, dried blood and all, in a tangled mess atop my head. On the streets of Shenzhen I'd have been taken for a madman.

"Back to your home country. I mean, you must be angry with us for what happened."

"Are they going to cancel my work visa?" I panicked.

But that wasn't what she meant. In fact, she wasn't the only one who later offered a sincere apology on behalf of all her fellow countrymen for my having been knifed. I was touched, but I was also determined.

"Do you see Nantian Towers over there?" I said, pointing to the series of wave-shaped blocks where I lived. "*That's* my next destination."

It had never occurred to me to leave China. I had been very happy in Shenzhen and it struck me as predictable that at some point I, like many others, would be randomly targeted by a robber here, the Street Crime Capital of China. Blame it on the lack of a feeling of belonging – almost everyone was a migrant – and the Special Economic Zone's own policies that spawned a "get-rich-quick" mindset.

★

I left the People's Hospital with a right hand that was next to useless, hypersensitive to the slightest touch and initially horribly scarred. But with the help of public hospital staff in Hong Kong and a miracle worker in Shenzhen – a beauty parlor masseuse who charged me just 20 yuan a session – over the next two years I would regain the ability to use my hand for things like grasping objects, typing on a computer, and thankfully, eating with chopsticks.

During the first six months of my convalescence, however, the blood-red wound on my palm was eye-catching and elicited comments every day. In particular, one characteristically Shenzhen conversation re-occurred countless times.

"What happened to you? Get robbed? Where at?"

"I was mugged, right here in Shenzhen," I'd reply.

"Did they catch the guy?"

"Nope."

"How much did he steal from you?"

"Whatever cash he found on me, that's nothing compared to this injury," I'd assert. "You can see it's my right hand that's been hurt, and I'm right-handed."

"Oh." A brief, awkward pause, inevitably followed by one more pointed query.

"But, honestly speaking, how much *did* he get off you?"

THINKING REPORTS

Dominic Stevenson

Dominic Stevenson is a Bangkok based writer and videographer. Since 1985 he has lived and traveled in various countries throughout the Far East, including China and Japan. In 2010, Mainstream Publishing published his first book, "Monkey House Blues: A Shanghai Prison Memoir."

THE FINAL SLURPS OF cabbage soup barely had time to go down before the Chinese were off to work again. A piercing noise resonated down the corridor as the work group leader yelled at the stragglers, still shoveling the last grains of soggy rice into their mouths. Amongst them, a new arrival called Zhou, a thief from Hunan, got a slap across the head from his group leader, partly for being late, but mainly for being new.

There was no time to waste, the biggest sweatshop in Shanghai was open for business, and the cadres could smell the money.

We were on the fifth floor of Eighth Brigade, one of 10 huge blocks of Shanghai Municipal Prison, built by the British at the beginning of the century. Downstairs was the punishment wing, where troublesome prisoners from across the jail were "re-educated." Below that, on the third floor, was death row, which, it was widely whispered, served the best food in the jail, allegedly to keep the condemned men's organs in shape for later harvesting.

After the cacophony of clattering mess tins subsided, the Foreign Unit – all five of us – sat waiting for the arrival of Captain

Ma, who had arranged the meeting the day before. Along with the foreigners, the oldest prisoner in our brigade, Jin Feng, had been summoned to translate.

A tall gangly man in his 70s, Jin had spent much of his adult life in prison for being a "sexual hooligan." The term covered everything from rape to pedophilia to being a bit of a playboy. We never knew what Jin had done, but he was liked and trusted by the guards and prisoners alike, and his command of English – which wasn't so much good as it was less-bad than the others – made him the obvious choice to liaise between the guards and the Foreign Unit.

He had studied at a Christian school in Shanghai before the revolution, and had not fared well in the People's Republic on account of his "suspect" class background. Jin lived on the landing above ours in what was known as the Intellectual Unit. The intellectuals were given work as translators and copywriters rather than the laborious manual tasks assigned to most other prisoners, and were highly educated compared to the majority of the other inmates...and staff.

All five of us foreigners were hash smugglers trying to make some cash along the ancient Silk Road. I myself had been caught getting on the ferry to Kobe, Japan, with less than half a kilo of dope, having travelled overland from Peshawar on the Afghan/ Pakistan border to Shanghai. I'd contracted hepatitis on the journey, and had staggered into the customs check at the border with mustard-yellow eyes and a one-way ticket to The Monkey House. I'd spent eight months on remand in Shanghai Number One Detention Center in a cell with two thieves. After that place, Shanghai Prison wasn't so bad after all.

Until the early 1990s, foreign lawbreakers in China were simply deported, but China had recently entered the War On Drugs and was eager to show its credentials as an international player. At the same time, its prisons were woefully unprepared to accommodate foreign inmates into a system that in many ways was a throwback to the Cultural Revolution.

★

"Here he comes," groaned Bob, a Welshman, as Captain Ma made his way down the corridor to our table.

"Stand for the Captain," snapped Jin Feng, taking the lead. The rest of us followed suit, but in a lazy, slovenly manner, a far cry from the eager, military-style stand-to-attention the Chinese were expected to perform.

Captain Ma looked flustered, pausing to take a handkerchief from his pocket and wipe the sweat from his brow. It was Monday, and he'd probably spent the weekend dreading the thought of having to take over as the officer in charge of the foreigners. His predecessor, Captain Yu, had got off to a bad start, and a mutual loathing had built up in the years before my arrival.

Yu had stated from the beginning that foreigners should not be in his prison, because they were unable to take part in the process of reform. It was a fair point. Tilan Qiao was no ordinary prison, but a model prison that specialized in ideological reform of inmates through labor. Not only were foreigners alien to the Chinese idea of "reform," but according to international human rights laws, we were not permitted to work either, since many of the products made in the prison were to be exported, via front companies, to Western countries.

Our otherness within the system was compounded by the fact that we were the only people in the prison who didn't wear uniform. While the guards wore olive green uniforms, and the inmate's grey and white stripes, we wore tracksuits, jeans and t-shirts. Even though some of us had long sentences, we all looked like we were just passing through; like tourists who'd taken a wrong turn – which in a sense we had.

Captain Ma shuffled his papers around nervously while wiping the sweat that oozed from every pore. He was a big man, but his head still looked too big for his body, while his green, tea-stained teeth protruded awkwardly from his flat face. He'd been a prison officer for many years but had only recently had dealings with the foreigners.

My Mandarin was very basic, and his English non-existent, but he had a kindly attitude towards prisoners, and seemed to consider himself to be in the caring profession, rather than simply a turnkey. He'd proudly show me photos of his two-year-old daughter, which he carried in his wallet, and I'd show him family photos in return. He'd even bought me some Western medicine from a local pharmacy when I'd been unwell. His shoulders bobbed up and down when he laughed, which he did a lot, and he lacked the cold officiousness of many guards at the jail.

Captain Ma was one of us really – just doing his time on the other side of the wall.

"The captain has an announcement to make," Jin Feng translated. "From today, foreign prisoners will be required to write Thinking Reports."

The foreigners all looked at each other vacantly until Larry, an American, refused point blank on the grounds it would breach our "human rights." This wasn't the first time the issue had arisen; indeed, Captain Yu had tried it when the Foreign Unit had first opened in 1991, but then abandoned the idea.

Thinking Reports had been one of the key features of Chinese Communism since the Party had triumphed in 1949, but while the practice had subsided in modern society, it remained at the center of prison life in Tilan Qiao. The reports had a quasi-religious, confessional tone to them, and were supposed to provide the guards with evidence that the wrongdoers were atoning for their crimes and on the long road to reform. A sort of window into our souls the guards could peep through at their leisure.

However, they were also the chief way in which inmates could snitch on each other, since the guards rarely even ventured into our wing other than to lock and unlock the cell doors in the morning and evening. It was an ingenious system that allowed the staff to monitor the goings on in the prison without having to leave their office.

Captain Ma leaned back on his seat, wiped his brow again, and took a deep sigh. He must have known it wasn't going to be easy converting the foreigners to the idea of Thinking Reports, but he had a job to do.

"Look, it's easy," explained Jin Feng, holding up a copy of a Chinese prisoner's report for us to see. "Here you write your name, number, brigade and date."

"What's the point?" asked Werner, a German hash smuggler. "Nobody reads these bullshit reports anyway. It's just a waste of time."

Ma listened to Jin Feng's choppy translation and came back with his carrot and stick answer. "If you don't write Thinking Reports, you can't reform." And then the ace up his sleeve: "Without reform you can't get a reduction."

The foreigners perked up. We had been to reduction meetings, which took place twice a year on average, but none of us had ever received a reduction in our sentences. We'd also noticed that those that did get them tended to be the "senior" prisoners – a small clique of Chinese inmates who effectively ran the wings while the guards drank green tea and chain-smoked in their office all day long. Regular prisoners rarely got reductions.

For the Chinese, Thinking Reports were only one of many requirements for getting a sentence reduction. The main criterion for qualification was the accumulation of merit points, which were related to work performance. Since the foreigners were not permitted to work, they could not be involved in the merit point system. The foreigners feared they were being sucked into taking part in an ideological program without any of the benefits.

Sensing we weren't buying the idea, Captain Ma began to explain the wider benefits of taking part in the scheme.

"Thinking Reports enable the prisoners to wash their brains, and become new!" he announced cheerfully. "Washing the brain is very important to your reform, and improving your real situation."

"I don't want my goddamned brain washed," sneered Larry, as the rest of us tried – unsuccessfully – to keep straight faces.

Ma looked perplexed. He didn't understand why we didn't want our brains washed, and felt we were turning down a golden opportunity to show our repentance. Neither did he understand how loaded the term "brain washing" was for Westerners. A chasm had opened up between us. He was proposing redemption, but all we saw *The Manchurian Candidate.*

Captain Ma decided it was time for the meeting to break, and went back to the officer's room for tea, leaving the foreigners to discuss the issue between ourselves. All five of us were convicted of hash offenses, and did not feel any great need for contrition. In a prison of 5000-plus inmates, we'd never met or heard of any Chinese being charged with a hash offense. There were a few heroin dealers, but the vast majority were thieves, violent offenders or sexual hooligans.

Prior to my own arrest, I'd seen weed growing freely on the side of railroad tracks across China, and assumed the plant was categorized as an herb. Cannabis had a long history of being used in Chinese medicine, and had only recently been criminalized as part of China's new global role as a "responsible" nation.

The arguments for and against writing Thinking Reports were heated, but at the end of the debate most decided we should do it. All that was required was 10 minutes of jotting something down on paper once a week, and it would keep the guards off our backs.

For me, with my two-and-a-half-year sentence it was irrelevant. I already knew I'd serve my full term. However, it made a lot more sense for the prisoners with longer sentences who would later be relying on reductions. I abstained from the vote, but three of the other four voted in favor of Thinking Reports.

Captain Ma was triumphant at the news. He'd succeeded where his superiors had failed, gaining face among his own prison hierarchy, while bringing the foreigners round to the

Chinese way of thinking.

★

"So what do you write in your Thinking Reports?" I asked Mr. Chew, an embezzler from Singapore serving 12 years. He was hunched over a desk with a pen in his hand, writing on a piece of prison-issue paper. "Today I'm writing about how I once stole a mango."

"Did you get caught?" I enquired.

"Oh, it's not true," he laughed, "it's just a story about how I used to be a bad person, but, thanks to the Party and cadres at the prison, I've been reborn. That's the sort of thing they like to read," he said, before adding, "*If* they bother to read it, which is unlikely."

I posed the same question to Mr. Sun, who was playing cards with his team of goons who effectively ran our wing. As the most senior prisoner, Sun had more reductions than anyone, and was looking at getting released soon after serving 15 years of an 18-year sentence for strangling his wife. It was unclear how he had avoided the death penalty, but he was popular with the guards, who felt that Sun's wife deserved it.

Mr. Sun waived his hand dismissively and gobbed a load of sunflower husks into the wet pile on the floor.

"Just write anything. They won't read it anyway," said another card player chomping on a chicken foot.

A hunchbacked friend was next. We spoke via the translation help of a mutual mate, a fraudster. Despite our inability to communicate, I liked the hunchback very much; he seemed to live in a parallel universe to the other inmates and kept to himself. In spite of his physical disability and withdrawn manner, word was he had killed a gang boss in Shanghai, for which he was doing 21 years.

"What do you write in your thinking reports?" I asked the hunchback.

"Nothing. He can't write," the fraudster answered for him after a brief consultation. "His friend writes them for him"

"So what does his friend write?"

"He doesn't know. He can't read either."

With the deadline looming, it was time to write my own Thinking Report, but since I'd already been told that I was going to complete my full sentence anyway, there was no reason to try and ingratiate myself with the guards, or their editors upstairs.

★

Captain Ma had a spring in his step as he arrived for the weekly meeting. Armed with an old Nescafe jar filled to the brim with steaming-hot green tea, he looked chipper as we stood to greet him. From under his arm he produced a file stuffed with our Thinking Reports, including paper-clipped translations, and began to address the group through Jin Feng.

"The foreigners have been very good, and have completed their Thinking Reports!" he announced, stating the obvious, an annoying habit of Chinese officials. "This is an important part of your reform and shows that you understand the real situation and are ready to become new again."

He shuffled through a few reports before coming to mine and raising his eyebrows. "What is this?"

"Excuse me?" I replied, looking at Jin Feng for help.

"Captain Ma wants to know why you have not written about your crime. I translated these reports myself, and there is no mention of your offense."

So they *do* read our reports, I sighed.

"I wrote about the crimes against Chinese wildlife, and the fine work the government is doing to eradicate them," I said, defending myself.

You see, an article in the English-language China Daily newspaper provided to foreign inmates had caught my attention. It concerned the smuggling of falcons from northern

Pakistan to the Xinjiang region of Northeast China, and on to the Gulf States. The Chinese were having a crackdown on the trade, so I wrote a short piece praising the Chinese Communist Party in its efforts to stamp out the illicit business. I also added that, while I was opposed to the death penalty, and felt sorry for those languishing on the floor below ours waiting to die, the CCP should be congratulated for taking a robust stand against Panda poaching.

Jin Feng relayed the information back to Ma, who leaned back in his chair and laughed his "Ho Ho Ho" laugh that reminded me of Father Christmas.

"But you're supposed to write about *your* crime," he said between fits of "Ho's."

"My crime was to be stupid, but these crimes are evil."

"You like animals?" chuckled Ma.

"Yes. Very much."

"So do I. Maybe that's why I work in a prison," he said winking, before looking at his watch and jerking his head back in an "is that the time?" kind of way.

Captain Ma returned to the officer's room, and Jin Feng went back upstairs to the Intellectual Unit. The Foreign Unit stayed put in the corridor where we lived, 24 hours a day, seven days a week, for years, but now with our consciences a little lighter, and our brains a little cleaner.

EMPTY FROM THE OUTSIDE

Susie Gordon

Shanghai-based writer and journalist Susie Gordon was born in the northwest of England in 1981. She moved to China in 2008, and writes for many of the city's English language publications, specializing in business and culture. She has published three guidebooks about Shanghai and Beijing, and is currently working on a novel.

FRIDAY NIGHT STARTED, AS many do in Shanghai, on the back of a motorcycle taxi. It's not the most glamorous way to travel, but it's the quickest, and here in fast-paced Shanghai, speed often takes precedence over show.

I'd already had a couple of drinks with a friend on my way to meet Zhou Ning, so the ride was tempered with a haze that was part inebriation and part neon, scoring lines of blue and orange and green with every traffic light we passed.

As we veered down Maoming Lu and down onto Julu, the streets became thinner; the fog of the day's pollution had gathered under the arc of the phoenix trees, tinted by the yellow streetlights. Smoke from the shaokao sellers' makeshift barbecues plumed in the air at the corner of Fumin and Changle, and their shouts were peppered by the yell of car horns.

Zhou Ning, my business partner, had invited me for drinks at a new wine bar on Yongfu Lu, to celebrate a deal he'd just signed. As always with Ning, the details were mired in his usual euphemism, but he had promised me that everything was above board, and the remuneration was worthy of a celebration.

★

The Yongfu bar strip was already busy by the time the motorcycle dropped me off. The street is almost exclusively foreigners and drug dealers, or foreign drug dealers, along with a ragged coterie of beggars clutching flowers and rattling grubby Styrofoam cups. Ning's venue of choice was typically grander, but he'd heard that this new wine bar carried some special vintages. He loved wine. Despite owning a well-stocked cupboard of expensive baijiu gifted by clients over the years, his most prized possession was his wine cellar, built into the foundations of his renovated villa.

He was already there when I arrived at the bar, smoking a cigar and texting on his phone. Beside him, also occupied with her phone, was one of his girlfriends: young and pale with bobbed black hair, an Hermès bag on the armchair beside her.

"Hao jiu bu jian, long time no see," Ning said to me when I approached his table. It had been a long time. Our business relationship was conducted by email and WeiXin, and we saw each other in person only every couple of months. That was unusual for a culture that prizes in-person proximity, but it worked for both of us. Ning spent a lot of time in Hong Kong and Singapore expanding his empire, and he had his sights set on Europe.

He summoned the waiter with an imperious jut of his wrist, and said something to him that I didn't catch. We lit cigarettes and talked about the deal (circuitously, as Ning, in typical Chinese business fashion, never gave too much away) while his girlfriend texted vapidly, her long legs crossed and one foot lolling indolently. A few minutes later, the waiter came with a bottle of red wine and a glass carafe.

We'd nearly finished the first bottle when Ning's son, Li, arrived with some friends. We saw them pull up outside the bar in a phalanx of low, humming sports cars. Li was classic "fu er dai," one of the many princelings for whom Shanghai was just a toybox. I had known Zhou Li and his brother Zhou Ming since they were in their early teens. Li was now 20, and didn't work. He didn't need to. Ning had given him a penthouse apartment in one of his properties as soon as he turned 16, and his life was a parade of late nights, later mornings, women and drugs.

The boys seemed keen to order spirits, but Ning insisted on more wine. Within three hours we'd worked our way through eight bottles.

"Are you coming with us for dinner?" Li asked me with his usual aloofness. Despite knowing me for many years, he was still slightly suspicious of my dealings with his father. It wasn't that Ning and I had ever been anything other than friends, but I sensed that Li resented me for my participation in the business, especially since I was a woman, and almost certainly because I was a foreigner.

As Li and his friends got up to leave, I peeked into the narrow black book that contained the bill. At first I thought the numerals were a telephone number or some sort of bar code, but then I realized – *each* bottle of wine we'd consumed had cost 60,000 yuan. Yet Zhou Ning hadn't even glanced at the bill before he put his card down.

On the way out of the bar, we were trailed by beggars and flower sellers as we made our way to Li's armada of cars down on Fuxing Xi Lu. Ning was returning his wallet to the chest pocket of his suit as he walked down the steps, and I watched to see if he would offer any money to the stooped men with their jangling cups and persistent grins. He elbowed them aside so he could pass. Despite the fact that we'd just spent more on wine than these beggars might ever hope to earn in an entire lifetime, their plight just didn't register with someone like Ning.

Catching my eye, he shrugged. "I don't have any change; I only have hundreds."

Ning's driver was waiting for us in his BMW, but Li wanted to show me his new car, so I rode in the front seat on the way to the restaurant. The interior was a cramped relief of black leather and swift air-con. Li spent most of the journey talking in Shanghainese on his phone to arrange a KTV session with some more friends after dinner, while I watched the city unfurl outside the window.

"So how's life?" I asked him in Mandarin when he hung up.

"Bu cuo," he replied – a phrase that literally means 'not bad' but actually means 'pretty good.'

"What are you up to these days?"

"The usual stuff."

"Not married yet?"

He gave an affable snort of laughter, knowing I was joking. It was the typical question to ask an eligible, unmarried man in his mid-20s. There was no reason for Zhou Li to get married – not now, at any rate. Guys like him were rich enough to stand away from the majority. When he felt like it, he would most probably find a girl like his mother: a businesslike beauty, already rich, who would provide him with a doe-eyed heir (or two; men like him could also contravene the One Child Policy with a red envelope full of Renminbi) before getting on with her life.

We went up onto the elevated highway at Maoming Lu, swathed in the eerie blue glow of neon from the strip-lights. The traffic was loose and sparse, and Li swung from lane to lane, one hand on the wheel. The elevated highway slices through the city, cutting past buildings at 10th-floor level, higher than the treetops in People's Park. At that time of night, before midnight, the city seems unreal. Empty from the outside, but teeming; warrens and labyrinths of life unseen.

★

Located on the Bund, overlooking the river and the neon shards of the Financial District, Crystal Room was one of the most exclusive restaurants in Shanghai. The private room that Li always booked had a minimum charge of several *wan* yuan, and served the sort of lavish traditional fare that's more for show than taste: abalone, bird's nest soup, shark fin...

Li's favorite banquet room was prepped for our arrival, and the eight of us arranged ourselves around the circular table under a chandelier that prickled and shimmered with yellow light. I knew better than to try and make any requests when it came to the dishes; Ning and Li did it all.

Before long, the revolving glass at the center of the table bristled with spirit bottles – the best rice wine, 60-year-old baijiu, Guizhou Moutai – and the toasts began. Regular baijiu strips your sinuses and tilts your vision back an inch when you swallow, but this stuff was different. We had knocked back about four shots each by the time the food came, but the effect was mellow and jovial. I didn't know how much each bottle cost, but it must have been in the tens of thousands. The food was equally luxurious and abundant, coming dish after dish, carouselling in front of us on the revolving glass.

I found this kind of banquet intriguing, not just for the wealth of the participants or the profligacy of their spending, but because, when it came down to it, they were no different than any other dinner taking place at that same moment in any other part of the city or country. Whether the guests were moneyed or peasants, whether the dish contained shark fin or Anhui vegetables picked out of the ground, whether they're toasting with century-matured maotai, or cheap, rank erguotou, the conviviality, the speeches and the exhortations are all the same:

"To health...to money...to happiness...to *more* money...to friends."

After we'd sunk the last of the spirits, Li rallied us for our next stop: a karaoke parlor that his friend Yu Haiming had just opened in Lujiazui across the river. The valets brought the cars up from the basement, and the soberest among us were assigned to drive. Li held his drink well, but I could tell that he was in no state to take the wheel, so I offered. His usual laconic self, he gave me the keys and got into the passenger seat. Ordinarily I would have been petrified at the thought of being pulled over by the police, not just for driving under the influence, but for being a foreigner without a Chinese driver's license, yet with the Zhous there was nothing that couldn't be fixed with a neat sheaf of red RMB.

I wasn't looking forward to KTV, but decided to go along because spirits were high, and I hadn't seen Yu Haiming for a couple of years, not since he came back from an extended sojourn to Europe. His father, Yu Zhiwei, had made his fortune in mining up in Henan Province, and like Zhou Li, Haiming didn't need to work. His KTV venture was a flight of fancy, and it was impressive.

A wide staircase with gilded banisters curved up from the marble hallway in both directions, with reproduction Michelangelo statues keeping vigil over the scatterings of rich-looking men who stood around smoking. Many of them gawked at me, no doubt wondering who I was and why I was there. That type of KTV was a man's domain; the only women were staff or prostitutes – usually both.

Yu Haiming was summoned from his office and greeted us in the foyer. He was plumper than I remembered, and had segued his style from wealthy hipster to louche businessman. He showed us to an elevator and took us up to the top floor, where the most exclusive room was waiting for us.

It was more discreet than other, less-lavish KTV parlors I'd been to. Instead of the usual parade of tired-looking provincial girls traipsing in for the men to choose from, Yu Haiming had personally selected six pretty, well-groomed women whom he knew the guys would like. It felt less sordid somehow, but still awkward, especially as the girls didn't seem comfortable with me being there.

The customary libation at KTV is whisky mixed with green tea, or watery beer from tall green bottles, but Yu Haiming's place was unsurprisingly different. He had two of the girls bring in a magnum of champagne, a little silver tray arrayed with slim white lines of powder that might have been coke but in all likelihood was ketamine, and pills nestled like candies in a brass bowl. At one point, I remember looking around at the girls, the men, the drugs and the money, and wondering how long this utopia could last: the Chinese dream, in its second, prodigal generation.

Zhou Li and his two best friends, Ma Qiang (also known by his self-appointed English moniker of "Powerful" Ma) and Lu Yiming, took to the microphone to posture with renditions of Mandopop songs. The two other guys, Song Mingsen and Kong Xun, sat either side of me, nodding their heads to the music, clearly zoned out on the drugs they'd inhaled. KTV girls sat indolently in a line on the sofas opposite, waiting for the guys to show interest. Eventually, Kong Xun summoned one of them, and off they went.

"Not to your taste?" I asked Song Mingsen. He shrugged. I knew, and he knew I knew, that he was gay. Zhou Li knew too, but he didn't care. Nobody did, really, except perhaps his parents. And in all likelihood it wasn't any moralistic issue; New China isn't shackled with the Judeo-Christian morals of the West. Like most of his generation, Song Mingsen was an only child, and his parents' priority was a grandchild.

"Not really," he replied absently. He was distracted by a cruising app on his phone that was popular among young gay guys (or tongzhi – literally meaning "comrades").

Not long after, one of the girls came up to Mingsen and began to sway in her own, tired rendition of seduction. He curled his lip and shook his head, but she didn't desist. Eventually, he got up, pushed past her, and went to the "men's side" of the room. Pouting, the girl sat down near me and folded her arms petulantly.

"Busy night?" I asked, a little awkwardly, as we were the only women in the room, and were there for very different reasons.

"Been here since six this evening," she said. "And I don't clock out until six in the morning"

"That's a long shift."

"At least I get tomorrow off."

"Where are you from?" I asked.

Her back stiffened defensively. "Why?"

"Just wondering."

"Guess."

"Anhui?"

She huffed, slightly insulted. "No."

"Henan?"

"No." She looked even more insulted.

"Guangdong?"

"Yes." She may or may not have been lying.

"How long have you been in Shanghai?"

"About two years."

Every month, every week, of those two years were evident in her face – the weariness around her eyes, the determined clench of her jaw as she watched the guys capering on the other side of the room.

"Do you make good money?" I asked audaciously, normally a question thrown at foreigners by locals, not the other way around.

"Not as good as you," she sniffed.

"Why do you say that?"

"You're laowai."

"That doesn't mean I earn more."

"But you don't have to do *this*."

And to that, I had no response. We sat, the silence between us louder than the tracks that blazed from the karaoke screen, illuminating the self-entitled profiles of Zhou Li and his well-to-do friends as they danced, drank and debauched the night away.

★

The party didn't end until the day did. Dawn was beginning to show through the dirty Shanghai sky behind the towers as we drove through the limpid streets. Li's penthouse took up the

268

top floor of his father's latest development on Huaihai Lu, and he called his dealer to meet him in the lobby. The rest of us went upstairs and opened more champagne.

The living room of the penthouse was wrapped completely in windows, making it a beacon at the top of the city, from which everything was visible – the saber-teeth of the Pudong skyscrapers bleached with the morning, the low, dark green of the French Concession and its red villa roofs, the span of People's Square ringed with buildings.

Song Mingsen had gone off to meet a "comrade" from the cruising app, so it was just me, Lu Yiming, Powerful Ma and Kong Xun who sat and supped bubbly from the bottles while we waited for Zhou Li to come up with the drugs. I was comfortable with those guys. I always had been.

"Found a boyfriend yet?" Powerful Ma asked me with enough lazy imperiousness for it not to be a come-on. These guys didn't see me as potential quarry, and our interactions were amiable. They were low-key, calm people, despite the bluster of their wealth. They weren't striving for anything, and that fact had shaped their characters into affability.

"Not yet," I said. "I'm not looking."

"We'll find you a rich man," laughed Kong Xun.

"She doesn't want rich – she wants true love," Powerful Ma jibed. "Good luck!"

When Zhou Li came up, he had his brother Ming in tow, and several slim red envelopes in his pocket – hongbao for a festival of excess. Before long, the chrome tabletop was crisscrossed with rails of various powders. Dark heads, one by one, bent to take their lines through rolled notes. Only Zhou Ming and I resisted – Ming because he'd once told me he didn't trust his brother, and me because it was a world I preferred to observe from the fringes. It's a dark industry, and its talons spread into underworlds that I'd rather not be part of.

The first few lines made the guys dance. Their reflections played in the glass windows – puppets on the neon backdrop of the city outside. As dawn began to dirty the sky, they arranged themselves on the sofas to smoke joints.

"I'm going home," I finally announced. "It's late."

"Early..." Zhou Li corrected.

"I'm coming down," Powerful Ma murmured beside me. His words seemed prophetic for larger socio-economic issues related to China's impending hard-landing, but I was currently too exhausted to give any further credence to this.

"We all are," confirmed Kong Xun.

I left them dozing, and went up onto the roof of the building to watch the sun rise behind the skyline.

People paint Shanghai with the clichés created for other cities, in an attempt to corral it into a comfortable metaphor that will make it more understandable. "The city that never sleeps", some say. That's not true. Shanghai is the city that never wakes; never rises from its reverie. And there's no reason why it should.

Unsavory Elements

Tom Carter

Tom Carter spent two years backpacking 35,000 miles across 33 Chinese provinces and regions, resulting in his first book, "CHINA: Portrait of a People." Tom was born and raised in San Francisco and has called China home since 2004. He presently divides his time between Shanghai and a farming village in Jiangsu Province. He is the editor of "Unsavory Elements."

Author's note: Names have been changed to protect the not-so-innocent

STANDING IN FRONT OF us in a suspect-style lineup were four heavily made-up girls gaudily attired in fluorescent floral dresses, flesh-toned stockings and scuffed heels. The aliases they gave us were Ni Ni, Mi Mi, Jie Jie and Jia Jia. They were young, they were willing and they were for sale.

Attractive was not in the equation. Pretty peasants looking to make easy money migrate to China's major metropolises to work at karaoke parlors or massage spas. Their plain-of-face counterparts in the countryside, however, are consigned to bottom-tier brothels, such as the one my friends and I were presently standing in.

"I'll take those two," Claude slurred drunkenly, pointing at Ni Ni, a girl with dyed rust-orange hair and a bad complexion, and her co-worker Jie Jie, plump and unable to control her nervous giggles. Neither had ever in their young lives seen a real-life foreigner before. Now they were about to have a threesome with one.

The Canadian whose going-away party we were celebrating could hardly contain himself. This was certainly going to be the highlight of Claude's year in China. Maybe the highlight of his life. The single 40-year-old had accomplished little in his lifetime, working a succession of minimum-wage jobs since college and living in his parent's basement before coming to China to teach English. Claude admittedly couldn't care less about Chinese culture; he was simply, like so many other foreigners in China – myself included – aimless and desperate for an income. These are exactly the qualifications Chinese schools starving for English teachers seek. New China: a refugee camp for the world's losers.

Claude, however, would soon be returning to his parent's basement in Canada, having utterly failed here. In one year, he had not managed, nay, bothered to learn a single phrase of Mandarin other than ni hao (hello) and zhegi (this). Whenever some unknowing pedestrian tried to start a conversation with him, as the genial Chinese are wont to do with strangers from another continent, Claude would nod his head dumbly and repeat "ni hao...ni hao...ni hao..." until the exasperated person was left scratching his head at how idiotic Westerners are. If Claude wanted something at the market, he imperiously pointed his finger and shouted "zhegi...zhegi...zhegi..." while the confused clerk scrambled to help him.

Grunting and gesturing his way through China, Claude was, in the eyes of the natives, something like a modern-day Neanderthal. The unruly thatch of chest hair, thrusting its way out of his open-collar shirt like foliage seeking sunlight, didn't help negate this perception.

At 40, he wasn't a bad looking laowai. His thinning hair could be overlooked for his rugged handsomeness, and his muscular physique made up for his short stature. Surely, I had once naively believed, out of a population of 1.3 billion there must be a soulmate just for Claude. Earlier in the year I had tried setting him up on a series of blind dates, but each one ended, how shall we say: anti-climactically. Most Chinese girls seemed to be turned off by Claude's crude mannerisms, such as the way he wetly blew his nose at the dinner table, spoke with a mouth full of food or lifted his leg to fart loudly.

"I'm just mimicking Chinese men!" he cried defensively following his latest dating disaster.

"Which is why she doesn't want to go out with you again," I attempted to reason. "If she wanted gas and mucus, she'd marry a Chinese."

Due to the lack of female companionship that year, Claude's pent-up *man*nerisms eventually got the best of him, causing him to develop an explosive temper. Once he threw a chair across a classroom while screaming how spoiled his primary school students were. Expats in China call such outbursts "getting your P.R.C. period." Claude got his period often. He became known among our Chinese colleagues as "Bai Bianpao," White Firecracker.

Yes, Claude needed to get laid, and badly. And as his faithful albeit weary friend, I was intent on facilitating it. But when it became obvious that Claude would never find a real girlfriend, we resorted to the only other option a single, desperate man in China has.

★

Claude's going-away party began at six that July evening at a barbeque buffet, where the all-you-can-eat spread and bottomless beer was enough to convince him to part with 30 yuan. I forgot to mention that my friend Claude was a major miser, which, in addition to his flatulence, was also his dating downfall. Chinese women are well aware of their culture's severe gender imbalance and like to be splurged on. Claude didn't believe in splurging.

I had invited several mutual acquaintances to join us for dinner, but truth be told, most people did not like Claude very much; only one other person showed up. His name was Bahati, an intelligent, friendly fellow from Kenya who spoke several languages, including nearly perfect Putonghua. He had been teaching English in various provinces around China for years, achieving superstar status amongst his students...and their parents. One housewife even seduced Bahati into having an affair with her in exchange for free English tutoring for her son.

At one point Bahati lived together with his Chinese girlfriend, but in an unusual reversal, this young lady was unwilling to commit to marriage with him and moved back home with her parents.

"I think she was just using me for sex," the Kenyan confided in us during dinner. "Chinese girls are not so concerned anymore about marriage or raising a family; they've been infected with Western amorality."

Bahati was now on the rebound, looking for some eastern immorality to soothe his broken heart. I told him I knew just the place to take him.

With Kenny G's *Songbird* blaring from the overhead speakers on nauseatingly infinite repeat, we drank and feasted for a few hours, regaling each other with stories from the past semester, and vague discussions about each of our even vaguer futures as lowly English teachers. When the last bottle of Laoshan had been drained to its dregs, it was time to move on.

A 10-yuan taxi later, we finally arrived. "There it is," I announced with a giddy flourish. "Teen Street."

Sprawling out before us was a row of no less than 20 white-tiled shops, each glowing a soft-pink hue from its frosted-glass doorway. This particular side-street had been forsaken by the squawking commerce and ceaseless foot traffic that characterizes every other thoroughfare in China. There were no awnings advertising the specialty of these shops; only the women who sat idly in the thresholds hinted at their trade.

On the books, prostitution is illegal in China. But the reality is that sex is for sale in just about every district in every large or small city across the People's Republic. Hundreds of millions of Chinese men will never have a wife or even a girlfriend due to China's dramatically imbalanced male to female ratio – a tragic result of a century of female infanticide, selective abortion and forced sterilizations. To accommodate the tinderbox of testosterone that is China, the Communist Party is willing to look the other way at prostitution, thereby keeping the male masses at bay.

Houses of Pleasure come in all forms here. High-end KTV bars and their stable of long-legged hostesses cater to wealthy businessmen and corrupt communist cadres looking to squander their embezzled funds, while massage spas attract a more middle-class clientele. Hair salons are the most common, and accommodating, and can be found in almost all neighborhoods, where any average Zhou with 50 yuan receives a quick shampoo before ducking behind a curtain for a quick something else.

And then there are the brothels. These hole-in-the-wall dens are found only on the outskirts of townships that lack transportation hubs or where the local economy cannot sustain upscale karaoke parlors. I had inadvertently discovered such a place during a drive into the countryside that surrounds the nondescript, third-tier town we had been living in the past year.

"Why do you call it 'Teen Street?'" asked Bahati, smoothing out the wrinkles of an all-white suit which contrasted sharply with his purple-black skin. The heavy summer air made his musky scent palpable. Pure gold jewelry hung heavily from his neck and wrists. I don't believe I ever saw an African in China who did not dress impeccably.

"Because the taxi driver told me that none of the girls in these brothels is over twenty years old."

"Then it is not just a street of teens," he affirmed logically. "It is also a young women street."

"Yes, Bahati, I'm aware of that," I answered as diplomatically as possible. That was one of the downsides of living abroad: most of my puns went right over the heads of my non-native English-speaking friends. "'But 'Young Women Street' doesn't sound as catchy as 'Teen Street.'"

Bahati scratched his fuzzy pate as he contemplated this.

"What happens to them after they turn twenty?" asked Claude with a genuine look of concern.

"According to the taxi driver, they're exiled to another neighborhood."

"Like a henhouse," snorted Claude, suddenly less empathetic.

And with that, the second part of our going-away party commenced. To the incidental music in our minds, the American, the Kenyan and the Canadian strolled side-by-side, slow-motion movie-style, down the fractured pavement of Teen Street. Claude ruined the moment by lifting his leg at an angle and breaking wind.

★

As if word of our presence had traveled telepathically down the entire street, heads immediately began peering out of the pink-lit dens, followed by audible whispers of "laowai laile!", "foreigners have arrived!" Chinese men, when they go mongering in the pink-light districts, are afforded a respectful degree of anonymity, whereas absolutely everything a foreigner in China does – from how we hold our chopsticks to what we buy at the supermarket – is pried apart like a virgin's legs for commentary and analysis by the general populous.

"Ni hao...ni hao...ni hao!" Claude called out, grinning and waving. I yanked his arm to keep quiet and keep his head down. Claude was like a hyperactive juvenile on a field trip.

Our perusal along Teen Street was spared further scrutiny when a middle-aged, potato-shaped woman with short salt-and-peppered hair slid open her door and urged us inside. We sheepishly followed behind her.

"What is this place?" Bahati inquired, as dubious as I was, for the grim interior hardly fit our preconceived, Hollywood-influenced expectations of what a brothel must be like.

"This place? This is a bar," she answered in a corrupted dialect. I translated for Claude.

"Good," Claude grunted, dropping into a lacquered-wood seat. "I'm thirsty! Tell her I want a bottle of Tsingtao, and none of that room-temperature crap like they serve at these stupid Chinese restaurants. It's summer! I want an ice-cold bottle of beer."

"Some beers, please," I relayed to the woman.

"We don't have beer," she said flatly while thumbing the hairy mole on her chin.

"Um, okay, then something else to drink."

"We don't serve drinks here."

I let out a little laugh of exasperation. "I thought you said this is a bar."

"Correct, it is a bar."

Puzzled, I glanced around the establishment. There was a counter, and stools, and decorative plastic foliage hanging from the rafters, and little private drinking rooms with half-curtains. Taped on the wall was a cardboard cutout of Santa Claus, the patron saint of seedy establishments across China. Surely this was some kind of bar, just as she said. Yet I realized there were no beverages on tap, no refrigerator, no music, no customers... no nothing.

"What do you serve, then?" I asked resignedly.

"Xiaojie," was the woman's matter-of-fact reply.

I rolled my eyes. The Chinese are notorious for talking in circles.

"Now I am as confused as a Chinese driver at a four-way traffic light," boomed Bahati in his baritone African lilt. "So where are these girls?"

"They live in a dormitory out back. I'm just the proprietress here. Have a rest and I'll call them over for you to look at."

Rather than make an excuse to leave, as more responsible foreign guests of China would have, our curiosity got the better of us.

Four minutes later, four females poured in through the back door and dutifully albeit timidly took their places in a lineup, as is the custom of this counterculture. Their nervous giggles were irrepressible; clearly these were peasants straight out of the deep countryside who had never encountered a foreigner before.

"Here are," introduced the proprietress, "Ni Ni, Mi Mi, Jie Jie and Jia Jia."

Their makeup was thick and their clothes garishly fluorescent, as rural Chinese girls with some disposable income yet no fashion sense have a tendency to dress. They were obviously young, and passably cute, but nobody would ever call any of them beautiful. In several years or less they would look as haggard as their matron, and rightly relegated across town to that neon-pink henhouse.

Eight single-lidded eye slits collectively focused on Bahati, who was sitting between Claude and me. "Wosai! Look at his skin," exclaimed one. "He's so dark," said another. "He smells strange," grumbled a third. "I wonder if his gold is real?" pondered the fourth.

"I can understand you," the Kenyan chuckled good-naturedly.

The four girls each blushed a bright scarlet through their powdered cheeks.

"What do we do now?" Claude asked.

I shrugged; this was my first time too. "I think you pick the one you want."

"Oh, just like at the buffet," he said, laughing loudly at his own joke.

Claude, convivially drunk on a 500-milliliter bottle of Changyu Sanbianjiu he had polished off on the ride over, struggled back up onto his feet and inspected each girl up close not unlike a Xinjiang camel trader.

"This one has dirt under her fingernails...this one has too many pimples...this one's teeth are decayed...this one smells like feet..."

For a man who had consistently struck out with women all year, he was surprisingly picky.

"I guess I'll take that one," he finally decided, pulling the plump girl with apple-red cheeks out of the lineup. Claude shouted at the proprietress as if she were deaf: "Zhegi!"

"She's a person, not a 'this,'" I corrected, feeling as embarrassed as the girl surely was.

"Whatever," Claude said dismissively. "How much does she cost?"

The proprietress paused to pick her nose while regarding the three foreigners. "One hundred."

Claude stomped his foot impetuously. I knew what was coming because I had been subject to it all year: he would overreact; say it was too expensive; insist that all Chinese were dishonest.

"That's way too expensive," Claude huffed, right on cue. "These Chinese are always trying to rip off Westerners, eh?"

I laughed inwardly: so predictable. And yet, he had unwittingly raised a valid point. 100 yuan was an obscene amount of money compared with what grade-school dropouts earned toiling in some factory. Even after the 40 percent that goes back to the house, these prostitutes would take home 60 tax-free yuan for just half an hour with a customer, which was a tremendous *ten* times higher than the average hourly salary in China!

No wonder prostitution is so rampant in this country, I mused as I watched the four girls watch us: why stand on your feet all day for slave wages when you can get rich on your back?

"Wait a second, mon," Bahati said calmly. "Let us all pull together. Firstly, where else in the world can you have a teen for just ten dollars? Not even in Africa is human life this cheap. Secondly, everything in China is negotiable. Allow me to handle this."

One minute of rapid-fire Mandarin later, Bahati and the boss had come to an easy arrangement, further solidifying Sino-African relations.

"She agrees to lower the price to eighty yuan each…"

"That's good news," I said, glancing over at Claude for his

consent.

"If," Bahati added ominously, "we *each* get a girl."

I felt everyone's eyes on me. "*I'm* not getting a girl," I scoffed, my back unexpectedly up against a wall; apparently my 'When in China' outlook had been misconstrued. "I...I...have a girlfriend!" This was actually true; I wasn't being a pansy, and I'm not just saying it because I am the narrator and de-facto moral compass of the story.

After some deliberation and counting the money in his fanny pack, Claude cleared his throat for the big announcement: "Fine. If it means getting a bargain, then I'll buy *two* girls."

I shot him a look of disbelief. He was either infected with lust or unbridled greed, because this was the first time I had ever witnessed Claude splurge. It reminded me of a story I'd once read about Chinese immigrants arriving in Gold Rush-era California who wore extra-large Western-sized shoes that didn't fit – simply because it used more leather, thereby making the shoe more valuable in their avaricious eyes. Claude was turning Chinese, I really think so.

"Sure you can handle two girls, mon?" Bahati asked him. "You've had a lot to drink tonight."

"Dude, that wasn't just any alcohol, that was Three Penis Wine, made from an assortment of animal genitalia: dog dick, deer dick and...I forgot the third dick, probably panda. It's supposed to boost virility, eh? You might think I don't know anything about Chinese culture, but I do. I've been waiting all year for this moment; I'm roaring to go. I'll take those two. Zhegi! Zhegi!"

The two giggling girls, whose names were Ni Ni and Jie Jie, lead Claude arm-in-arm out the back door. He looked over his shoulder and winked at us. I resisted the temptation to make a wisecrack about "double happiness," but I was optimistic that we would never have to suffer an outburst from White Firecracker again.

Of the two remaining prostitutes, Bahati decided on Jia Jia, a slender creature who had trouble walking in her platform heels, like a daughter playing dress-up in mommy's closet; like a developing China struggling to cope with its own self-imposed modernization. The two of them disappeared together; the last girl returned dejectedly to her dorm, leaving me alone with the frowning proprietress.

"I have a girlfriend," I reasserted, grinning nervously, a habit I picked up from the Chinese. "I'll just wait here, in this lovely lacquered seat…is this real wood, or…?"

Arching a tattooed eyebrow at probably the only man who had ever turned down a teenager, she courteously turned on a dusty television set for me to watch and slid a VCD-format disk into a digital player. Whether it was meant to entice, or merely preoccupy, me I couldn't say, but a Japanese porno blinked on and the lady left me alone.

★

Two runny-nosed children wandered into the bar… No, this isn't the start of a bad joke, though in a way it kind of is. The boy and girl looked up at me with innocent mystification, then simultaneously over at the pixilated porn, then back at me. I leapt up and quickly smacked off the television set.

"Shouldn't you be asleep?" I asked the grubby little kids, more likely cousins than siblings, recalling the Communist Party's ruinous one-child policy that drove Chinese men to prostitution out of sheer mortification of conceiving with their own wives. "Where's your mama?"

"Don't know," the girl shrugged indifferently.

I should preface here that it was my intention to locate the proprietress about the two unattended tots wandering around her brothel, but, as the reader will soon see, the events that quickly unfolded distracted me from my altruistic course.

Exiting out the back door into a courtyard webbed with clotheslines dripping with drying bras and panties, I was immediately bombarded with a melody of moans drifting down from the second floor of the building. Admittedly curious, I followed a steep stairwell up into a dark hallway of a series of rooms. Each room had a window frosted with adhesive film facing into the hall, and the blurred silhouettes of my friends and their female companions were visible in the first two rooms. Listening to the animalistic panting and faux-orgasmic screams, I could hardly contain my laughter.

Shouting suddenly erupted from one of the rooms, shaking me out of my reverie. Two sets of shrill voices were arguing against one very angry foreigner. I was all too familiar with this linguistically-impaired temper tantrum: Bai Bianpao had returned.

"Oh no," I groaned, expecting a chair to come crashing through the window at any moment.

Instead, the window slid open, revealing a stark-naked fat girl. It was Jie Jie, even less appealing with her clothes off.

"What are you doing here?" she screeched, startled by my lurking presence. "Where's the boss?"

"I was just looking for her, too." It was a half-truth.

"Your friend is drunk!"

"So?" I said lamely, distracted by her extremely large and bare breasts; I am, after all, a male of the species.

"So he can't perform!" she whined, unconcerned with her modesty. "He's taking too long!"

I looked over at Claude the mounted Canadian panting on top of poor Ni Ni. His tortured face was dripping with sweat – either from the summer heat or out of sheer frustration. From what I saw, and without going into detail, it was obvious that Three Penis Wine had not had the intended effect.

"Having some trouble there, Claude?" I laughed not a little cruelly.

"It's not my fault! I can't concentrate. These stupid girls keep rushing me!"

"You've already been up here for half an hour, bro. We told you not to drink so much."

At this moment, the window to the adjacent room opened. It was Bahati in all his Swahili glory.

"What's going on, mon?" asked the three-legged African.

"Oh, nothing. Just Claude is unable to cum–..."

"We're only giving him five more minutes!" warned Jie Jie, gnashing her rotten-brown teeth. "We've got other customers, you know."

"...plete the task at hand."

Leaving the window open, Jie Jie crawled across the king-sized mattress back over to Claude and Ni Ni and began spanking my friend's hairy hiney in a fruitless effort to arouse him. I cannot recall seeing a more absurd sight in my life.

I turned my attention back to Bahati and Jia Jia. "How's it going with you guys?"

"This girl is annoying me, mon. She wants to take a photo of my manhood with her mobile."

"Why do you want to take a picture of it?" I asked the tiny teen, lying on her stomach with her feet up, unabashedly nude except for hose-socks. Her face was ghostly white from bleaching creams and cheap makeup, but her golden-brown body betrayed her rustic roots. A constellation of cigarette burn scars marred her left arm. She tossed her orange-hued hair and ignored me, then began playing Jocie Guo's *Bu Pa Bu Pa La* on a bejeweled pink cell phone to drown out our conversation.

"She said she wants to show her friends," Bahati answered for her. "But I refused, so now she is pouting. This is the problem with young Chinese these days; they're so spoiled, even the prostitutes!"

"As long as your face isn't in the picture, what do you care?" I laughed, wholly impressed at how these little women – these peasant grrrls – had retained complete control of their respective circumstances. "This is probably the most exciting thing that has ever happened to her."

"True, true," Bahati agreed, looking over at Jia Jia affectionately. "She is kind of cute. Reminds me of my middle-school students.

Maybe I can even make her my girlfriend."

I was about to make a tasteless joke about the Total Physical Response teaching method, when another young girl and a bloated Chinese man with a flattop, mismatched suit and plastic dress shoes exited a room down the hall. I presume they had just finished. The man cleared his throat grotesquely, spat on the floor, then withdrew a pack of Shuang Xi from his man-purse and lit up a cigarette. They squeezed past me in the narrow hallway, first peering into Bahati's open window at the naked African posing for pictures, then Claude's room, upon the most ill-fated threesome ever.

As the customer and his consort descended the stairs, I heard him say to her: "Foreigners are crazy."

This was probably true. Or at least the ones who come to China are.

"That's it, we're leaving!" growled Jie Jie as she hooked her hot-pink D-cup bra back on. Ni Ni followed suit.

"Did you, um, finish?" I asked Claude through the window. The small room reeked of hualushui oil and ass.

The furry foreigner wiped the perspiration from his forehead. "No, I didn't! Tell mother hen to send up another girl. I'm not leaving here until I get my money's worth!"

"I don't think it works like that, bro. We're not at the buffet. You had your chance. Best just to go quietly without making trouble. These kinds of places are operated by unsavory elements."

Unsavory elements. I'd heard that phrase used by the communist propaganda machine, but I never had an opportunity to say it myself until tonight – though at this point I wondered if the only unsavory elements here were us.

The two girls, fully dressed now, stomped their platform heels down the stairs and disappeared into the dark courtyard.

"Dumb hairy caveman!" one of them, probably Jie Jie, yelled once they were free and clear.

Claude cocked his head like a confused dog. "What did she say?"

Letting out a long sigh, I sat on the edge of the befouled bed and studied my friend's furious face. He had brought this on himself: Claude was crass, complaining and culturally insensitive, characteristics that have no place in a country as complex as China. Still, I felt a little sorry for him. He was probably the only man to never have been properly pleasured here.

But that's the thing about being a foreigner in China: it either makes you or breaks you; you either get it, or you don't. There are no gray areas.

"Tell me what she said!" Claude demanded, this time more irritably. I predicted another P.R.C. period coming on.

"Hmm? Oh, she just said 'thank you, please come again.'"

Epilogue

Simon Winchester

Simon Winchester was a Hong Kong-based Asia-Pacific correspondent for *The Sunday Times* and later for *The Guardian*, from 1985 until the colonial retrocession in June 1997, returning regularly to China in the years since. He has written several books based on his experiences in the region, including "Korea" and "Krakatoa." He spent several months traveling the length of the Yangtze between Shanghai and the Tibetan plateau to write "The River at the Center of the World" and followed in the footsteps of British scientist-Sinologist Joseph Needham to research his work, "The Man Who Loved China." Winchester, who was made Officer of the Order of the British Empire in 2006, now lives in the US.

"THE SILK ROAD, LIKE much of the world today, just isn't what it used to be."

I wrote that small piece of not-very-deathless prose as the opening line for an American magazine article a few years ago – and now cringe each time I am reminded of it. Because of course it isn't what it used to be. Nothing is, anywhere in the world. To make this kind of observation is the laziest kind of journalism – although a writerly fault to which all of us, at one time or another, are prey.

Except that in China, this kind of truism is more true than perhaps anywhere else on earth. For rare must be the country that has changed as much, and in so short a time, as modern China has.

I first came out in 1979, aboard a Royal Air Force VC-10. It was carrying a long-forgotten British minister to conduct some early soundings about the future of Hong Kong. We arrived in Peking, as every non-Chinese sensibly called the capital back then. I remember it as being a place of deathly quiet. We sped into the palace guest house without seeing any measurable traffic. There were police everywhere. When I went walking I was greeted by a palpable sense of fear in the hutongs, no one wanting to speak to me. The city's main boulevards were wide and dusty and filled at rush hours only with bicycles, on which oceans of blue-clad figures of indeterminate gender washed serenely to and fro, like animations from a Fritz Lang epic.

I had two friends in the city at the time, a married couple, both of them famous translators. He was Chinese, she English, and they had met at Oxford while studying, in the 1930s. When I first met them at home they wore terrible scars of the Cultural Revolution, which had sputtered to close only a decade before; not the least of their miseries was the suicide of their only son in England, which had taken place just days before I left.

He had been dreadfully affected by his parents' fate: during the turmoil they had each been jailed for seven years, neither knowing the fate of the other, nor the children knowing anything. And yet in spite of it all, when I went to them in their quiet and dusty offices in the Foreign Languages Press, they seemed good-humored, hospitable, tolerant, kindly and quite forgiving of the excesses of a country that, despite what its leaders and their zealots had done to them, they still loved, unwaveringly.

Their offices have long gone now, and tall skyscrapers designed by famous European architects have risen in their place. They have gone too, she dying in the 1990s, he just a few years back. Their tireless efforts in translating the Chinese classics are recognized now by just a few scholars – a class of people who are no longer as revered as once they were, before China began its spectacular modern ascent into the economic stratosphere. Scholars were once the cream of society: now successful businessmen are, and it can fairly be said, were it not for writerly laziness to do so, that scholarship in China just isn't what it used to be.

The thousands of miles I traveled through China in the intervening years have thrown up scores of moments like this – moments that I knew would never see their like again, or which on later visits offered proof that what I had once seen had long since vanished.

I used to spend quite a lot of time in Manchuria, for example – I had the idea once that, given its importance in the beginning of the Japanese war, it was one of history's cockpits, and deserved a book. Maybe it was: but the book went unwritten. That didn't stop me wandering all over the three provinces, though – I found Liaoning and Jilin not especially interesting, but Heilongjiang, up by the Russian border, was entirely enthralling, if very, very cold in wintertime.

On one occasion I spent many days living with an encampment of the Oroqen people, an ethnic minority made somewhat famous by the memorable Kurosawa film *Dersu Uzala*, which was shot on the Soviet side of the great Amur River, which separates the two countries.

That sojourn was memorable enough: living inside a salmon-skin tent, drinking unbearable quantities of local maotai, and being compelled (out of politeness, mainly) to dance with an amazingly obese ethnic Chinese political commissar assigned to the camp. He had come from southern China, hated the cold, drank himself silly each night and possibly thought that dancing with a Westerner might earn him enough trouble to get thrown out and sent home. He was there a year later, though; the ploy hadn't worked.

But what interested me more was the sight of Russia across the river. The Amur, the Black Dragon, is half a mile wide here. On this side, the Chinese side, all back then was dusty, silent, half-empty, poor. Everyone in the drab little town of Heihe dressed the same, everyone looked the same. But there were telescopes mounted on the riverbank, and for 10 fen or so you could stare for hours – as many Chinese did – at the unfolding drama that was the Soviet Union, so close and yet so far.

I remember once seeing a crowd of blue-suited old men gathered at the eyepiece, gazing into the town of Blagoveshchensk, watching minutely the details of Russia's everyday life. It seemed so *rich*, one man said to me. Life seemed so much better than on the Chinese said. Then there was a sudden commotion, and when I asked why I was pushed to the lens: a group of Russian footballers, most of them blond young men, were kicking a ball about on the riverbank. It was the hair that astounded everyone: to see another man sporting a crop of fair-colored hair – why, to most Chinese of the time, he might as well have been a Martian.

All has changed now, utterly. Heihe today is a sprawling city of skyscrapers and neon, its glow lighting up the horizon for miles. Blagoveshchensk across the river has now decayed to the point where it is as Heihe once was: dull and dusty, a relic of a failed state, a dingy place of threadbare grass and broken roads. Russians come across on boats to buy what they can in China – and everything is available. Few Chinese bother to cross the other way, and if there are Nordic-looking types playing football on the far side, it matters little...unless they are potential customers.

The Chinese want to build a bridge across the Amur. But Russians don't, fearful of being swamped by neighbors more aggressive, more successful than they are ever likely to be. Russia, in comparison with China, just isn't what it used to be.

In common with all this swift and steady change, matters have altered just about everywhere – as I was to find out one gale-swept winter's evening, out on the old Silk Road.

Five years or so ago this fabled highway was just a worn and rock-strewn trail, spearing along what was called the He Xi corridor, northwest of the terribly polluted town Lanzhou. It ran between mountain ranges and across pitiless deserts. Not uncommonly you would encounter Arab traders and Uyghur camel trains laden with treasure, plodding slowly along for mile after patient mile between Kashgar and Chang'an.

Today all is quite different. For much of its length the Road is now a billiard-table smooth divided highway, with flyovers and cloverleaf junctions. It is well on its way to being equipped with electronic tollbooths, and it is crowded with massive eighteen-wheeler trucks and shiny new cars – like my rented and Shanghai-made Volkswagen Passat, in which I was humming along at a steady 70.

At least, it was as modern and characterless as this – until the moment I reached the old Ming Dynasty fort at Jiayuguan. Here, and suddenly, the road changed back into its celebrated old self. West of the fort the Silk Road became suddenly quite hellish. Huge rocks littered its surface, there was a rash of potholes that could conceal a bus, and swelling waves of gritty Gobi sand blew in from the north, turning the road's surface into a vile porridge of grey grit. I slewed this way and that, I bumped and cursed, the stiff and cold north wind blowing sharp needles of sand into my eyes, making it difficult to see.

And then suddenly there came a sharp crack, a lurch, and an assortment of red warning lights promptly snapped on in the cabin. *Oil pressure low and falling*, said one. *Engine overheating*, said another. I stopped the car, got out into the gathering darkness and the maelstrom of Gobi sand, and shone a flashlight up into the engine. A black tide of oil was gushing out onto the roadway: I had cracked the sump, and within seconds the engine was unlubricated and then stopped dead, never to go again. And I, all of a sudden, was going precisely nowhere.

By now it was almost dark. A cold wind was whipping up from the north. There was no traffic. The closest village was 40 miles away, and the hotels and service stations in the cave-city of Dunhuang were getting on for 200 miles off. I was well and truly, not to put a too fine a point on it, *buggered*. Through the gloom I could glimpse the skeleton of a large mammal – a horse, I thought, perhaps a camel. It had died of thirst: and now, I fancied, so might I.

Except. The Chinese build their infrastructure well these days, and one of the first things they have created in making their new nationwide transportation system – long before finishing the roads, in other words – is a cell phone network. And not just ordinary cell phones: the signals put out from the cell towers here, even in the middle of the Gobi desert, were of a kind that allowed, incredibly, *my iPhone to work*. It wasn't the kind of signal that allowed mere voice transmission. It allowed data, and lots of it.

I had been sitting in the back seat twiddling with what I assumed was a useless hunk of plastic – wondering how many days before I might try to eat it – and lo! It sprung into life. Its lights came on. Its screen showed signal, good, strong, data-ready signal. And that being the case I realized that I could get the internet. I could get Google. I could get rescued!

Which is exactly what I did. I tapped in Google. I searched for 'Hotels, Dunhuang, China.' And it was plenty fast enough; just two minutes later I had found a hotel. I scrolled down to its phone number, called, and then said the following, in the best Chinese I could muster:

"Excuse me. I'm stuck on the Silk Road with a busted sump (very tricky in any language, let alone this), two hundred and sixteen miles from you. If I come to stay with you – and I can give you a credit card number – will you come and rescue me?"

There was a pause. A whispered discussion. The phone was evidently handed around the room. Then came the loveliest voice I have ever heard. A young woman's voice, clear above the gale.

"Hello, my name is Merry," said the angelic voice. "This will not be a problem. We see on the map just where you are. So I have asked for two cars. It will take us five hours. My recommendation is that you go to sleep. Leave the flashing lights on. We will be there before dawn. And when you get here come and say hello. My name is Merry Zhang. Just ask for Merry."

And just before four in the morning, two sets of headlights blazed out of the western night. One set belonged to a crane, which winched up the broken car and hurried her away. The other had two drivers inside, a six-pack of cold Tsingtao beer, a thermos flask of noodles, and another insulated container with a bowl of soup. "I hope you like donkey," said one driver. "We eat donkeys in Dunhuang."

Well, anyway, suffice to say that five hours later I was in Dunhuang, sitting at a table topped with white linen, eating a donkeyburger for breakfast. With Merry. She was as pretty as she sounded. I told her that I was now as happy as Larry, and more delighted than it is possible to imagine. I was glad that I had an iPhone, and that I didn't have to eat it. Even donkey is better than that.

The more important point, I added, was the simple existence of that cell phone signal. My life had been saved, I said, by the simple existence of that precious signal, pulsing out from a faraway chain of towers, unseen, unknown, but already built and set down in the sand. For out in the Gobi desert, long before the new road was built, the Chinese had arranged for the data links that would one day be so necessary – arranged for them to be constructed first, and not as a casual afterthought.

China, it struck me that morning over breakfast, is becoming so successful precisely because it not a casually planned society any more. It is not at all like, as someone once wrote of Calcutta, *chance directed, chance-erected*. It is all now so very planned, so well thought-out, so carefully-made. Charmless, maybe, but now on an unwavering road to success.

Such planning, such a sea-change, and the results are everywhere to see and feel. Whether out here on the Silk Road, or up in the rivers of the Manchurian north, or in the great cities where the dreamy scholars of Confucian lore are fast yielding ground to the hard realities of the market place – the old China just isn't what it used to be. And for that very reason the whole world should tremble.

I saw a sign once, in far western China, written in English on a huge poster beside the highway. *Without fear, without haste, China will rule the world.* For sure; and in our lifetime, too.

Editor's Acknowledgements

Like all things in China, this anthology, took its own sweet time to materialize. First conceptualized in a third-tier Chinese town in 2011, it was not until meeting publisher Graham Earnshaw in Shanghai the following year that *Unsavory Elements* finally found a home.

I am much obliged to all the contributors herein for agreeing to participate in this grassroots publication. The following individuals also played a part in making this book what it is: Dominic Johnson-Hill at Plastered T-shirts for suggesting the brilliant cover art; Susan Blumberg-Kason, the best beta-reader ever; Suzanne Edwards and Team Earnshaw for their production assistance; Tina Mani Kanagaratnam at AsiaMedia and Michelle Garnaut at M Restaurant Group for inviting us to debut during the 2013 Shanghai Literary Festival; Chris Cottrell, David Green, Jade Gray, Jamie Barys, Jerry Chan, Jules Quartly, Kristianna & Robert Foye, Lee Mack, Lloyd Lofthouse, Lonnie Hodge, Matt Muller, Paul French, Pete Spurrier, Richard Perez and Ryan McLaughlin for their suggestions and support.

And of course my wife, Hannah Hong Mei, who for the past auspicious eight years has resolutely remained at my side as we backpacked together across all of China, and then all of India, before embarking on our biggest adventure yet – parenthood – with her giving birth to our first child at our local public People's Hospital as I, not a little distractedly, edited this anthology.